Immigration and Integration Policy in Europe

The role of political parties in immigration control and integration policy in Europe is underestimated, and parties on the centre-right are particularly important and interesting in this respect. They make up many European governments and therefore help determine state and EU policy. Moreover, even before the rise of the populist radical right, immigration and integration were matters of genuine ideological and practical concern for Europe's market liberal, conservative and Christian Democratic parties. Exploiting such issues for electoral gain may make superficial sense, but too hard a line risks alienating their supporters in business and in civil society, as well as undermining party unity. It is a difficult balance, but one that makes a big difference both to the parties involved and the public policies they help produce. This volume brings together experts on both migration and political parties – fields that have not always interacted as much as they could or should have done – in order to study the impacts, dilemmas and trade-offs involved.

This book is based on the special issue of the *Journal of European Public Policy*.

Tim Bale is a Senior Lecturer in the Department of Politics and Contemporary European Studies, University of Sussex.

Journal of European Public Policy Series

Series Editor: Jeremy Richardson is a Professor at Nuffield College, Oxford University

This series seeks to bring together some of the finest edited works on European Public Policy. Reprinting from Special Issues of the 'Journal of European Public Policy,' the focus is on using a wide range of social sciences approaches, both qualitative and quantitative, to gain a comprehensive and definitive understanding of Public Policy in Europe.

Immigration and Integration Policy in Europe

Why Politics – and the Centre-Right – Matter

Edited by Tim Bale

Routledge
Taylor & Francis Group

LONDON AND NEW YORK

First published 2009 by Routledge
2 Park Square, Milton Park, Abingdon, Oxon, OX14 4RN

Simultaneously published in the USA and Canada
by Routledge
270 Madison Avenue, New York, NY 10016

Routledge is an imprint of the Taylor & Francis Group, an informa business

© 2009 Edited by Tim Bale

Typeset in Sabon by Value Chain, India
Printed and bound in Great Britain by Biddles Ltd, King's Lynn

British Library Cataloguing in Publication Data
A catalogue record for this book is available from the British Library

ISBN10: 0-415-46834-5
ISBN13: 978-0-415-46834-3

Contents

Turning round the telescope. Centre-right parties and immigration and integration policy in Europe[1]

Tim Bale

A recent 'state of the art' review of the political science literature on migration notes that myriad studies 'have provided evidence that a range of actors influence policy outcomes. They include organised interest groups, courts, ethnic groups, trade unions, law and order bureaucracies, police and security agencies, local actors and street-level bureaucrats and private actors' (Lahav and Guiraudon 2006: 207). Missing from the list (although, to be fair, they later make a brief appearance in a table as 'conduits of public opinion') are actors that one might have expected to have had some say in the matter. Their absence, however, is not unusual even if it is curious: as a contribution to one recent edited collection puts it, 'political parties have received relatively short shrift among students of the politics of migration'; they 'enter the story as minor characters with undefined roles' (Triadafilopoulos and Zaslove 2006: 171, 176).

This is almost certainly because, with a handful of exceptions (Hammar 1985; Perlmutter 1996; Schain 1999, 2006; Geddes 2003; Givens and Luedtke 2005; Williams 2006 and, interestingly, Lahav 2004), the political science communities working on asylum and immigration, on the one hand, and parties, on the other, have traditionally sat at separate tables. Leading migration scholars have rightly nodded to the need to understand how the arrival of newcomers and their families impacts on attitudes and electoral politics (see, for example, Hollifield 2000: 170–1). But very few treat the parties that fight those elections as a vital source of state and European Union (EU) policy – policy which for some time now has been moving towards an emphasis on restriction and cultural integration that borders on the coercive (see Joppke 2007a). Meanwhile, scholars of contemporary party politics often talk about the backlash against migration and multiculturalism. But they do so largely in two limited contexts. The first is research into the phenomenon of far-right parties (see, for example, Carter 2005; Norris 2005; Rydgren 2005; Mudde 2007). The second – in a manner reminiscent of arguments concerning public opinion and party positions on European integration – is the question of whether the debate on migration and multiculturalism cross-cuts traditional constructions of the left–right dimension or, as would seem to be the case, is collapsed into it (see Gabel and Anderson 2002; McElroy and Benoit 2007).

Policy people, in other words, do not really do parties, while party people do policy only insofar as it affects party competition and positioning. This talking past each other is a great pity for those who, in general, see merit in joined-up political science rather than the logic of specialization that encourages us all to know more and more about less and less. Few of us, after all, have given up completely on the notion that there is a real world out there that we have some kind of mission to explain. Often we do this by using heuristics that make our task more manageable and our findings easier to communicate. But, if so, we need to ensure that we extract full value from the explanatory frameworks we employ. Hence, if, as experts on political parties, we believe that their motives and dilemmas can be usefully modelled by declaring they must trade off between 'policy, office, and votes' (Müller and Strøm 1999), we need to take the first every bit as seriously as the other two. By the same token, if we believe, as many who study migration policy believe, that we need to focus on 'the liberal state' (Hollifield 2000: 146–50) or on organized interests calculating costs and benefits (Freeman 1995) or on more or less inertia-prone institutions (Hansen 2002), it seems only sensible to pay attention to the 'critical nodes' (Triadafilopoulos and Zaslove 2006: 189) that connect, influence, and are influenced by, all these things, namely political parties.

WHY (MAINSTREAM CENTRE-RIGHT) PARTIES MATTER

Political parties matter to European public policy on migration because 'the nation-state is ... where the majority of the migration action lies' (Lahav 2004: 10) but they will continue to do so even if the action moves elsewhere.

Recent work by migration scholars emphasizes the capacity and desire of EU member states not to cede competence in such a sensitive area unless it suits them (see, for example, Geddes 2003; Messina 2007). But even those scholars more inclined to look for evidence of Europeanization, selective and otherwise (see Faist and Ette 2007; also Joppke 2007b), routinely emphasize that it involves the 'uploading' of policy to the EU by member states as well as its 'downloading' to the member states by the EU (Börzel 2002). Given that the direction and detail of state policy demonstrably depends on who governs (Schmidt 1996; Imbeau *et al.* 2001), this means that parties are highly likely to count for something on immigration and integration irrespective of whether states refuse or decide to cede (or at least share) sovereignty in those areas. And should things move even further beyond the state, parties will still count for something. Immigration and integration may eventually become subject not just to instrumental intergovernmental co-operation but to full-blown community competence. Even, then, however, they will be amenable to influence by political parties that are increasingly coherent and cohesive at the transnational level (see Hix and Noury 2007). In other words, it is not just in (migration) policy-making that one finds Europeanization (see, for example, Lavenex 2006): parties, too, are eventually affected, albeit in an equally uneven, contested and normatively problematic manner (see Mair 2006). As long as representative politics remains a feature of both the nation-state and that which transcends (or at least enmeshes) it, there is no escape from parties.

The logical corollary of acknowledging the potential influence of parties on public policy in this and other areas is to look first at those parties which have spent most time in government, either singly or in coalition. One study (Givens and Luedtke 2005) takes a promising step in this direction, even if its discovery that there is more difference between left and right governments on integration policy than on immigration has to be tested on a wider range of countries (and over a longer timespan) before it can be regarded as anything more than indicative. For some reason, however, most of those who have dealt with the issue of party impact have chosen to look, as it were, down the wrong (or at least the other) end of the telescope: they explore the putative influence of 'fringe' or 'extremist' parties rather than that more obviously exercised by the 'mainstream' parties which by and large have kept them (and continue to keep them) out of government. Clearly, the issue of whether these smaller parties have – often indirectly – influenced public policy on immigration and integration is both interesting and important, as a number of stimulating studies, both recent (Schain 2006; Williams 2006; Triadafilopoulos and Zaslove 2006) and slightly older (Minkenberg 2002), have demonstrated. It is about time, however, that we turned the telescope around and trained it, too, on the parties that have a more direct impact on public policy at and beyond the level of the state. In this respect, parties of the centre-right, which, despite their crucial importance to the past, current, and future governance of the continent, have enjoyed nowhere near the scholarly attention of their more radical counterparts, are an obvious point of departure.[2]

Many mainstream parties that have a chance of forming – or helping to form – governments in contemporary Europe are under pressure to take a harder-line, more restrictionist and 'assimilationist' stance on issues of immigration and inte-gration. The sources of such pressure obviously include real-world problems such as increased labour migration and asylum-seeking, stretched border security, welfare and criminal justice systems, the threat of terrorism, and the evident – though hardly novel (see Lucassen 2006) – unease about cultural differences in some segments of the self-styled 'native' population. Mainstream parties are also under pressure from radical, populist alternatives, from a media that 'compares immigrants in generous moments with thieves, in less generous moments with sewage' (Hansen 2003: 32), and from their own members, sup-porters and electorates, with considerable feedback between each of these forces. Clearly, the perceived problems and the apparently pressing need for solutions are in part cued and constructed by political (and especially government) actors (see, for example, Statham 2003: 170–1, 175). Demand is not independent of supply, as any successful entrepreneur – electoral as well as economic – knows. Nor does one need to buy wholesale into constructivism or postmodernism to realize that, when it comes to how voters think about immigration and asylum, 'perception is reality' – particularly when it comes to the numbers involved (see Sides and Citrin 2007). But all this is true only up to a point. If we are to gain an understanding of the policy pursued by mainstream political parties, we have to acknowledge what for some of us may be uncomfortable realities.

In other words, even if we discount for the inflated figures bandied about by opponents of immigration, the decades since the end of the Cold War have seen large numbers of people hoping to work, or take refuge from persecution, in western Europe (see Penninx et al. 2006). Since 2004 these numbers have been swelled by the accession to the EU of ten Central and Eastern European states and may in a decade or so be boosted even further by the entry of Turkey. While the numbers may be small relative to the existing population, they are – or can be made to look – huge in absolute terms, especially if the faces, languages and cultures of the migrant population and their descendants seem very different. By the same token, only a minority of entrants rely on, or even abuse, Europe's welfare systems. But some of course do, either because they are encouraged to by a benefits regime that requires little in return for the assistance it provides or because they are trapped into doing so by overt and covert discrimination that prevents them from escaping depen-dence. Similarly, it may well be that ethnic minorities, who are either the des-cendants of migrants or migrants themselves, are overrepresented in the criminal justice system not just because they are poor but also because law enforcement agencies pay them an inordinate amount of attention and hand them down tougher sentences. But overrepresented they are. Equally, they are not the only people to be involved in terrorism in Europe, and the threat may indeed be exaggerated out of all proportion. Yet, the most recent and most high-profile attacks have indeed been instigated by extremists from (or with roots) outside Europe – and their atrocities have been all too real. It is the real world, then, and not just the fevered imaginings of demagogues and ill-informed, culturally threatened voters, that poses real policy questions for politicians.

Parties operating on the centre-right – our focus here – are perhaps particularly preoccupied with such questions. In other words, we should expect them to care irrespective of (or at least in addition to) electoral considerations. Part of their *raison d'être*, after all, is to defend the socio-economic and cultural status quo to which the entry of large (or at least highly visible) numbers of migrants would appear to present something of a challenge. Just as traditionally, they are in favour of keeping tax low, ensuring law and order is maintained and national security is protected – all aims that are apparently threatened by ethnic minorities that have for some time been overrepresented in the welfare rolls and crime statistics (Joppke 2007a: 6), and now, in the era of 9/11, and the bomb attacks on Madrid and London, are thought to present an even more dramatic threat (see Karyotis 2007; also Collyer 2006 and Hampshire, forthcoming). Parties of the centre-right also have an ambivalent relationship with the parties that play up such threats: on the one hand, the far-right may eat into their vote-share (the preoccupation of much of the literature); on the other, it may help them into office by joining or supporting governments that they lead (Bale 2003). Accordingly, calling for the tightening of borders and sounding off against the evils of multiculturalism might serve to counter the electoral threat from radical right-wing populists or, by boosting the salience of the issues that such forces thrive on, it might increase their vote-share and help the more respectable right to win back or maintain office (Bale 2003; see also Meguid 2005). Whatever, a hard-line stance must be quite a temptation, especially if it is consonant with, or no more than a logical extension of, one's own ideological position.

Some migration scholars, however, would deny that there is much of a correlation between being on the right of centre and greater concern about inflows and greater insistence on integration; immigration, apparently, 'is located at the crossroads between two very different semantics: those based on economic or functional issues ... and those based on culture, identity and tradition', thus rendering 'the distinction between conservative and progressive' problematic if not meaningless (Sciortino 2000: 224–5). This is highly debatable – both institutionally and ideologically. Notwithstanding their concern about public anxiety over immigration and integration, 'progressive' parties cannot help but notice that those of immigrant origin vote for them in disproportionate numbers (see Messina 2007), while the trade unions with which they continue to enjoy links seem to have decided that they can best avoid their members being undercut by recruiting rather than rejecting newcomers (see Haus 2002; ETUC 2005). Meanwhile, the idea that immigration and integration cross-cuts left and right also seems to be contradicted by empirical evidence: Lahav (2004: 126–32) shows that there is a clear ideological and party distinction between the conventional left and right on these issues and that one does not have to look too far along the right-hand side of the divide before attitudes become restrictive and suspicious (see also Lahav 1997). Put bluntly, centre-right voters and the parties they vote for are indeed more preoccupied about immigration and integration, are more likely to kick up over such issues, and have been for quite some time, even in the absence of a significant far-right threat (Perlmutter 1996). Expressing the desire to protect 'us' from 'them', whoever or whatever 'them' (or 'the other') may happen to be at the time, is in what Panebianco (1988) calls the 'genetic code' of many mainstream centre-right parties – and arguably, given the 'racialized' nature of European society and history, their centre-left counterparts cannot claim to be totally immune either (see Garner 2005: 125).

This is a very important point. Framing the centre-right's (and indeed the centre-left's) stand on immigration control and immigrant policy as purely, or at least primarily, a strategic response to the populist radical right implies that Europe's mainstream parties are somehow incapable of coming to their own conclusions on the seriousness of the issues and the policy direction they should take on them. This is not only potentially patronizing, it is misleading – as even scholars determined to find far-right influence are wise enough to acknowledge in the small print (see Williams 2006: 69–70). Moreover, given the fact that more 'progressive' parties are under as much, if not more, pressure from populist entrepreneurs aiming to steal their voters, the 'far-right pressure' frame does not explain why it has so often been the centre-right that has made the running on immigration control and more aggressive integration rather than the centre-left – even if the centre-left does tend to play catch-up (see Bale *et al.* 2007). If political competition is indeed about 'issue ownership' and campaigning about 'selective emphasis' – about parties talking past each other because they are preoccupied with moving the agenda on to issues on which they are 'strong' (see Budge and Farlie 1983) – then the centre-right has had a claim to own the issues we deal with here for some time.

LITTLE PRODDING NEEDED: THE RECORD OF THE CENTRE-RIGHT ON IMMIGRATION AND INTEGRATION

To read or hear some accounts, both in the media and in more academic work, however, one would think that it is only since the 'rise of the far-right' that countries – and by implication centre-right parties – have been worrying about and taking action on immigration and integration. But the now familiar notion that there was a more or less bipartisan (and ultimately counterproductive) 'conspiracy of silence' on the part of the mainstream that created 'a political space' for the anti-immigrant extreme which now needs closing down (see, for example, Messina 2007: 86–7) is, notwithstanding its status as common wisdom, highly problematic. It did not require, for instance, a far-right threat to bring about the almost pan-European 'immigration stop' in the early 1970s. It is abundantly clear, for example, from the policy debate and measures in post-war France that 'mainstream' politicians, especially (though not exclusively) on the centre-right, have been active in this area for well over 30 years.

True their efforts and rhetoric intensified after, first, 1986 and then 1993, when the *Front National* was clearly seen as an electoral threat. But we have to remember that the latter year also marked a dramatic increase in anxiety about the security threats allegedly posed to France by (Algerian) migrants (see Collyer 2006): no one who saw or heard Charles Pasqua – France's Minister of the Interior who spearheaded the government's hard line on immigration and integration – in action would have argued that he was reluctantly driven into such a stance simply in order to head off Le Pen. We also need to recall that it was 1974, under Giscard (and Chirac) and long before Le Pen was taken so seriously, that 'marked a seachange' which saw immigrants regarded 'more as a liability than as an asset' (Hollifield 1994: 155).

But France was by no means alone in seeing the centre-right taking immigration and (albeit to a lesser extent) integration seriously before, and not wholly because of, the far-right (or, for that matter, Osama bin Laden). Entzinger's fascinating account of the (note, pre-Pim Fortuyn) retreat from multiculturalism – inasmuch as it ever really existed as official policy (see Joppke and Morawska 2003: 1) – may not mention parties as much as some of us think it might (Entzinger 2003). But it does serve as a useful reminder that it was the leader of the market- or conservative-liberal VVD (People's Party for Freedom and Democracy), Frits Bolkestein, who, in September 1991, triggered a national debate by declaring the incompatibility of Islam and 'Western values' and insisting that immigrants should adapt to the host culture rather than the other way around. Unless we are willing to label a future European Commissioner (1999–2004) as a populist radical right-wing entrepreneur *à la* Blocher, Haider *et al.*, we have to acknowledge that, if it was this intervention that in part provoked the Dutch government to re-direct its efforts away from minority promotion and toward integration, it came from the mainstream not the extreme.

Germany is another case in point. The Christian Democratic Union–Chrsitian Social Union–Free Democratic Party (CDU–CSU–FDP) coalition won the first election of the 1980s 'in part on the grounds that it would "do something" about immigration' (Martin 1994: 203); at that point, however, there seems to have been relatively little anxiety about a resurgent far-right. Some will, of course, argue that German politicians are, for obvious historical (and indeed diplomatic) reasons, hyper-vigilant about such a resurgence, and that even its possible (as opposed to actual) occurrence can therefore be wheeled in as an explanation of their growing determination to crack down since, say, the late 1970s. But this does not explain, first, why they did not act in the late 1960s when fears of the far-right were more apparent. Nor, second, does it explain why it was the centre-right rather than the centre-left (presumably every bit as sensitive to the far-right threat) that over the last 30 years has taken a harder line.

The argument that Germany's centre-right acts because it fears the far-right dovetails with a wider presumption that mainstream politicians somehow require public opinion to be channelled or mediated by a populist political entrepreneur before they act – even when that opinion is clearly running in one direction and can in part be explained by a massive absolute increase in numbers coming (or trying to come) into the country, as well as the fact that some minorities already there are clearly not well integrated. Just as importantly, it ignores the indisputable point that in Germany the far-right never seems to make the breakthrough into national politics that in other countries – not least France – is apparently responsible for policy shifting towards restriction and intolerance. Perhaps if we could see beyond Germany's Nazi past, we might be able to locate its mainstream politicians' attitudes and actions on immigration and integration in the party system that the country currently has rather than in the one that some fear it might one day have again. Doing this might lead us to look at, for example, Germany's constituency-based electoral system. If such a system is indeed part of the reason why British politicians respond so quickly to public anxieties about immigrants (see Money 1997), might it also explain why their German counterparts pick up on them too?

It is perhaps no accident that it is in the UK, with its two (or two-and-a-half) party system and absence of a fascist past, that policy and parties have been most closely tied together by migration specialists (see, for example, Spencer 1997). But the UK should not be alone – something that becomes obvious the more one thinks about it. Given the examples of radical right-wing populist involvement in government in Italy and Austria (and we would also include Denmark where minority governments of the centre-right have in recent years relied on parliamentary support by the populist radical right), Garner (2005: 133) might be overstating the case when he argues that the racialized nature of immigration control and immigrant policies in Europe is quite simply 'a result of mainstream politics'. But he has a point: even outside the UK, what he calls 'the logic of defence' (2005: 133) was around long before the far-right became a force to be reckoned with once again.

The predictable retort to this counterblast is that any failure of the extreme right in the UK (or indeed Germany) is, at least in part, testimony to the fact that a hard-line stance by the mainstream right works to close down the issue space: cue endless misquotations of soon-to-be prime minister Margaret Thatcher's famous remark to a television interviewer in the late 1970s concerning people's fears of being 'swamped' – a remark which, to read some accounts, seems to have single-handedly done for the National Front, forerunner to the today's British National Party (BNP).[3] In fact, closing down the space in this way rarely has the desired effect: once the toothpaste is out of the tube, the can of worms opened, the issues rarely go away – for at least four reasons.

First, such issues are very real, or at least very threatening, for many millions of people (see Sides and Citrin 2007). Second, they are (to coin a phrase) media-sexy, consonant with classic and contemporary 'news values' (see Brighton and Foy 2007) as well as dovetailing nicely with the political agenda of some media owners. Third, there are enough mainstream politicians prepared to help keep the issues on the boil – even, as Hansen and Koehler (2005: 635–41) show, in Germany, where they are supposedly so determined to head off extremists by offering an apparently more responsible rhetoric on immigration and integration. And, fourth, those politicians do so – at least in part – because they think the problems warrant talking about and see it as their democratic duty to do so. As Thatcher said, in the same television interview in 1978, 'We are not in politics to ignore people's worries: we are in politics to deal with them.'

There is, in fact, a fundamental question of representation here. Matthew Gibney's highly stimulating attempt to bring together the ethics and politics of asylum gives only the briefest of nods to the *party* politics surrounding (and possibly also driving) policy and public debate on the topic. But when it does so it leads him to assert that the increasing climate of restriction exists 'in part because of the behaviour of irresponsible political elites prepared to use every card in the deck to stay in or to come to power'; instead, he suggests, political leaders should reduce their 'electoral vulnerability' to intolerant and arguably anti-humanitarian public opinion by, among other things, a concerted 'attempt to establish greater political bipartisanship on asylum issues' (Gibney 2004: 245). Only a fully paid-up populist, of course, would interpret this as a call for a cosy élite conspiracy designed to deny the people's will, albeit apparently in their own best interests. But it does run the risk of sounding a little like a plea for a kind of 'permissive consensus' that denies the right – and some would say the responsibility – of politicians and their parties to articulate (and perhaps even help to call forth) widespread public anxiety. This is risky: after all, the clash of socially embedded (and, yes, socially constructed and often ill-informed and illiberal) opinion lies at the heart of even the thinnest conception of representative democracy and the good (or at least best-available) governance that is supposed to arise from it. Mainstream parties should not – and, despite the putative 'end of class voting' and 'partisan dealignment', do not (see Thomassen 2005) – float entirely free of supporters who expect those parties to reflect their sometimes suspicious and even hostile attitude to immigration and the cultural heterogeneity that comes with it.

This genuine (and yet at the same time generated) suspicion and hostility explain why it is not just the issues that hang around. So, too, in many cases do the parties that the centre-right's hard line is supposedly so cleverly designed to defeat. This is partly because, by talking about and acting on issues of immigration and integration, the mainstream parties help to maintain their salience and therefore the traction of their more extreme counterparts. Whether this is by accident or by design – especially in the case of centre-right parties which stand to gain in terms of their opportunities to form governments – is a moot point (see Bale 2003). Certainly, there are few centre-right parties that have showed much reluctance when it comes to talking up the issues concerned – the Swedes (notwithstanding the country's retreat from multiculturalism as detailed by Soininen 1999) and, until the mid-1990s perhaps, the Italians (Calavita 1994, 2004, though see Perlmutter 1996: 380–1) being the exceptions that seem to prove the rule. Whether acknowledging this fact, and offering up as further evidence the more detailed contributions to the rest of this volume, will ever make an impact on the gnomic pronouncements of the *galacticos* of the global intellectual circuit is another matter. Francis Fukuyama, for example, will no doubt continue to insist that Europe, mired in political correctness, has failed to rise to the challenge of an honest and robust debate on integration – particularly of Muslims – because 'political parties on the center-right that should drive such a discussion have been intimidated by the left through accusations of racism and old-style nationalism; they fear above all being tarred by the far right. This is a huge mistake. The far right will make a big comeback if mainstream parties fail to take up this issue in a serious way' (Fukuyama 2006: 18).

But back to reality, to the continent where the debate conducted by main-stream parties over immigrants and immigration was in the mid-1990s already being called 'chronically populist' (Brubaker 1995: 908) by one of the many American scholars who really do know what they are talking about. The main point, then, is that to privilege 'reacting to the far-right' as the expla-natory variable for policy change on migration and multiculturalism effected (or urged on other parties) by the centre-right is a mistake. It is no more sensible than, for example, suggesting that migration flows themselves or public anxiety about them – both factors which have an impact on parties' policy pos-itions – are determined by the economic logic of late modern liberal capitalism or globalization à la, for instance, Saskia Sassen or Alejandro Portes (see Hollifield 2000: 155–7; though see also Sassen 2006). Most migration scholars reject such a simplistic analysis when it comes to political economy, so why settle for less when it comes to political competition?

INTERNAL DILEMMAS AND OTHER INFLUENCES

Talk of economics and liberalism, however, does serve as a useful warning. We should not allow our desire to question the common wisdom that the main-stream right finds it difficult to talk and act on immigration and integration because they are cross-cutting issues (Sciortino 2000: 224–5; and see Perlmutter 1996: 377) to go too far. A very clear hard-line stance does indeed jar, poten-tially at least, with some of the core values of centre-right parties. An obvious example would be charity and internationalism for Christian Democrats, who have always been concerned to turn 'strangers into friends' (Hanley 1994). Another is (economic) freedom from interference by big government for Con-servatives and Liberals. These tensions between what we might call the 'identity right', the 'paternalistic right' and 'the business right' exist more in some parties, and in some countries, than in others. They are also played out against a context in which both personal and factional ambition loom large, and in which links with traditionally friendly interest groups also matter. Italy is a particularly interesting case because the 'mainstream' centre-right (in the guise of *Forza Italia* plus sundry smaller centrist and Christian Democratic parties) has actually governed alongside the more 'extreme' right, the *Lega Nord* and the (increas-ingly 'respectable') *Alleanza Nationale* (see Ignazi 2005). Prior to the election of 2001, Berlusconi was counselled by his advisers to 'ride the tiger' of immigra-tion (Calavita 2004: 362); after it, he sometimes appeared to be 'contracting out' policy to Bossi and Fini. Yet the resulting, and apparently harsh, immigration law that bore their names was almost certainly diluted according to a tradition whereby the needs of employers and the pleas of charities, both echoed by other parties in the right-wing coalition, led to multiple amendments (see Zaslove 2006) and unreliable implementation – a tradition which Berlusconi did little or nothing to change in this case (or in many other cases).

Whether the centre-right's traditional 'will to power' (which might suggest a hard line to match public opinion) will automatically trump its 'conscience' or at least its ambivalence on immigration and integration (which might lead to something a little softer) is a moot point – especially since everything we know about parties tells us that they are not wholly (or at least not wholly office-seeking) rational actors. We also know that, however much we are convinced that we can sort individual organizations in each country into cross-national 'party families', the differences between them often occur, and are due in no small part to their being the products of places as much as ideas. While neither geography nor history is destiny, any trade-off made by centre-right parties between restriction and permissiveness, and between votes and values, is path-dependent and therefore in part contingent on the following: on whether the centre-right parties in question operate in traditionally sender or receiver countries; on their welfare state regimes; on the vulnerability of their physical borders; on their traditions of assimilation or multiculturalism; on other national traditions like Commonwealth or republican solidarity, or self-definition as an asylum country; on the extent to which security from, for example, terrorist attack is an issue; and, of course, on their attitude to EU enlargement, actual and potential.

CASES AND QUESTIONS

Hence we have tried in this issue to select cases from countries that vary as much as possible on these variables, although research on migration policy and politics in Central and Eastern Europe, we reluctantly concluded, was not yet sufficient for us to expand our exploration beyond the 'old' member states. Two examples of the latter, it is hoped, provide an illustration of the range that our selection provides: Germany has a 'continental' insurance-based welfare system, is extremely vulnerable to land-based incursion, received immigrants as guest-workers rather than former colonials, previously had one of the world's most generous asylum regimes, has so far avoided an attack by Islamist terrorists, and worked hard for the 2004 enlargement but is distinctly cagey about Turkish entry; Great Britain, on the other hand, has an Anglo-Saxon welfare regime, is an island, became multicultural as a result of its imperial past, saw 'Her Majesty's opposition' propose withdrawal from the 1951 United Nations Convention on Refugees at the 2005 general election, has suffered multiple terrorist attacks in recent years, suffered a public backlash against a supposed 'flood' of Eastern European workers following enlargement, but continues as a strong supporter of Turkish entry.

The immediate aim of this issue is to map and explain the conduct and stance of the centre-right parties in a number of European countries (and in Europe's unique trans- or supranational setting) on the issues of immigration and immigrant integration. In so doing it acknowledges, indeed it stresses, variation – not just according to geography and history, but also according to changing flows and, indeed, foes. Positions or actions taken by parties will, then, fluctuate over time, even if we can claim to detect some underlying ideological consistency. Shifting perceptions of what works, both electorally and in terms of inter-party alliances, also make a difference: the Swedish Liberals, for instance, did well out of campaigning for language tests in 2002 and then said virtually nothing about them in 2006, partly in order to ensure their membership (and the stability) of the centre-right's pre-electoral (and, as it turned out, post-electoral) pact. Meanwhile, the British Conservatives (who are apparently anxious to learn as much as they can from the Swedish example) seem unlikely to 'bang on about' immigration next time as they did in 2005: whatever else their then leader, Michael Howard, did for the party, he surely tested to destruction that particular route back to power, although his successor, David Cameron, will almost certainly hear calls for a return to populism if his Swedish-style modernization does not appear to be delivering the electoral goods.

But that, of course, is a very particular matter. We are more interested in more general questions – ones to which we return in the conclusion. First, while we, no more than others, 'believe that parties are the sole determinants of migration forces' (Triadafilopoulos and Zaslove 2006: 189), have we established that they are indeed more important than some give them credit for? Second, how much is the role and behaviour of centre-right parties in particular more than a function of the threat posed by parties on their far-right flank? Third, what are the internal tensions and dilemmas they face?

Last but not least, we need to assess whether the attempt to bring together our 'separate tables' – or at least some of the diners – is a useful one. Does it make sense for those interested in political parties to get their head around public policy? Those interested in migration have won their battle to 'bring the state back in' when it looked at one stage as if it might disappear under the fashionable weight (and essentially 'apolitical logic') of globalization theory (see Hollifield 2000). Having done so, is it worth their taking more seriously an institution that in liberal democracies is charged with steering that state and providing (however inadequately sometimes) linkage with the citizens from which it supposedly derives its legitimacy and authority? In short, is it time for those who do policy to think, as a stimulating but all too brief contribution written over a decade ago (Perlmutter 1996) put it, about 'bringing parties back in'?

NOTES

1 Thanks to Martin Schain for helpful comments and to Jeremy Richardson for guidance through the editorial process.
2 This issue began as a workshop in an ESRC-funded seminar series on the Contemporary Right in Europe which was organized out of the University of Sussex but which also met at University College London, and the Universities of Antwerp, Cambridge and Leiden, thanks to (among others) Sean Hanley, Steven Van Hecke and Sarah de Lange, Julie Smith and Petr Kopecky. Details can be found at http://www.sussex.ac.uk/sei/1-4-9.html. Whether the relative neglect of the centre-right is due to what are widely assumed to be the more left-wing preferences of political scientists, or to the definitional problems surrounding a space in the political spectrum that is shared by a number of party families (the subject of another workshop in the series), is a moot point. Here we take a 'big-tent' approach: by centre or mainstream right we include market (but not social) liberal parties, Christian Democrats and conservative parties – in short, those party families (excluding Agrarian/Centre and Regionalist parties) which tend to score five or above on most expert surveys but which are not part of the populist radical right (or simply far-right) party family.
3 Anyone interested in reading the full text of the interview in January 1978 can find it at http://www.margaretthatcher.org/speeches/displaydocument.asp?docid= 103485. At the time, it seemed clear to most observers that the remarks, inasmuch as they had a strategic purpose, as well as presaging what within a year or two became a government policy, were intended to target working-class Labour voters in general rather than those who were flirting with the National Front in particular (see http://www.time.com/time/magazine/article/0,9171,948011,00.html).

REFERENCES

Bale, T. (2003) 'Cinderella and her ugly sisters: the mainstream and extreme right in Europe's bipolarising party systems', *West European Politics* 26(3): 67–90.
Bale, T., Green Pedersen, C., Krouwel, A., Luther, K.R. and Sitter, N. (2007) 'If you can't beat them, join them?'. Unpublished MS.
Börzel, T.A. (2002) 'Member state responses to Europeanization', *Journal of Common Market Studies* 40(2): 193–214.
Brighton, P. and Foy, D. (2007) *News Values*, London: Sage.
Brubaker, R. (1995) 'Comments on "Modes of immigration politics in liberal democratic states"', *International Migration Review* 29(4): 903–8.
Budge, I. and Farlie, D. (1983) *Explaining and Predicting Elections: Issue Effects and Party Strategies in Twenty-Three Democracies*, London: Allen & Unwin.
Calavita, K. (1994) 'Italy and the new immigration', in W.A. Cornelius, P.L. Martin and J.F. Hollifield (eds), *Controlling Immigration: A Global Perspective*, Stanford: Stanford University Press.
Calavita, K. (2004) 'Italy: economic realities, political fictions, and policy failures', in W.A. Cornelius, T. Tsuda, P.L. Martin and J.F. Hollifield (eds), *Controlling Immigration: A Global Perspective*, 2nd edn, Stanford: Stanford University Press.
Carter, E. (2005) *The Extreme Right in Western Europe: Success or Failure?*, Manchester: Manchester University Press.

Collyer, M. (2006) 'Migrants, migration and the security paradigm: constraints and opportunities', *Mediterranean Politics* 11(2): 255–70.

Entzinger, H. (2003) 'The rise and fall of multiculturalism: the case of the Netherlands', in C. Joppke and E. Morawska (eds), *Toward Assimilation and Citizenship: Immigrants in Liberal Nation States*, Basingstoke: Palgrave.

ETUC (2005) *Towards a Pro-active EU Policy on Migration and Integration*, http://www.etuc.org/a/1159.

Faist, T. and Ette, A. (eds) (2007) *The Europeanization of National Policies and Politics of Immigration: Between Autonomy and the European Union*, Basingstoke: Palgrave.

Freeman, G.P. (1995) 'Modes of immigration politics in liberal democratic states', *International Migration Review* 29(4): 881–902.

Fukuyama, F. (2006) 'Identity, immigration and liberal democracy', *Journal of Democracy*, 17(2): 5–20.

Gabel, M.J. and Anderson, C.J. (2002) 'The structure of citizen attitudes and the European political space', *Comparative Political Studies* 35(8): 893–913.

Garner, Steve (2005) 'The racialisation of mainstream politics', Ethical Perspectives 12(2): 123–40.

Geddes (2003) *The Politics of Migration and Immigration in Europe*, London: Sage.

Gibney, M.J. (2004) *The Ethics and Politics of Asylum: Liberal Democracies and the Response to Refugees*, Cambridge: Cambridge University Press.

Givens, T. and Luedtke, A. (2005) 'European immigration policies in comparative perspective: issue salience, partisanship and immigrant rights', *Comparative European Politics* 3(1): 1–22.

Hammar T. (ed.) (1985) *European Immigration Policy*, Cambridge: Cambridge University Press.

Hampshire, J. (forthcoming) 'Disembedding liberalism? Immigration politics and security in Britain since 9/11', in G. Freeman, T. Givens and D. Leal (eds), *Immigration and Refugee Policy in a Post-9/11 World*, Basingstoke: Palgrave.

Hanley, D. (1994) 'Christian Democracy as a political phenomenon', in D. Hanley (ed.), *Christian Democracy in Europe: A Comparative Perspective*, London: Pinter.

Hansen, R. (2002) 'Globalization, embedded realism and path dependence', *Comparative Political Studies* 35: 259–83.

Hansen, R. (2003) 'Migration to Europe since 1945: its history and its lessons', *Political Quarterly* 74(1): 25–38.

Hansen, R. and Koehler, J. (2005) 'Issue definition, political discourse and the politics of nationality reform in France and Germany', *European Journal of Political Research* 44: 623–44.

Haus, L. (2002) *Unions, Immigration, and Internationalization: New Challenges and Changing Coalitions in the United States and France*, Basingstoke: Palgrave.

Hix, S. and Noury, A. (2007) 'Politics, not economic interests: determinants of migration policies in the European Union', *International Migration Review* 41(1): 182–205.

Hollifield, J.F. (1994) 'Immigration and republicanism in France: the hidden consensus', in W.A. Cornelius, P.L. Martin and J.F. Hollifield (eds), *Controlling Immigration: A Global Perspective*, Stanford: Stanford University Press.

Hollifield, J.F. (2000) 'The politics of international migration: how can we "bring the state back in"?', in C.B. Brettel and J.F. Hollifield (eds), *Migration Theory: Talking Across Disciplines*, London: Routledge.

Ignazi, P. (2005) 'The extreme right', *South European Society and Politics* 10(2): 333–49.

Imbeau, L.M., Pétry, F. and Lamari, M. (2001) 'Left–right party ideology and government policies: a meta analysis', *European Journal of Political Research* 40(1): 1–29.

Joppke, C. (2007a) 'Beyond national models: civic integration policies for immigrants in Western Europe', *West European Politics* 30(1): 1–22.

Joppke, C. (2007b) 'Transformation of immigrant integration: civic integration and antidiscrimination in the Netherlands, France and Germany', *World Politics* 59: 243–73.

Joppke, C. and Morawska, E. (2003) 'Integrating immigrants in liberal nation-states: policies and practices', in C. Joppke and E. Morawska (eds), *Toward Assimilation and Citizenship: Immigrants in Liberal Nation-States*, London: Palgrave Macmillan.

Karyotis, G. (2007) 'European migration policy in the aftermath of September 11: the security migration nexus', *Innovation* 20(1): 1–17.

Lahav, G. (1997) 'Ideological and party constraints on immigration attitudes on Europe', *Journal of Common Market Studies* 35(3): 377–406.

Lahav, G. (2004) *Immigration and Politics in the New Europe: Reinventing Borders*, Cambridge: Cambridge University Press.

Lahav, G. and Guiraudon, V. (2006) 'Actors and venues in immigration control: closing the gap between political demands and policy outcomes', *West European Politics* 29(2): 201–23.

Lavenex, S. (2006) 'Asylum policy', in P. Graziano and M.P. Vink (eds), *Europeanization: New Research Agendas*, Basingstoke: Palgrave Macmillan.

Lucassen, L. (2006) *The Immigrant Threat: The Integration of Old and New Migrants in Western Europe Since 1850*, Champaign: University of Illinois Press.

Mair, P. (2006) 'Political parties and party systems', in P. Graziano and M.P. Vink (eds), *Europeanization: New Research Agendas*, Basingstoke: Palgrave Macmillan.

Martin, P.L. (1994) 'Germany: reluctant land of immigration', in W.A. Cornelius, P.L. Martin and J.F. Hollifield (eds), *Controlling Immigration: A Global Perspective*, Stanford: Stanford University Press.

McElroy, G. and Benoit, K. (2007) 'Party groups and policy positions in the European Parliament', *Party Politics* 13(1): 5–28.

Meguid, B. (2005) 'Competition between unequals: the role of mainstream party strategy in niche party success', *American Political Science Review* 99(3): 347–59.

Messina, A.M. (2007) *The Logics and Politics of Post-WWII Migration to Western Europe*, Cambridge: Cambridge University Press.

Minkenberg, M. (2002) 'The new radical right in the political process: interaction effects in France and Germany', in M. Schain, A. Zolberg, and P. Hossay (eds), *Shadows Over Europe: The Development and Impact of the Extreme Right Wing in Western Europe*, Basingstoke: Palgrave Macmillan.

Money, J. (1997) 'No vacancy. The political geography of immigration control in advanced, market economy countries', *International Organization* 51(4): 685–720.

Mudde, C. (2007) *Populist Radical Right Parties in Europe*, Cambridge: Cambridge University Press.

Müller, W.C. and Strøm, K (eds) (1999) *Policy, Office, or Votes? How Political Parties in Western Europe Make Hard Choices*, Cambridge: Cambridge University Press.

Norris, P. (2005) Radical Right: *Voters and Parties in the Electroal Market*, Cambridge: Cambridge University Press.

Panebianco, A. (1988) *Political Parties: Organization and Power*, Cambridge: Cambridge University Press.

Penninx, R., Berger, M. and Kraal, K. (eds) (2006) *The Dynamics of International Migration and Settlement in Europe*, Amsterdam: Amsterdam University Press.

Perlmutter, T. (1996) 'Bringing parties back in: comments on "Modes of immigration politics in liberal democratic societies"', *International Migration Review* 30: 375–88.

Rydgren, J. (2005) *Movements of Exclusion: Radical Right-Wing Populism in the Western World*, New York: Nova.

Sassen, S. (2006) 'The de-nationalization of the state and the re-nationalization of political discourse over immigration', in M. Giugni and F. Passy (eds), *Dialogues on Migration Policy*, Lanham: Lexington Books.

Schain, M. (1999) 'Minorities and immigrant incorporation in France', in C. Joppke and S. Lukes (eds), *Multicultural Questions*, Oxford: Oxford University Press.

Schain, M. (2006) 'The extreme-right and immigration policy-making: measuring direct and indirect effects', *West European Politics* 29(2): 270–89.

Schmidt, M.G. (1996) 'When parties matter: a review of the possibilities and limits of partisan influence on public policy', *European Journal of Political Research* 30(2): 155–83.

Sciortino, G. (2000) 'Toward a political sociology of entry policies: conceptual problems and theoretical proposals', *Journal of Ethnic and Migration Studies* 26(2): 213–28.

Sides, J. and Citrin, J. (2007) 'European opinion about immigration: the role of identities, interests and information', *British Journal of Political Science* 37: 477–504.

Soininen, M. (1999) '"The Swedish model" as an institutional framework for immigrant membership rights', *Journal of Ethnic and Migration Studies* 25(4): 685–702.

Spencer, I. (1997) *British Immigration Policy since 1939: The Making of Multicultural Britain*, London: Routledge.

Statham, P. (2003) 'Understanding anti-asylum rhetoric: restrictive politics or racist publics?', *Political Quarterly* 74(1):163–77.

Thomassen, J. (ed.) (2005) *The European Voter: A Comparative Study of Modern Democracies*, Oxford: Oxford University Press.

Triadafilopoulos, T. and Zaslove, A. (2006) 'Influencing migration policy from inside: political parties', in M. Giugni and F. Passy (eds), *Dialogues on Migration Policy*, Lanham: Lexington Books.

Williams, M.H. (2006) *The Impact of Radical Right-Wing Parties in Western Democracies*, New York: Palgrave.

Zaslove, A. (2006) 'The politics of immigration: a new electoral dilemma for the right and the left', *Review of European and Russian Affairs* 2(3): 10–36.

Politicizing migration: opportunity or liability for the centre-right in Germany?

Christina Boswell and Dan Hough

Immigration policy has emerged as an important area for European centre-right parties to assert their distinctiveness in the battle for votes. Indeed, the centre-right has consistently championed more restrictive approaches than its left of centre counterparts. Such positions appear to offer extensive possibilities for mobilizing electoral support and in many ways sit comfortably with the culturally conservative and patriotic values of many such centre-right actors. Yet, a focus on these issues carries its own risks. Conservative and Christian Democratic parties may lose legitimacy or electoral support from ethnic minority voters by 'playing the race card'; anti-immigrant positions may run counter to human rights or humanitarian values that are traditionally defended by the Christian church; and restrictive policies may conflict with a range of policy goals embraced by the centre-right – especially in the areas of economic policy and free trade (Boswell 2007). Moreover, a range of institutional constraints can impede governments from implementing restrictionist goals, with the result that they may fail to deliver on their electoral promises (Hollifield 1990). Given these risks, there is no golden rule stating that Conservatives or

Christian Democrats will automatically move to occupy the space available for populist mobilization on migration issues; or, if they do so, that this will yield electoral dividends.

Perhaps the most obvious framework for exploring these questions is offered by the literature on political opportunity structures – POS (Koopmans and Statham 2000; Tarrow 1998). The POS approach holds that political institutions, cleavages and alliance structures shape the opportunities, or 'space', for political mobilization. However, while the focus on opportunities is clearly important, we argue that the POS approach fails to explore the risks associated with occupying this space. It is fairly indisputable that centre-right parties have opportunities for political mobilization on immigration issues, and indeed that they have frequently used them. But how do they assess and respond to the perceived risks of occupying this space? While the question of political costs is in principle captured by the POS framework, it nonetheless remains under-theorized.

In our contribution we develop a typology of the potential costs, or risks, of anti-immigration mobilization to help explain how the German Christian Democratic Union (CDU) has positioned itself on migration issues over the past two decades. These risks are understood in terms of the legitimacy deficits that may be created by this type of mobilization. We also – briefly – analyse the CDU's interactions with two other broadly centre-right actors, the Christian Social Union (CSU) and Free Democratic Party (FDP). Our contribution is divided into two parts. In the first part we explain the political opportunities and risks opened by the rise to prominence of immigration issues since the 1980s. In the second part we analyse the positions that the CDU has taken on immigration and asylum questions between 1982 and 2005. Focusing on this period allows us to trace the emergence of immigration as a political issue in the 1980s, and to examine how the CDU responded to this new political opportunity. It also provides scope for comparing the party's strategy in government (1982–1998) and in opposition (1998–2005); as well as variations in its strategy in response to the radical upheaval linked to reunification, and a phase of growth in support for the far-right (1989–1994).

OPPORTUNITIES AND RISKS OF ANTI-IMMIGRATION POLITICS

The POS literature seeks to explain strategies of political mobilization in terms of a party's perceptions of the costs and benefits of occupying a given 'space' – in this case, that of restrictive, conservative or anti-immigrant positions. The concept of 'space' presupposes the existence of a set of preferences amongst sections of society that have not been adequately represented within the existing configuration of party positions. By occupying this space, a party provides the opportunity to articulate such claims, with the intention of garnering electoral support.

The notion of political space would appear to be highly pertinent in the case of immigration. In the decades after World War II, migration policy in many European countries was characterized by élitist or clientelistic forms of policy-making (Hammar 1985; Freeman 1995). At least until the 1980s, policies on the recruitment of migrant labour, immigrant integration and citizenship acquisition tended to be the object of cross-party consensus and/or corporatist forms of decision-making. Such policies were designed to meet labour market needs and to promote social cohesion, but were not necessarily responsive to (generally more anti-immigrant) public preferences. Once political parties did start mobilizing support on immigration issues in the 1980s, it became clear that large parts of the electorate held considerably less tolerant views *vis-à-vis* immigration. In this sense, the relatively limited range of views being represented by the dominant political parties created space for anti-immigrant mobilization. And a number of parties, including centre-right parties, began to adjust their programmes accordingly.

However, attempts to mobilize support by articulating anti-immigrant views also carried risks. One danger flagged in some of the literature is that airing such views can bolster support for parties further to the right, by increasing the salience of these questions, or by making such positions more credible (Bale 2003). In this sense, occupying anti-immigrant space may not prove to be a wise strategic move for centre-right parties. Less explored in the literature, however, is a second type of risk, linked to the potential for a party to undermine the legitimacy of its own position. We can distinguish between three types of legitimacy that centre-right parties may put at risk through mobilization on migration issues.

Value legitimacy

This is the perception on the part of party members, (potential) supporters and relevant societal groups, that the party's rhetoric and programme correspond with ethical norms espoused by these constituencies. Centre-right parties tend to be catch-all parties, usually uniting disparate sets of voters, many of whom are fairly moderate in their views. Unlike in the case of far-right parties, we can assume that the mainstay of support is not susceptible to more radical positions. This means that centre-right parties need to be careful not to deviate from mainstream societal expectations about appropriate norms governing treatment of immigrants and ethnic minorities. In the case of Christian centre-right parties, the Church may be a particularly influential source of critique of populist approaches, typically espousing more humanitarian approaches to immigrants.

Programmatic coherence

The party's legitimacy also rests on its capacity to put forward and implement a coherent set of goals, avoiding excessive contradictions between different interests and policies. The restriction of migrant entry, rights of residents, or asylum policy can contradict human rights commitments; it may conflict with business interests in prolific and cheap supplies of labour, or with the goal of attracting a highly qualified work-force; and it may be incompatible with other foreign policy goals, such as European provisions on free movement, or bilateral relations with sending countries. Moreover, where restrictive positions imply mobilizing anti-immigrant sentiment, this can be socially divisive. Where these conflicts become explicit, or where certain goals are prioritized at the expense of others, parties may lose support.

Practical credibility

The third point concerns the capacity of centre-right parties to deliver on their promises of restrictive policies. Electoral guarantees to restrict immigration, reduce numbers of asylum seekers, or crack down on irregular migration, may not be feasible and once in power centre-right parties risk losing credibility if there is too pronounced a gap between rhetoric and action. We can distinguish between two types of factors that constrain the implementation of restrictive policies once a party is in power. The first is more formal: states are signed up to various constitutional commitments, treaties, and international agreements, which are often difficult to modify. They may impede attempts to deliver more restrictive measures. The second constraint is less formal, taking the form of path dependency. Policy choices in the past create a certain 'stickiness', or resistance to change, even where incumbents are keen to introduce a change in direction (Hansen 2000). These constraints can lead to a failure to implement electoral promises, thereby undermining the credibility of governments.

Different centre-right parties may be more or less susceptible to these potential problems of legitimacy; and, of course, they may be more or less astute in their assessment of, and reaction to, the risks involved. In some cases, centre-right parties, or factions and individuals within them, have badly misjudged these preconditions for legitimacy, and have suffered a loss of support as a result. Moreover, as we shall see later, the decision to occupy this anti-immigration 'space' can appear to be driven by the ideological proclivities of party members who may be out of tune with targeted voters. In short, while parties may hope to derive electoral advantages from mobilizing on migration issues, parties that do so also run the risk of losing legitimacy and credibility, especially over a longer period of time. And this in turn can have (sometimes severe) effects on their performance at the polls in future years.

THE CENTRE-RIGHT IN GERMANY

There are a number of parties in Germany which may be regarded – either now or at some point in their history – as being 'centre-right'. The CDU is the party that has traditionally fitted this ideological space. In the formative years of the

Federal Republic of Germany (FRG) the party became unambiguously associated with many of the country's success stories; the FRG's economic recovery, its embeddedness within the European Union (EU) and its successful return to the league of respected nations. The CDU's founders explicitly sought to incorporate both sides of the sectarian divide in a party which remained broadly conservative, broadly pro-church and largely supportive of pro-business policies. The strong 'social Catholic' wing (with especially robust representation in the Rhineland) and a more conservative Catholic wing in the south nonetheless exerted particular influence on many of the social and economic policies during the Adenauer years. The CDU's aim was, however, not to 're-Christianize' an increasingly secular Germany, but to apply a rather generalized set of Christian principles and values to practical politics. This involved a strong commitment to an organic model of society and a stress on integrating different social groupings into a unified, harmonious whole (Huntington and Bale 2002: 45). The leaders of the CDU, and Konrad Adenauer in particular, were expressly keen to stress that the CDU was subsequently a catch-all party of the centre, and not of the right. Adenauer built a broad coalition based on anti-socialism and Christian values, without extenuating the importance of ideology or class in the CDU's self-understanding. The CDU of the 1950s and 1960s therefore stressed social responsibility and a clear commitment to the social-market economy, ensuring that its main opponent, the Social Democratic Party (SPD), was inevitably forced leftwards.

The CDU dominated party politics until the mid-1960s and – no matter how one chooses to measure this in quantitative terms – was very much at the centre of Germany's ideological spectrum. To vote against the CDU was seen in many quarters as voting against many of the successes of German post-war democracy. In programmatic and ideological terms the CDU was therefore as much a party of the centre as of the centre-right. Through the 1980s, and certainly post-unification, this perception of the CDU's ideological position began to change; it became more clearly a party that was right of centre, mainly because of its positions on non-economic issues. Even now, the CDU's economic policies have more in common with what citizens of the UK would regard as the centre-left (i.e. Labour) than the centre-right/right. It no longer automatically dominated the 'centre' of the party system and it certainly did not occupy the pivotal point that it had done previously (the SPD took over this mantle). A reduction in the space afforded to socio-economic interventionism and a heightened interest in culturally traditionalist themes characterized a drift into what was – in a spatial sense – subsequently more 'classic' centre-right territory.

Germany has two further parties that certainly deserve some sort of brief discussion in this context; the CSU and the FDP. Both have, in different ways and at different times, been a part of the broadly defined German centre-right. The CSU is, of course, in rather a unique position. As the CDU's sister party, it only stands for election in Bavaria (where in turn the CDU does not compete) and has traditionally been more conservative, and yet also rather more 'social', in its orientation than its Christian Democratic partner. It has developed a unique role for itself as both a very successful Bavarian regional party, and a nationally significant actor. Although separate political organizations, the CDU and CSU sit together in the federal parliament and have proved to be a potent electoral force. Together they have embraced a broad alliance of voters as they prospered, in particular, in the elections of the first three post-war decades; it would therefore appear opportune to deal with these two distinct actors concurrently.

The only small party to initially forge a niche for itself in the German party system was the FDP, developing away from its original national-liberal ethos and articulating both greater economic liberalism and also a strong defence of civil liberties. It traditionally had a base that was composed mainly of middle- and upper-class professionals, and it has frequently been mocked as a party of dentists and doctors as well as 'Yuppies' and 'Dinkys'. The FDP's strategic position between Germany's two big *Volksparteien* saw it, until the late-1980s at least, reside firmly in the centre of the political spectrum with a traditional liberal ethos of protecting civil liberties and pushing for a liberalization of Germany's regulated social market economy. The position of the FDP has become much less comfortable in recent years and it is for this reason that it merits some discussion as a party that – at least spatially (if not necessarily ideologically) – has a link with the centre-right. We will therefore analyse its positions in passing.

THE CASE OF GERMANY: CDU MOBILIZATION ON MIGRATION ISSUES

Like other Christian Democrat parties, the CDU (although not the CSU) has seen a significant erosion in its voter support base since the mid-1980s (Dalton 2003). It has lost its position as the median party and it is faced – thanks to the stabilization of the Greens and *Die Linke* in the national party system – with a structural majority of left-leaning voters (Lösche 2003). Eastern Germans in particular are more inclined to vote for the SPD and *Die Linke* than are western Germans and this has forced the CDU to reassess its entire political strategy. Under these conditions, it was hardly surprising that the party would look for new issues with which to mobilize lost support. As with many other Christian Democratic parties, it was particularly drawn to two new directions: the embracing of a more liberal (if not neo-liberal, despite what its critics claim) economic policy; and appealing to more restrictionist policies in areas such as migration.

The CDU in power, 1982–1998: attempts to restrict immigration and asylum

It was only from the early 1980s that the Christian Democrats began to thematize the issue of immigration control. This was, in many ways, a clever choice. First, it was certainly an issue that was beginning to have popular resonance. Polls from 1982 suggest that two-thirds of German voters agreed that the guest workers recruited in the post-war period should return to their countries of origin, and only 11 per cent agreed that there should be intensified efforts to promote their integration (Schönwälder 1996: 166).

In addition to its popular appeal, highlighting the costs of migration provided a superficially plausible explanation for many of the country's socio-economic ills. Non-nationals could be depicted as competing with Germans for scarce jobs, housing, welfare assistance and social services. Probably more importantly for Christian Democrat voters, immigration-related issues fitted well with established traditions of defining membership of the German nation around ethno-cultural criteria (Brubaker 1992). This pattern of identification was arguably sustained after World War II as a justification for Germany's continued political claim to reunification and the inclusion of the Germans in the German Democratic Republic (GDR) and minorities in the rest of central and eastern Europe within the German nation (Joppke 1998). Clearly, this was not the only available philosophy of membership, but it certainly appealed to more conservative supporters, and, from the early 1980s onwards, Chancellor Helmut Kohl was willing to capitalize on this. This is therefore not a case of the Christian Democrats merely reacting to the perceived policy choices/political challenges of others (i.e. the far-right). CDU and CSU politicians chose this course not just for its hypothesized electoral expediency; they also did it out of (at least a degree of) conviction.

In his 1982 government statement, Kohl announced that immigration policy would be one of the four priorities for his new administration. Reaffirming the mantra that Germany was 'not an immigration country', he announced that his government aimed to reduce the number of resident non-nationals by promoting their return to their home countries, as well as preventing further inflows (Herbert 2001: 250). Above all, the pronouncement was targeted at Turkish non-nationals. Many Christian Democrat politicians emphasized what were considered to be the particular problems in integrating immigrants of Muslim background, who, unlike Italian or Greek immigrants, were considered incapable of integrating into German culture. Interior Minister Friedrich Zimmermann subsequently introduced financial incentives to encourage non-nationals to return 'home'. The government also attempted to reduce so-called 'family reunion' through restricting possibilities for non-national children to join their parents already resident in West Germany. Neither policy proved to be a success. In the case of return policy, the incentives were largely ineffectual (Herbert 2001: 255). Christian Democrat attempts to restrict family reunion, meanwhile, ran into strong opposition from its coalition partner the FDP, as well as from the churches, which pointed to the constitutionally enshrined duty of government to safeguard the family (Article 6 of the Basic Law). A subsequent attempt to modify the Foreigners Law in 1988 to impose a more restrictive system of residence permits also failed, largely owing to pressure from within the government.

Throughout its first term in office the government continued to encounter major hurdles in implementing its programme. The FDP maintained its resistance to plans to restrict rights to family reunion, and the government failed to produce a bill on this during its first term in office. When the bill was finally introduced in 1987 it provoked heated debate, encountering heavy criticism not just from the left but also internally, and it did not become law until a full three years later (and then only in diluted form). There was further tension over the question of the rights of Turkish workers to free movement. An Association Agreement between Turkey and the European Community contained a clause allowing free movement from 1986 onwards, and the CDU and CSU were keen to revoke this. This was fiercely resisted by FDP foreign minister Hans-Dietrich Genscher who at one stage even threatened to resign if the government failed to respect its commitments to Turkey. All in all, and despite the tough rhetoric of 1982–83, immigration did not become a central plank of government policy over this period, and the Kohl government clearly did not deliver the restrictive agenda that it had promised.

From around 1986, political attention began to switch away from immigration to the question of asylum. Throughout the 1950s and 1960s West Germany received relatively few asylum applications, but, during the late 1970s, the number increased rapidly to reach a high of 107,000 in 1980. While many applicants did not qualify for asylum under the definitions set out in the German Basic Law or the Geneva Convention on Refugees, a substantial number were able to prolong their stay by making use of West Germany's generous provisions for appeal. They were subsequently granted the right to stay on humanitarian grounds (Green *et al.* 2007: 95). Some in the CDU (and the CSU) argued that Germany would only be able to keep numbers manageable and prevent abuse of the system if it amended its constitutional commitment to the 'right to asylum'. However, major reform proved to be politically unfeasible, hence the government contented itself with the introduction of new procedural restrictions. While these measures may have contributed to a reduction in applications during the mid-1980s, the number of asylum seekers rose again in the latter years of that decade to reach 121,000 in 1989.

In 1987 the CDU debated whether or not to make asylum an election theme. The party's General Secretary, Heiner Geißler, warned that making asylum into an electoral issue would 'provoke an escalation of emotions and feelings', and raise expectations that the party would never be able to fulfil (cited in Herbert 2001: 271–2). But Geißler was in a minority; the prevalent view was that asylum had become a political issue that the CDU could not afford to ignore, and that it was legitimate to respond to voters' worries. The problem of asylum 'abuse' subsequently became a central issue in the campaign.

The number of asylum seekers reached crisis levels following the end of the Cold War. With united Germany lying at the heart of Europe, it continued to receive by far the largest share of asylum seekers in the EU, with over 1.2 million applications between 1990 and 1993. The sense of crisis in German immigration was exacerbated by events in the new *Länder*. As part of the reunification treaty, from December 1990 20 per cent of asylum seekers were dispersed to the eastern states – a policy that was introduced with minimal preparation and at a time of substantial social and economic upheaval in these areas. At the same time, hundreds of thousands of *Aussiedler*, ethnic Germans from eastern Europe, were also arriving in the Federal Republic. In areas of eastern Germany tensions escalated into shocking incidents of anti-immigrant violence (notably in Hoyerswerda and Rostock). In the west, meanwhile, there was a widespread perception of an asylum crisis, and panic about a mass influx of refugees and *Aussiedler*. There were also sporadic outbreaks of anti-immigrant violence there too (most notably in Sollingen and Mölln). A poll of 1991 suggested that more than 70 per cent of western Germans considered the question of refugees and immigration to be 'very important' political issues; unemployment scored only 10 per cent (Betz 1994: 69).

The far-right were able to exploit this panic, and the German People's Union (DVU) began to make electoral ground in eastern Germany whilst the Republicans continued to mobilize rather more in the western states. The CDU publicly attributed rising right-wing extremism and violence to the 'unresolved asylum problem', holding the SPD responsible because of its continued resistance to a constitutional amendment (Berg 2000: 199). Under considerable pressure, the SPD accepted a compromise on the asylum question in December 1992, agreeing to amend the right to asylum in the Basic Law. They secured concessions from the CDU not just to ease rules on naturalization of non-nationals, but also to fix a quota for the number of *Aussiedler* relocating to Germany each year (for a discussion, see Thränhardt 2000).

It is important to note that the Christian Democrat positioning on asylum was not driven exclusively by perceived electoral gains. Right up until 1998, leading figures from both the CDU and CSU, including successive Interior Ministers, continued to argue that Germany was *not* a country of immigration. This rigid cultural conservatism prevailed not because they thought that it was an 'electoral winner', but rather as many party stalwarts simply believed it to be true. They claimed that Germany had never sought, and indeed still did not seek, actively to recruit permanent migrants to settle in the country, in the way that countries such as the United States and Canada had done in the past. Many within these parties viewed immigration from non-European or non-Judeo-Christian cultures as potentially undermining social cohesion, and they opposed notions of multiculturalism. Cultural conservatism on this issue may not be as strong as it was pre-1998, but it certainly still exists, and continues to shape approaches to immigration and integration policies (Boswell 2000).

The CDU in opposition, 1998–2005: citizenship, *Leitkultur* and the Immigration Law

Shaken by its defeat in the 1998 election, the CDU appeared subsequently to be more willing to make use of populist forms of mobilization. Writing in 1998 about possible new strategies for the CDU, Konrad Schuller, for example, pointed out the advantages of focusing on issues of national identity: the CDU would be able to attract voters in both western and eastern Germany through capitalizing on the 'newly awakened theme of ethnic homogeneity' (Schuller 1998: 114). And this is indeed what the party did. The CDU quickly seized the opportunity to mobilize support against the SPD–Green government's attempts to reform and update Germany's (at times antiquated) citizenship and naturalization laws. From late 1998–1999 it launched a major campaign to mobilize German citizens against dual citizenship, under the leadership of then CSU Bavarian Minister-President Edmund Stoiber. In fact, the practice of dual citizenship had been widely tolerated throughout the 1990s, and the law simply aimed to codify this in a more systematic way (Joppke 2000: 153). The scale of the campaign, and the rhetoric used, far surpassed previous CDU campaigns. The Christian Democrat parties managed to gather 5 million signatures against the law, which was described by Stoiber as 'more dangerous to Germany's domestic security than the terrorism of the Red Army Faction in the 1970s and 1980s' (Joppke 2000: 155). It was widely perceived that the CDU were able to win the Hesse *Land* election in February 1999 through mobilization on this platform (Benthin 2004: 170). The mobilization strategy therefore appeared to have reaped significant electoral dividends at the regional level, at least in the short term.

A second significant area for mobilization was the Red–Green government's proposals to ease restrictions on labour migration. The debate was triggered by the introduction of a 'Green Card' programme in Spring 2000, designed to attract high-skilled information technology (IT) workers to Germany. The CDU opposed the programme on the grounds that Germany should invest resources to train indigenous workers to fill vacancies, rather than recruiting foreigners – a position captured in the famous slogan for the May 2000 North Rhine-Westphalia elections, 'Kinder statt Inder' ('Children instead of Indians'). The SPD–Green government, however, persisted in its attempts to open up a public debate on labour migration. In 2001 it established an independent commission headed by the liberal-oriented CDU politician Rita Süssmuth. The Commission's report, which was issued in July that year, recommended a number of channels to recruit high-skilled workers to Germany. Many of the Commission's proposals were incorporated into a draft Immigration Law, which was approved by the lower chamber but subsequently blocked by the Bundesrat in March 2002, where the Red–Green coalition had a majority of just one.

The publicity attracted by this dramatic vote, as well as the controversial cross-party negotiations on the bill in 2003–2004, gave the CDU ample opportunity to air their views on migration. A persistent theme was the CDU's opposition to the government's plan to lift the foreign worker 'recruitment ban' of 1973: a largely symbolic change given that there were already multiple exceptions to it. But warnings about the consequences of lifting the ban evoked fears of a return to the pre-1973 era of large-scale, low-skilled labour migration. Another prominent theme was the irresponsibility of admitting more immigrant labour in a situation of high unemployment in Germany; with 4.5 million unemployed, the priority should be to train Germans rather than to recruit more people from abroad. Characteristically, the old concerns about multiculturalism and identity re-emerged. Many CDU politicians stressed the need to integrate already resident non-nationals before admitting new ones. Wolfgang Bosbach, for example, deputy chair of the CDU/CSU parliamentary party, considered that Germany had already reached the limits of its absorption capacity. Peter Müller, Minister-President of Saarland, meanwhile, was concerned about the 'socio-demographic profile of many immigrants', and their limited capacity to integrate (CDU-Bundesgeschäftsstelle 2003).

There have also been several fairly isolated episodes of mobilization on issues of integration and German identity. In October 2000, the CDU politician Friedrich Merz announced that the CDU/CSU parliamentary group, of which he was then leader, would make immigration a central theme of the next national election. In this context, he called upon immigrants to adapt themselves to German 'Leitkultur'. The CDU attempted to define this fuzzy concept more clearly in its subsequent report on immigration, listing loyalty to the constitution, knowledge of the German language, and acceptance of human rights and the equality of women (Hentges 2002). But the concept provoked considerable criticism, and met with derision from large sections of the media. Other attempts at mobilizing support for more robust assimilation of non-nationals revolved around the issue of the poor performance of their children in the German education system; and concerns about Muslim immigrants, especially in the wake of the September 11 terrorist attacks.

Perhaps surprisingly, immigration did not feature as a central issue in the national election of 2002 or 2005. So while the CDU's stint in opposition clearly provided an opportunity to advance more restrictive policies on areas such as citizenship, labour migration and integration, it chose not to emphasize these positions in national election campaigns. This may be partly because of the lack of political space left by the government: the SPD Interior Minister Otto Schily earned a reputation as being tough on crime, terrorism and immigration. And the government had backed down from more liberal positions on citizenship and immigration, with the result that the CDU was not able to capitalize on these differences when it came to national polls. As we shall see, however, there are a number of other explanations, linked to the political risks faced by adopting more populist stances.

POLITICIZING MIGRATION: OPPORTUNITY OR LIABILITY?

As suggested above, there are three ways in which the centre-right risks a loss of legitimacy through mobilizing on migration issues: it may create a deficit of value legitimacy in the eyes of party members or (potential) voters; it may produce an impression of incoherence because of inconsistency with other policy goals; or it may engender a loss of confidence in the party's capacity to implement election promises once in power. Drawing on the account above, it is interesting to consider which, if any, of these problems the CDU has encountered as a result of its attempts to exploit political opportunities to lobby on migration issues.

Value legitimacy

The Christian Democrats have shown themselves to be vulnerable to criticism from the Church, and the possible loss of support from its more socially oriented wing. This was probably most clear on issues of asylum and refugee policy, including the 1992 constitutional compromise (Bösch 2002: 274). High-profile electoral successes that were built on platforms where anti-immigration rhetoric played a significant part (such as the Hesse election of 1999) did not blind CDU leaders to the inherent dangers of alienating more liberal parts of their membership and electorate in the longer term. The Christian Democrats have lost face through a number of (less successful) popu-list manoeuvres. The debacle triggered by the 'Children instead of Indians' slogan proved this beyond all doubt, with the party severely criticized for the racist overtones of its campaign. The *Leitkultur* debate is also illustrative of this, highlighting how CDU politicians can be adept at retreating quickly from less tenable positions when this proves politically expedient.

However, the CDU also benefits from a relative lack of societal disapproval when it comes to ethnocentric discourse: it is still quite legitimate within large sections of society to reject multiculturalism, or to label certain groups as unable to integrate. In comparison to countries such as the UK or the Netherlands, there is a wider acceptance of the type of more ethno-nationalist rhetoric that CDU politicians periodically produced. Linked to this, the CDU has also benefited from the absence of a strong ethnic minority or immi-grant vote. Because of low naturalization rates (less than 5 per cent of voters fall into this category), most of the guest-worker generation and their descendants cannot vote and have little interest in going down the long and expensive route that would enable them to do so (Green 2005). Indeed, the majority of citizens who acquired citizenship between 1989 and 1998 were *Aussiedler*, a group which is classified as being ethnically German and which tends to have rather more conservative political views (Wüst 2004: 342). They therefore pose few problems for the CDU and CSU in terms of value legitimacy and immigration policy. *Aussiedler* are not just ethnically German, they also tend to be more religious (generally meaning more Catholic), and it should come as no surprise that around 70 per cent of ethnic Germans from the terri-tory of what was once the Soviet Union, 60 per cent from Romania and over 50 per cent of those originally from Poland support the CDU/CSU (Wüst 2004: 346, 351).

The CDU's unwillingness to support ideas of multiculturalism or religious pluralism may not prevent it from attracting *Aussiedler* votes, but it clearly does not assist it in attracting support from other groups of naturalized citizens; Andreas Wüst indicates that over 60 per cent of naturalized Turks tend towards the SPD, whilst barely 11 per cent favour the Christian Democrats. Thus, any concerns the Christian Democrats may have about value legitimacy have certainly not been pressing enough to prompt them to embrace culturally pluralist or even multicultural positions that might attract more conservative German citizens of Turkish origin (Wüst 2004).

Programmatic coherence

The Kohl government did encounter problems with its policy of promoting the return of Turkish *Gastarbeiter* and its attempts to modify European Community commitments to free movement of Turkish nationals – both of which created tensions in bilateral relations with Ankara, as well as within the coalition government. These concerns were voiced most articulately by the FDP foreign minister of the time, Hans-Dietrich Genscher, illustrating the important role that the Free Democrats played in de-radicalizing some of the Christian Democrats' more contentious policy rhetoric. As the CDU increasingly embraces a more liberal economic policy, we can expect further tensions to emerge between economic and immigration policies. This may well be a more serious problem, particularly in the longer term, with projected demographic trends almost certainly generating acute labour shortages in coming decades. Although the Immigration Law of January 2005 marked a significant turning point in German immigration policy, it would clearly be wrong to conclude that it is the end of the story. CDU immigration and citizenship policy is caught between the need to attract more high-skilled labour and manage what is effectively cultural pluralism whilst not neglecting the political imperative to emphasize restrictionist credentials to the electorate.

Programmatic tensions also stem from another source: the EU. The EU is a major source of policy content in the area of immigration. The trend towards greater Europeanization of many policies is likely to continue, and yet Germany – and the Christian Democrats in particular – may not be as traditionally supportive of this agenda as they once were. When EU-level co-operation in immigration and asylum was formalized in the 1992 Maastricht Treaty, Chancellor Kohl's government was a major driving force behind this initiative (Green *et al.* 2007: 109). Kohl hoped to 'export' the asylum issue, which at that stage was completely dominating domestic politics, to the EU arena (Henson and Malhan 1995). However, by the time the Amsterdam Treaty, which brought immigration and asylum under the so-called 'first pillar', came into force in 1999, support for a full Europeanization of this policy area had dropped in temperature from red-hot to decidedly tepid (Hellmann 2006). The reason for this lay in the fact that, by then, Germany had instituted its own measures to restrict asylum under the 1992 reforms. Yet at European level, German negotiators were now being confronted by countries adopting positions which were frequently more liberal than their own, especially in asylum and family reunification policy. Germany's – and the CDU's (and CSU's) – concerns that its own standards, which it perceives as rigorous, could be 'hollowed out' have made it reluctant to support the full harmonization of policy necessary to make this policy area work at EU level (Green *et al.* 2007: 109–10).

Practical credibility

The asylum compromise of 1992 demonstrated that where there is a clear interest in 'regaining sovereignty' even constitutional constraints can be overcome in the area of immigration control (Joppke 1998). However, the Kohl government was not able to reverse constitutional provisions that allowed for the expansion of rights of long-term residents in, for example, rulings on the right to family reunion, or protection from deportation. Moreover, the constraints of coalition politics – ruling with the more liberal FDP – meant that the Christian Democratic parties were unable to implement large parts of their 1983 programme on migration.

The demands of business for migrant labour and migrant communities themselves have evolved at a much faster rate, leaving public policy to play a more or less perpetual game of 'catch-up'. Thus, the effectiveness of the 'Green Card' programme of 2000 was severely compromised by the bureaucracy's highly restrictive approach to any new labour migration, even of high-skilled workers. This programme subsequently represented nothing more than a tentative first step in the direction of liberalization. It is likely that employers will continue to press for expanded opportunities for recruiting foreign labour in sectors facing acute shortages. This is likely to raise serious dilemmas for any future CDU government, forcing the party to juggle its business-friendly leanings with a more populist restrictionist stance.

Finally, it is worth pointing out a particular problem faced by opposition parties in the German political system. Even where anti-immigration positions do garner support from voters, the consensual system of decision-making means that this does not always translate into electoral gains. Because of the need to pass legislation through the upper chamber (which is often composed of a majority of opposition parties) incumbents must continuously adjust their policies to meet opposition criticisms. By the time it comes to the next national election, a compromise may already have been reached, and there is limited opportunity for the opposition party to capitalize on its critical position. This was clearly the case with the CDU(/CSU)'s opposition to the Immigration Bill of 2001, which became the object of a compromise deal in Spring 2004, thereby removing it from the electoral agenda in Autumn 2005. The same was true of their critique of the Citizenship Law of 1998, with the compromise being reached in May 1999, well before the next election of Autumn 2002 (although the 1998–1999 debate did contribute to local electoral gains). Paradoxically, then, opposition parties would benefit electorally from a concentration of legislative power in the hands of the incumbent government.

CONCLUSION

The CDU has, by and large, been keen to tap into the perceived electoral advantages of anti-immigrant positions. This can to a large extent be understood as a calculated strategy to articulate popular anxieties about the economic and social impacts of immigration in Germany. The concern to occupy this 'space' was in theory rendered more urgent by the rise of the Republicans and DVU (and latterly the National Democractic Party – the NPD) on their right flank, with these parties displaying no qualms about using anti-immigrant language. The anti-immigrant violence in the early 1990s undoubtedly led to greater interest in immigration issues. Yet, whilst there is evidence that the CDU/CSU did indeed harden policy stances as a result of specific, high-profile events, it is far from clear that this was done because of specific worries about the far-right mobilizing support on account of them. The Republicans in particular may well have been an electoral threat, but there was also a strong feeling that something also had to be done to change failed policy choices. It was that worry that drove CDU/CSU policy development rather than the need to head off political extremists at the pass. The centre-right's propensity to adopt more restrictionist positions was therefore not simply a case of reacting to public opinion or the tactics of their far-right competitors. Many in the CDU (and CSU) were personally committed to the rather more hard-line rhetoric that they espoused, regardless of political expediency.

The more interesting question is therefore whether the CDU will rediscover its traditional ability to win elections frequently or whether it will – much as has happened to the British Conservatives – choose to articulate restrictive positions on issues such as immigration which appeal to some of its core supporters but in reality may not be so attractive to more liberal/left-leaning social democratic oriented voters. The considerable number of veto players in the German political system makes implementing tighter immigration policies difficult, and even the more right-wing members of the CDU are aware that balancing more restrictive policies with the 'social' ethos of their parties, as well as business interests, will be politically tricky. More overtly, there seems to be little evidence that the CDU's intransigence over immigration reforms has won it many voters in the *national* arena. While ideological differences between left and right are frequently only expressed indirectly, there can be little doubt that there is clear water between the centre-right and its more left-wing opponents in this area. And yet voters seem unwilling to cast their ballots on this basis (the Hesse regional election of 1999 being a notable exception). Having said this, there may well be one issue which potentially serves to ratchet up the debate another notch: the impending question of Turkey's prospective membership of the EU, and the issue of free movement of Turkish nationals. This may serve to ignite the party political touch-paper in the coming years.

We have highlighted the complex nature of the immigration issue for the centre-right in contemporary German politics. On the one hand, the CDU sees genuine electoral opportunities in granting this issue-complex an increased profile in its election campaigning. A significant number of its members genuinely believe in restrictionist and, in many ways, decidedly antiquated notions of citizenship and integration. Cultural conservatism thus remains a significant part of the CDU's (and CSU's) political DNA. The POS literature nevertheless highlights both the limitations and risks that the parties face in articulating these demands too fiercely. The CDU has a strongly Christian core and is moving (if only slowly) in the direction of free markets, implying that restrictionist stances on issues such as labour migration and asylum are likely to generate concerns about value legitimacy and programmatic consistency. The successive attempts of Christian Democratic administrations to revise German immigration laws have also illustrated how difficult it can be to implement coherent sets of policies that chime with the party's original programmatic claims. Talk, for many in the CDU on this issue, remains much easier than action. And this is something that is likely to remain true for many years to come.

ACKNOWLEDGEMENTS

Drafts of this paper were initially presented at an ESRC seminar in Cambridge (January 2005) and a follow-up meeting in Cambridge in June 2007. We would like to thank participants of both workshops for their extremely helpful comments, and especially Tim Bale and Julie Smith for organizing the events. Tim Bale also provided thorough and extremely helpful comments on a number of versions of this paper. Finally, we would like to thank the anonymous reviewers for their insightful comments and suggestions.

REFERENCES

Bale, T. (2003) 'Cinderella and her ugly sisters: the mainstream and extreme right in Europe's bipolarising party systems', *West European Politics* 26(3): 67–90.

Benthin, R. (2004) *Auf dem Weg in die Mitte: Öffentlichkeitsstrategien der Neuen Rechten*, Frankfurt-am-Main: Campus.

Berg, H. (2000) *Politische Mitte und Rechtsextremismus: Diskurse zu fremdfeindlicher Gewalt im 12. Deutschen Bundestag (1990–1994)*, Opladen: Leske & Budrich.

Betz, H.-G. (1994) *Radical Right-wing Populism in Western Europe*, New York: St Martin's Press.

Bösch, F. (2002) *Macht und Machtverlust: Die Geschichte der CDU*, Stüttgart: Deustche Verlags-Anstalt.

Boswell, C. (2000) 'European values and the asylum crisis', *International Affairs* 76(3): 537–57.

Boswell, C. (2007) 'Theorizing migration policy: is there a Third Way?', *International Migration Review* 41(1): 75–100.

Brubaker, R. (1992) *Citizenship and Nationhood in France and Germany*, Cambridge, MA: Harvard University Press.

CDU-Bundesgeschäftsstelle (2003) 'CDU/CSU-Innenpolitiker geschlossen gegen rot-grünes Zuwanderungserweiterungsgesetz', 2 April.

Dalton, R.J. (2003) 'Voter choice and electoral politics', in S. Padgett, W.E. Paterson and G. Smith (eds), *Developments in German Politics 3*, Basingstoke: Palgrave, pp. 60–81.

Freeman, G.P. (1995) 'Modes of immigration politics in liberal democratic states', *International Migration Review* 29(4): 881–902.

Green, S.O. (2005) 'Between ideology and pragmatism: the politics of dual nationality in Germany', *International Migration Review* 39(4): 921–52.

Green, S.O., Hough, D., Miskimmon, A. and Timmins, G. (2007) *The Politics of the New Germany*, London: Routledge.

Hammar, T. (1985) *European Immigration Policy: A Comparative Study*, Cambridge: Cambridge University Press.

Hansen, R. (2002) 'Globalization, embedded realism, and path dependency: the other immigrants to Europe', *Comparative Political Studies* 35(3): 259–83.

Hellmann, G. (ed.) (2006) *Germany's EU Policy on Asylum and Defence: De-Europeanization by Default?*, Basingstoke: Palgrave.

Henson, R. and Malhan, N. (1995) 'Endeavours to export a migration crisis: policy making and Europeanisation in the German migration dilemma', *German Politics* 4(3): 128–44.

Hentges, G. (2002) 'Das Plädoyer für eine "deutsche Leitkultur" – Steilvorlage für die extreme Rechte?', in C. Butterwegge (ed.), *Themem der Rechten – Themen der Mitte: Zuwanderung, demographischer Wandel und Nationalbewusstsein*, Opladen: Leske & Budrich, pp. 95–121.

Herbert, U. (2001) *Geschichte der Ausländerpolitik in Deutschland: Saisonarbeiter, Zwangsarbeiter, Gastarbeiter, Flüchtlinge*, Munich: Verlag C.H. Beck.

Hollifeld, J.F. (1990) 'Immigration and the French state: problems of policy implementation', *Comparative Political Studies* 23(1): 56–79.

Huntington, N. and Bale, T. (2002) 'New Labour: new Christian democracy', *Political Quarterly* 73(1): 44–50.

Joppke, C. (1998) *Immigration and the Nation-state: The United States, Germany, and Great Britain*, Oxford: Oxford University Press.

Joppke, C. (2000) 'Mobilization of culture and the reform of citizenship law: Germany and the United States', in R. Koopmans and P. Statham (eds), *Challenging Immigration and Ethnic Relations Politics: Comparative European Perspectives*, Oxford: Oxford University Press, pp. 145–61.

Koopmans, R. and Statham, P. (2000) 'Migration and ethnic relations as a field of political contention: an opportunity structure approach', in R. Koopmans and P. Statham (eds), *Challenging Immigration and Ethnic Relations Politics: Comparative European Perspectives*, Oxford: Oxford University Press, pp. 13–56.

Lösche, P. (2003) 'The German party system after the 2002 Bundestag elections', *German Politics* 12(3): 66–81.

Schönwälder, K. (1996) 'Migration, refugees and ethnic plurality as issues of public and political debates in (West) Germany', in M. Fulbrook and D. Cesarani (eds), *Citizenship, Nationality and Migration in Europe*, London: Routledge, pp. 159–78.

Schuller, K. (1998) 'Zwischen Kalten Krieg und neuer Republik: Die Berliner CDU auf der Suche nach Identität', in T. Dürr and R. Soldt (eds), *Die CDU nach Kohl*, Frankfurt: Fischer, pp. 98–114.

Tarrow, S. (1998) *Power in Movement: Social Movements and Contentious Politics*, Cambridge: Cambridge University Press.

Thränhardt, D. (2000) 'Conflict, consensus, and policy outcomes: immigration and integration in Germany and the Netherlands', in R. Koopmans and P. Statham (eds), *Challenging Immigration and Ethnic Relations Politics: Comparative European Perspectives*, Oxford: Oxford University Press, pp. 162–86.

Wüst, A. (2004) 'Naturalised citizens as voters: behaviour and impact', *German Politics* 13(2): 341–59.

Il rombo dei cannoni? Immigration and the centre-right in Italy[1]

Andrew Geddes

INTRODUCTION

> *'Io voglio sentire il rombo dei cannoni . . . altrimenti non la finiamo più'* ('I want to hear the sound of cannons . . . otherwise this story will never end'), Umberto Bossi, Leader of the Lega Nord, *Corriere della Sera*, 16 June 2002.

Why did governing centre-right parties in Italy led by Silvio Berlusconi between 2001 and 2006, which at times employed strident anti-immigration rhetoric and introduced apparently highly restrictive immigration legislation, preside over record levels of immigration and the most generous regularization in Italian – if not European – history? The period 2001–06 saw the largest growth in the legally resident immigrant population in Italian history from 1.3 million in October 2001 to 2.67 million in January 2006. This included

646,000 people who had their status regularized in 2002–03 (ISTAT 2006). Yet, elements within the governing coalition continued to employ hard-line anti-immigration rhetoric and even threaten military action against immigrants, as the above quote from Bossi illustrates.

The key immigration measure introduced by the centre-right was the Bossi–Fini law of 2002 (Law No. 189 of 30 July 2002), which has been understood in a number of ways: as containing harsh and repressive elements (Einaudi 2007), as racist (Ballerini and Benna 2002), or as a far more ambiguous mix of extremism, tempered by implicit moderation and provoking unintended consequences, that was only a 'pallid echo' of proposals made during the CdL's (Casa delle Libertà's) 2001 election campaign (Colombo and Sciortino 2003). Pugliese (2006) sees contradictory elements in that the Bossi–Fini law made it easier for immigrants to regularize their status, but more difficult for them to renew a residence permit. The period has thus been seen as characterized by contradictions and paradoxes (see also Zincone 2006).

This contribution's argument is that party system and governmental variables underpin these apparent paradoxes and contradictions. While the gap between rhetoric and reality could be presented as paradoxical or as some kind of puzzle, it is really nothing of the sort. The 'gap' is actually a standard outcome across Europe (and other liberal states) (Cornelius *et al.* 1994, 2004) and is suggestive of political and institutional limitations on state capacity to regulate international migration. Such limitations are by now a well-established theme in the immigration literature (Geddes 2003). At a more specific level, this contribution shows how, why and when the Italian political system mediated the relationship between the party political debate about immigration and the development of legislation. It also addresses a point made by observers of migration policy-making that policies often 'fail' in that they do not achieve restrictive objectives (Calavita 2004; Castles 2004a, 2004b). Such accounts tend to read back from policy outcomes to account for policy failings without specifying political processes that generate 'failure'. To address this point, this contribution distinguishes between three interrelated aspects of the political process characterized as 'talk', 'decision' and 'action' (Brunsson 1993, 2002). While interrelated, each of these three stages can be governed by different logics; for example, by electoral positioning and appeals to core party supporters that may induce tough talk on immigration. For instance, the Lega's 'often vulgar' expression (Cotta and Verzichelli 2007: 49) was evident in the discursive construction of immigration policy within the coalition, but extreme rhetoric was difficult to integrate when intra-coalition negotiations occurred as pressures were brought to bear by key social interests.[2] Neither 'talk' nor 'decision' need correspond with 'action' as shifts to implementation reveal differences between 'institutional' and 'technical' environments (Meyer and Rowan 1977). The former signifies structures, processes and ideologies within the political process while the latter refers to practical issues associated with regulating highly complex, diverse and fast-changing migratory phenomena in a relatively new country of immigration such as Italy. While the focus is on the political-institutional environment, there are significant practical constraints on Italy's ability to regulate immigration as there is a need for migrant workers, the country is proximate to major sending countries and regions, and it has long, hard-to-police coastal borders.

There are specific elements of Italian politics that inhibit the comparative reach of this contribution's analysis, particularly the dislocation in the party system following the political crisis of 1992–94 that created space for apparently anti-system parties such as the Lega Nord. That said, Italy was identified by Freeman (1995) as a 'critical case' for the new immigration countries in southern Europe. By this he meant whether or not Italy would confirm his supposition that new countries of immigration would conform with a general tendency towards expansive and inclusive immigration policies (Freeman 1995: 893). Expansiveness would occur because the concentrated beneficiaries of migration (business interests and pro-migrant groups) would have a stronger incentive to organize than diffuse cost bearers (the general public). In the mid-1990s Italy was seen to have a hostile public, expansionist policies and major parties that were largely silent on the issue, seemingly fearful of providing opportunities for the right.

This contribution analyses the centre-right in Italy since 1994, explores centre-right 'talk' about immigration prior to and during the 2001 election campaign, presents an overview of recent immigration to Italy and then focuses on intra-coalition negotiation, the content of the Bossi–Fini law and the subsequent regularization. The shift from 'talk' to 'decision' is central to the argument in order to show how and why party system and governmental variables generate supposed policy failure, which, from the point of view of some political actors, may be seen as successes.

THE CENTRE-RIGHT IN ITALY

The heterogeneous and fragmented *Casa delle Libertà* (CdL, House of Freedoms) coalition that won the 2001 general election comprised four centre-right parties: the 'business party' of *Forza Italia* (FI) led by 'the knight of anti-politics' Silvio Berlusconi (Pasquino 2007), the 'post-fascist' *Alleanza Nazionale* (AN) led by Gianfranco Fini; the northern-based regional populists of the Lega Nord led by Umberto Bossi and the *Centro Cristiano Democratico–Cristiani Democratici Uniti* (Ccd–Cdu) who fought the 2001 election as the *Biancofiore* (white flower coalition) and formed the *Unione dei Democratici Cristiani* (UDC). The Ccd–Cdu represented the 'old' within the 'new' in the sense that they were the more direct inheritors of the once dominant Christian Democratic party (*Democrazia Cristiana*, DC). The 'compound' identities of FI and Ccd–Cdu/UDC became apparent as this analysis develops with FI containing both 'radical' and 'liberal' elements while Ccd–Cdu has strong links with Caritas and other Church organizations. While AN and Lega Nord dominated policy debate and led calls for tough immigration legislation, the Ccd–Cdu/UDC played a key role in negotiating the content of legislation and found some sympathy within FI. As Ignazi (2003: 994) puts it, the Christian Democrats 'succeeded in gaining the role of the moderate and bargaining-oriented component, thus acquiring far more relevance in the political arena'.

While the contemporary centre-right in Europe tends to be defined by some combination of economic liberalism with traditions of solidarity, the Italian centre-right is far more heterogeneous and fragmented. There were no parties in Italy using the centre-right label until 1994. The right-wing descriptor was not used by mainstream parties during the first republic when the 'white' and 'red' cultures of the DC and Communist Party (PCI) dominated Italian politics (Diamanti 2003; Cotta and Verzichelli 2007). Right-wing politics was associated with extremism and the more explicitly fascist *Movimento Sociale Italiano* (Italian Social Movement, MSI), which has since largely morphed into the AN (Ignazi 1994, 2002; Fella and Ruzza 2006).

The leading party on the centre-right was FI, created, led and symbolized by Berlusconi who 'went on to the pitch', as he put it, to defend the centre and the right against post-communists (Poli 2001; Ginsborg 2004). At the 1994, 1996 and 2001 general elections, Berlusconi was the centre-right's undisputed leader and fought a highly personalized campaign in which his power and patrimony as Italy's richest man were made evident as he offered a *contratto con gli italiani* (a contract with the Italian people). Billboards across the country showed a photo of Berlusconi informing Italians of his commitment to decrease taxation, reduce the size of the state, increase expenditure on public works in the south, cut crime, reform the judicial system and, significantly in the context of this analysis, control illegal immigration while welcoming migrants who came to work (Newell 2002).

The emergence of FI on the centre-right together with AN and Lega Nord is illustrative of new phases of party development as the mass parties of the Italian first republic were challenged by 'autonomous formations' such as FI and Lega Nord that placed less emphasis on social roots and more on media presence and the replacement of ideology with loyalty (Diamanti 2003: 16). FI has been seen as 'the most innovative element of the new political landscape by virtue of its nature and its political structure' (Cotta and Verzichelli 2007: 59). While ostensibly new, FI does also bring together elements of the old DC, plus some socialists, republicans and liberals from the older governing majority. It has become the largest party in Italy in terms of popular votes, but has not been able to govern alone.

At the May 2001 general election, FI were confirmed as the largest party in the centre-right coalition with nearly 30 per cent of the popular vote and 60 per cent of the centre-right vote (see Table 1).[3] During the 'first republic', Italian politics was characterized by centrifugal pluralism (Sartori 2005). The electoral system introduced in 1993 induced centripetal dynamics prior to elections as parties coalesced on the centre-left and centre-right. Post-election, however, there continued to be centrifugal dynamics, as parties entered into pre-election coalitions in order to maximize seats, but were not bound to honour agreements

Table 1 Results of the 2001 Italian general election

	Chamber of Deputies		Senate	
	Vote (%)	Seats	Vote (%)	Seats
Casa delle Libertà				
Forza Italia	29.4	178		
Alleanza Nazionale	12	99		
Ccd–Cdu	3.2	40		
Lega Nord	3.9	30		
Nuovo PSI	1	3		
Total	**49.5**	**350**	**42.5**	**176**
Ulivo				
DS	16.6	138		
Verdi & SDI	2.2	17		
Margherita	14.5	80		
PdCI	1.7	9		
Total	**35**	**244**	**39.2**	**128**
Rifondazione Comunista	5.0	11	5.1	4
Others	10.5	4	13.2	7

Source: Adapted from Ministero dell' Interno http://politiche.interno.it/ and Ignazi (2002).

beyond the election. Thus parliamentary dynamics continued to be centrifugal (Bardi 2007). Within government, ideological and territorial divisions within the parties have meant fragmented coalitions.

FI served as a 'point of convergence' on the centre-right for different territorial and political identities (Diamanti 2007: 736). FI attracted support from both the north and south of Italy whereas this was a source of division between other coalition partners. FI's appeal was also distinct because its supporters tended to be less interested in politics, more susceptible to media influence and more motivated by the personal appeal of leaders.

AN and Ccd–Cdu drew support from the south where there is higher unemployment, a larger role for the public sector in the economy, scepticism about federalism, as well as immigration into the informal economy. The Lega, on the other hand, draws its support from areas such as the Veneto in north-east Italy where small firms are the bedrock of the economy and there is reliance on migrant workers to sustain flexible production models. By 2001, the Lega had developed and subsequently altered strategy during its relatively brief history to call for federalism, confederation, secession (with the creation of Padania proclaimed – albeit to little effect – on 15 September 1996) and then '*la devolution*'. Despite its stance as both anti-system and anti-party, the Lega managed to place itself at the heart of debate and to play a key role in setting the political agenda at élite level and more broadly. Diamanti (1996: 7) characterizes this as polymorphism, by which he means that the Lega functioned as a 'prism that projected the many faces of the Italian crisis' of the early 1990s: between society, economy and polity; between north and south; within the north between peripheral areas and the traditional centres of capital and finance; between the decline of mass parties and the emergence of new parties and new forms of political participation. The Lega was thus a 'telescope' and a 'detonator' (Diamanti 1996: 7).

This highlights the significance of the territorial dimension to voting – and to Italian politics more generally. Territory serves as far more than a base for political and administrative organization, but also possesses a symbolic dimension as the reference point for political identity because it possesses 'a material, spatial notion establishing essential links between politics, people and the natural setting' and serving as a 'psychosomatic device ... related to the human striving for security, opportunity and happiness' (Gottmann 1971: 9–10). The Lega, for example, played on the threat to the 'hard-working north' from what they called '*Roma ladrona*' (Rome the big thief) and, from the late 1990s, immigrants. In such terms, Diamanti's (1996: 672) argument that the Lega redefined the concept of territory acquires a particularly profound resonance in contemporary Italian immigration politics. Territory is more often indicative of division rather than of cohesion or integration in Italian politics.

In terms of their respective stances on immigration, both the Lega and the AN have been characterized as anti-immigration with the AN seen as being on the 'opportunistic right' and the Lega an 'ethno-national' party (Messina 2007). The opportunistic right comprises parties that pursue an anti-immigration strategy motivated by the desire to win votes that is woven into a larger critique of the existing order. Such parties also have a 'pliable' ideological identity which highlights the importance of the party leadership in the ideological positioning of the party (Fella and Ruzza 2006). The opportunistic right will thus be oriented towards the mainstream (Messina 2007: 69), as has indeed been the case with the AN under the leadership of Gianfranco Fini.

The AN, led by Gianfranco Fini, was founded following the dissolution of the MSI in the mid-1990s. Fini has been determined to reposition the AN as a modern, mainstream European centre-right party while also trying to position himself as a future leader of the Italian centre-right (Ignazi 1994, 2002). This has meant distancing himself from the fascist origins of the MSI through, for example, his visit to Israel and denunciation of Nazi and Fascist crimes, his membership of the Convention on the Future of Europe, his support for more liberal rules on assisted human fertilization and, as we see later, his support for local voting rights for immigrants. Fini was also closely linked to Berlusconi, who had aided his entry as a legitimate figure on the national political scene by backing Fini's unsuccessful 1993 bid as MSI leader to become Mayor of Rome. Fini's modernization strategy has occurred within a party that is itself heterogeneous, that has seen contestation of his more liberal initiatives and some departures on its right-wing flank that adheres most closely to the AN's roots in the MSI.

The ethno-national right – within which Messina locates the Lega Nord – can also be ideologically flexibile, but at its core is an ethno-national movement denoting group solidarity based on ethnicity rather than territory. This does raise questions about whether the Lega is a territorial or an ethnic party given diversity within its 'northern' heartlands and some difficulty specifying where the north begins and ends. Messina (2007: 72) goes on to argue that, because of its ethno-national identity, immigration will not be to the fore in Lega activity. Anti-immigration appeals 'merely complement and reinforce the traditional agenda of the ethno-national right by explicitly linking the economic, cultural and political "penetration" of the periphery (the traditional regions) by the metropole (i.e. central government)'. The Lega would also appear to be hard to accommodate within government 'because governing from Rome challenges its very *raison d'être*' (Tambini 2001: 148). The Lega was, however, accommodated within the governing coalition for five years even though, at times, its behaviour within government – particularly its rhetoric – was more like that of an opposition party.

It would have been possible for Berlusconi to establish a centre-right government in 2001 without Lega support as the Lega's seats were superfluous to a parliamentary majority. The 2001 general election results were a major setback for the Lega with just 3.9 per cent of the vote and a sharp fall in its share of the vote in its northern heartlands of Lombardy, Piedmont, Veneto and Friuli Venezia-Giulia (Albertazzi and McDonnell 2005: 954). Nevertheless, the Lega had an influence within the governing coalition that was disproportionate to its share of the vote because of Berlusconi's concern about the potential impact on his coalition and support for FI if the Lega were once again to leave the governing coalition, as they had done in 1994. The 'axis of the north' centred on Berlusconi and Bossi became fundamental to the centre-right coalition and meant that Berlusconi tended to support the Lega over AN and UDC within the coalition while the Lega were strong supporters of Berlusconi (Diamanti 2007: 747). This relationship only began to weaken following Bossi's stroke in March 2005 and FI setbacks in the 2004 European Parliament and 2005 regional elections when increased support for the AN and UDC saw Fini and Pierferdinando Casini become rivals to Berlusconi. The March 2005 reconstitution of the centre-right coalition in Berlusconi III contained stronger cabinet representation from AN and UDC and marked the growing presence of Casini and Fini.

While emphasizing security and advocating 'guest workers'' recruitment, FI were keen to respond to business concerns about adverse effects of draconian immigration legislation on labour supply. The Ccd–Cdu were particularly influential because they mobilized both business and Catholic Church concerns about the restrictive aspects of legislation. On the issue of immigration there was thus heterogeneity within the coalition that would need to be accommodated as the focus moved from 'talk' to 'decision'.

Table 2 shows attitudes of centre-right voters to immigration at the 2001 general election and illustrates that the immigration issue's salience was higher than the average across all parties for supporters of FI, AN and particularly Lega Nord while lower for Ccd–Cdu voters.

Table 2 Immigration issue salience by party vote, proportional ballot for election to Chamber of Deputies, 2001

	AN	Ccd–Cdu	FI	LN	Total for all parties
Very important problem	68.9	60.0	70.9	83.6	65.1
Fairly important problem	23.8	32.5	21.4	10.9	25.1
Not a very important problem	6.3	5.0	5.6	5.5	7.3
Not really a problem	1.0	2.5	2.1	0	2.5
Total	100	100	100	100	100

Source: Italian National Election Survey (ITANES) 2001.

Table 3 shows that FI, AN and, in particular, Lega Nord voters at the 2001 election were far more likely than average to see immigration as a threat to national identity, employment and public order. Voters thus mirrored the rhetoric employed by party leaders. Ccd–Cdu supporters were CdL outliers in the sense that they were far less likely to see immigration as a threat in such terms. As will be seen, it also jars with legislative outcomes, particularly the 2002–03 mass regularization. The data thus provide support for the thesis that public attitudes and stances of parties seem to have less impact on migration policy outcomes than more specific mobilization by organized interests and the effects of these on inter-coalition negotiations, as analysed more fully later in this contribution.

ITALY AS AN IMMIGRATION COUNTRY

Italy only became a country of immigration in the early 1980s with an acceleration in numbers during the 1990s (Calavita 2004; Pugliese 2006; Bonifazi 2007; Einaudi 2007). In common with other south European immigration countries, there has been a tendency for migrants to enter irregularly (the main route being to overstay an entry visa) and to find work in the informal economy (Reyneri 1998). Migrants did not create this economic informality, but the presence of large numbers of flexible and low-paid migrant workers has become an important structural component of the Italian labour market

Table 3 Attitudes towards immigration by party vote, proportional ballot to Chamber of Deputies, 2001

Agree completely that immigrants are a threat to:	AN	Ccd–Cdu	FI	LN	Total for all parties
Our culture and identity	17.3	5.0	20.0	20.4	13.6
Employment	23.7	2.5	23.5	23.6	17.5
Security and public order	33.8	15.0	28.1	44.4	23.4

Source: ITANES 2001.

and economy, replacing to some extent more traditional south–north intra-Italian movement, which declined in scale. This labour market presence and its relationship to the welfare state demonstrates the importance of internal regulation and is not simply a matter of ever tougher external frontier controls (Geddes 2006). As Einaudi (2007: 371) notes, the 2002–03 regularization of nearly 650,000 people who were already in the country 'drew attention to the dimensions of the substitution of welfare state services by provision of private welfare for families thanks to the work of carers and domestic workers from abroad, above all from eastern Europe'.

The foreign population in Italy is heavily concentrated in the areas where support for FI and the Lega Nord has been strong, where immigrants have been 'wanted' for work, but not always 'welcome' in terms of their social impacts (Zolberg 1987). European Union (EU) widening to include ten central and east European countries has created new opportunities for 'community' migration to Italy. On 1 May 2006, Italy lifted restrictions on labour market access imposed on A-8 nationals that joined the EU on 1 May 2004, but maintained restrictions on labour market access for the A-2 (Bulgaria and Romania) (Geddes 2008). The majority of Italy's legally resident foreign population live in northern Italy with 36.6 per cent of the foreign population in north-west Italy and 27.4 per cent in the north-east. Around a quarter (24.9 per cent) of the foreign population live in Lombardy, particularly in the province of Milan (10.9 per cent of the total foreign population in Italy). In the south, only Abruzzo has a sizeable presence of legally resident foreigners and then only 3.4 per cent of the total foreign population (ISTAT 2006). Table 4 shows the size of the legally resident foreign population in Italy and the ten most significant origin countries. There has been substantial growth in intra-EU migration, particularly by Romanians.

Table 4 Total numbers of migrants in Italy and main countries of origin

Country	% of total foreign population
Albania	13.1
Romania	11.1
Ukraine	4.0
Serbia-Montenegro	2.4
Morocco	12.0
Tunisia	3.1
Senegal	2.1
China	4.8
Sri Lanka	1.9
Ecuador	2.3
Total for top 10 source countries	56.8
Total foreign population ('000)	2,670,514

Source: ISTAT 2006.

POSITION-TAKING BY THE CENTRE-RIGHT ON IMMIGRATION DURING THE 'LONG' ELECTION CAMPAIGN

The centre-right set the agenda on immigration during the 'long' campaign prior to the 2001 general election with a strong focus on the supposedly lax approach of the centre-left coalition to illegal immigration. AN were keen to position themselves as a modern European centre-right party and to avoid accusations of xenophobia. This led them to focus on illegal immigration and criminality, which connected with their more general focus on law and order. In 1999 the AN-sponsored Fini–Landi bill proposed to make clandestine entry a criminal offence. Fini argued that immigration functioned as a 'picklock' that could destroy social order while also creating a new lumpenproletariat of immigrant voters ready to support the left (cited in Colombo and Sciortino 2003: 203).

While outside the CdL in 1999, the Lega had proposed a referendum against the centre-left government's 1998 Turco-Napolitano law (Law No. 40, 27 March 1998), an initiative ruled invalid by the *Cassazione* (Supreme Court) because revocation would have been incompatible with the Schengen agreement. The EU in this specific instance served as an external constraint on domestic immigration politics. During the period of centre-right government there was, however, a distinct Eurosceptic tinge to the FI and Lega's 'axis of the north' with Bossi, for example, likening the EU to a 'Stalinist superstate'. Quaglia and Radaelli (2007: 933) see a 'negative reference' in centre-right debate about immigration, with the EU seen as not tough enough. Consequently, while the EU has been represented in terms of the strategic choices of Italian policy-makers as a *vincolo esterno* (an external lock-in) that binds (willing) domestic policy-makers (Dyson and Featherstone 1996), in this case limited EU jurisdiction for labour migration coupled with Euroscepticism meant that EU effects were marginal. There were, however, significant EU migration flows as a result of the Union's May 2004 and January 2007 enlargements. EU effects were more evident as flows than policy.

Lega opposition to Turco-Napolitano, and to immigration more generally, included prime examples of the 'vulgar' politics to which Cotta and Verzichelli (2007) refer. There were, for example, Lega threats to fertilize land with pig manure near the proposed site of a mosque in Lodi, near Milan, while the Lega Mayor of Treviso proclaimed his intention to dress immigrants as hares and declare 'open season' (cited in Zincone 2006: 357–8). Links between the AN and Lega Nord have been apparent at local level, such as in Treviso where post-fascists of the AN's *destra sociale* (social right) faction are ideologically more consistent with the party's fascist roots. AN supporters in Treviso have supported the controversial Lega Nord Deputy Mayor, Giancarlo Gentilini, also known as *sceriffo* (sheriff) Gentilini, who has become notorious for his verbal attacks on immigrants, homosexuals and other minorities. On the Lega's re-entry to the CdL coalition prior to the 2000 regional elections, Bossi joined with Berlusconi to propose a guest worker system that would break the connection between work and residence by linking the presence of immigrants in Italy to their employment.

During the long campaign prior to the 2001 general election there was opposition from the centre-right both to illegal immigration and to the permanent settlement of migrants in Italy, with immigrants stigmatized as destructive of social order. Colombo and Sciortino (2003) note the electoral usefulness of a rhetorical commitment to tough action on immigration, but note too that this would be less helpful as an approach to governing. There is a core tension for the Italian centre-right as 'security'-oriented claims to stringently regulate immigration threaten to open the 'Pandora's box' of internal controls that would not only impact on immigrants who as foreign nationals cannot vote but on Italian citizens such as business owners who can vote, exert influence through their associations and form part of the centre-right's core constituency (Sciortino, 1999). Zincone (2006) argues that labour market regulation to tackle illegal immigration has the potential to be a 'political boomerang' impacting on small businesses that were the bedrock of FI and Lega support.

The centre-right was aided in its politicization by what Colombo and Sciortino (2003: 204) refer to as 'moderate opposition' to immigration from those such as Giovanni Sartori in his *Corriere della Sera* editorials and the Archbishop of Bologna, Cardinal Biffi, who argued that there should be preference for Christian immigrants. During the 2001 campaign the Ulivo coalition seemed ashamed of Turco-Napolitano and hardly tried to defend it (Colombo and Sciortino 2003).

THE CENTRE-RIGHT IN POWER 2001–06: BOSSI–FINI AND ITS AFTERMATH

Attention now shifts to the composition of the CdL coalition and to how the accommodation of inconsistencies derived from the ideological and territorial heterogeneity of the Berlusconi II government rendered problematic the translation of talk into decision.

The Berlusconi II government came to power on 10 June 2001. Berlusconi was Prime Minister (and Foreign Minister for 11 months in 2002 following the resignation of Renato Ruggiero and prior to the appointment of Franco Frattini). Fini was appointed Deputy Prime Minister and represented Italy on the Convention on the Future of Europe before being appointed Foreign Minister in November 2004 when Frattini became a European Commissioner. The key immigration policy implementation ministries were the Interior Ministry where Claudio Scajola (FI) served until his resignation in July 2002 when he was replaced by Giuseppe Pisanu (FI) and the Work and Welfare Ministry held by Roberto Maroni (Lega).

In contrast to the Berlusconi I government in 1994, immigration was immediately identified as a priority for the new government, with a draft immigration law sent to the Council of Ministers on 2 November 2001. While dominant within the coalition, FI were not the key players in the development of immigration and asylum legislation. The most vocal parties at the 'talk' stage were Lega Nord and AN. The proposals came from Bossi and Fini with both keen to be seen to lead on this issue. As the focus switched to negotiation the Ccd–Cdu/UDC and its leader, Marco Follini, became more influential.

The first draft of the law was presented to the cabinet in July 2001. Einaudi (2007) notes that the mode in which the legislation was presented was rather particular as it was basically a combination of measures proposed separately by FI, AN and Lega Nord with no consultation at EU level or with local and regional actors. Also excluded from consultation was Foreign Minister Ruggiero, despite the potential foreign policy implications of these measures. There were, for example, proposals to favour re-entry by Italians abroad while major reductions were proposed in 'privileged flows' from countries such as Nigeria (Einaudi 2007). This affirms the point made by Zincone (2006) that Bossi–Fini emerged from within restricted party political circles with little civil society involvement. The proposed law was approved by the cabinet on 14 September 2001 with *La Padania*, the Lega newspaper, greeting it with the headline 'Finally Italy is a serious country'.

Opposition to Bossi–Fini came not only from the centre-left, but also from Ccd–Cdu, which pushed from within the coalition for a regularization. The Ccd–Cdu were particularly quick to identify counterproductive aspects to the law as domestic workers (*colf*) and carers (*badanti*) who were highly valued could easily fall foul of the proposed tough line on irregular migration and the more restrictive approach to labour migration. Bossi–Fini proposals were for guest worker recruitment based on a *contratto di soggiorno* (residence contract) that would expire when a migrant came to the end of her employment or lost her job (Livi Bacci 2002; Bonifazi 2007). Further proposals from Work and Welfare Minister Maroni in July 2001 required employers not only to conduct extensive labour market checks to see if there were unemployed Italians who could do the job, but also provide accommodation and travel costs for immigrants to return to their countries of origin at the end of a contract of employment. All this made recruitment of migrant workers a potentially lengthy process and effectively tied their presence in Italy to their employment, creating bonded labour. There were also proposals in Bossi–Fini for restrictions on family migration, the end of sponsorship schemes for new migrants, tougher border controls, increased expulsions and ten new *Centri di Permanenza Temporanea* (temporary detention centres).

From the outset, the notion of '*si entra in Italia solo con un contratto di lavoro in mano*' (entry only on the basis of a labour contract) was not going to be the case because a number of routes including family migration, study, asylum, health care, and religion remained open. EU legislation also meant that non-EU migrants (*extra-comunitari*) would have six months to find new employment after a previous contract of employment had ended.

The Ccd–Cdu leader Marco Follini made it clear that the government could not rely on his party's support for the more repressive aspects of the proposed legislation, such as restrictive work and residence requirements and the proposed limits on family reunification. This did not mean that the legislation would be lost, but meant that Ccd–Cdu were active opponents within the governing coalition of the proposed legislation. The Ccd–Cdu Minister for Europe, Buttiglione, received proposals to ameliorate aspects of the legislation from the *Fondazione Migrantes* of the *Conferenza Episcopale Italiana* (Conference of Italian Bishops). Business interests also contested the proposals with Innocenzo Cipolletta, the Director General of the Italian employers' confederation, *Confindustria*, disputing the idea of immediate expulsion at the end of a migrant's labour contract (cited in Einaudi 2007: 310). This helped the Ccd–Cdu to turn opposition from within the coalition to aspects of the legislation into a bargaining role because of the importance to the centre-right of the interests that were being mobilized.

Tensions within the coalition between the AN and the Lega and the Ccd–Cdu, meant that the bill presented to the Senate on 2 November 2001 had a provisional feel to it, as it was based on a combination of the Fini–Landi and Bossi–Berlusconi proposals, plus other proposals that had been made subsequently with various imprecise articles or ambiguities (Colombo and Sciortino 2003: 205). There were also some immediate concessions. Clandestine entry was not made a crime, the right to family reunion was maintained without quotas or an increased waiting period. There was to be an extension of the period before permanent residence could be acquired from five to six years, although this was less than the eight proposed by Fini–Landi.

Between December 2001 and January 2002 there were two key meetings of CdL coalition leaders on immigration (Einaudi 2007). At these meetings the Lega conceded a regularization to *colf* and *badanti* because of their role in supporting the family while excluding a wider regularization. Colombo and Sciortino (2003: 208) argue that it is at this point that we see the Lega exchange the potential benefits of a regularization with the launch of further high-profile repressive measures. So, on 2 February 2002, proposals were made for the use of naval force against boats carrying immigrants while, on 7 February 2002, proposals were made for a regularization of *colf* and *badanti*. Similarly, in May 2002, proposals were made for the collection of biometric data when immigrants applied for or renewed residence permits. Colombo and Sciortino (2003: 211) see the use of the navy and collection of biometrics as devices to maintain the public focus on the repressive aura of the legislation and not on what they call its 'strategic contradictions'.

These strategic contradictions become more evident when it is noted that Ccd–Cdu started pushing for a wider regularization than *colf* and *badanti* with support from business organizations and the Church. As Einaudi (2007: 317) puts it: 'inch by inch, the Lega and the tougher elements of the AN were obliged to cede ground to the Catholics, under pressure from the ecclesiastical hierarchy and the employers' organizations'. In January 2002, Follini pushed for broader application of the regularization. In the same month, between 150,000 and 250,000 people demonstrated in Rome against the proposed legislation. The Ccd–Cdu Minister for Europe, Rocco Buttiglione, announced that 'with Bossi–Fini we have decided to regularize not only the *colf* but all the immigrants that are already working' (*Corriere della Sera*,

20 January 2002). In order to save face, the provisions for a more general regularization were actually made in the name of Ccd–Cdu member of parliament, Bruno Tabacchi. Colombo and Sciortino (2003: 209) offer three explanations for this apparently paradoxical situation. First, 'democratic common sense' as all previous regularizations began with restrictive criteria but ended up being less restrictive for reasons of fairness, as how could domestic workers be included while those working in small and medium enterprises were not? Second, there was a need to proceed on a consensual basis within a fragmented coalition. Here, as we have seen, the role of Ccd–Cdu as the bargaining-oriented component of the coalition and the vehicle for representation of business and Church interests was crucial. Third, the regularization actually 'confirmed rather than contradicted' (Colombo and Sciortino 2003: 210) the government's immigration policy in the sense that it reduced the role of consultation and established more discretionary power to shape responses to migration. Discretionary powers were, for example, evident in the actions of Maroni, who sought to take sole control of immigration quotas in order to try and ensure temporary migration and minimize dialogue with regional and private actors with a stake in this issue. Maroni issued authorization for 'small contingents' through ministerial decrees in, for example, February, March, May and July 2002. There was a growth in seasonal migration and an increased reliance on central and eastern European migrants. There were big cuts in non-seasonal migration from 50,000 to 19,000 in 2002. In 2003 only 11,000 non-seasonal migrants entered Italy (Einaudi 2007: 324).

Inconsistencies within the centre-right coalition were also evident during the continued debate about immigration's effects while the CdL coalition was in office. After the 9/11 attacks on the USA, increased attention was paid to Muslim immigration. The political debate became more heated following a long article entitled *la rabbia e l'orgoglio* (The Anger and the Pride) in the *Corriere della Sera* on 29 September 2001 by Oriana Fallaci, who took Huntington's points about a clash of civilization to write of an attack on freedom and civilization by Islam. In extended book form, Fallaci sold more than a million copies (Fallaci 2002). Berlusconi said that he shared Fallaci's views and, at a Berlin press conference, declared that 'we have to be aware of the superiority of our civilization that has provided for well-being and respect for human rights; things that are not found in Islamic countries.' Ambiguities within the governing coalition were evident in the actions of Interior Minister Pisanu, who did not follow this path of confrontation, but combined tough measures on immigration and border security with dialogue with Italy's Islamic communities, culminating in 2005 with the creation of the *Consulta per l'Islam* (Consultative Committee on Islam). This attracted the ire of *Corriere della Sera* columnist Magdi Allam, who became an ardent and prolific critic of what he saw as misconceived notions of dialogue with organizations such as the *Unione delle Comunità ed Organizzazioni Islamiche in Italia* (Union of Islamic Communities and Organizations in Italy), which he saw as fundamentalist (Allam 2005).

Potentially even more significant was Fini's call for local voting rights to be ceded to migrants when he argued that the rigour of action against illegal immigration needed to be combined with an openness towards the integration of those migrants already settled in Italy (*Corriere della Sera*, 7 October 2003). This is an example of Fini seeking to reposition the AN as a mainstream centre-right party and himself as a future leader of the centre-right. Not surprisingly, the proposals attracted opposition from within the AN and from Lega Nord and were not successful. In this case, however, 'talk' was very important in terms of Fini's strategic repositioning of himself and his party.

By 2006, we have seen the airing in public debate by centre-right parties of ideas for stringent regulation of migration including much tougher action on irregular/illegal immigration and the attempt to create a guest worker system. What we have also seen is how party system and governmental variables mediate the relationship between policy inputs and outputs. The shift from 'talk' to 'decision' within the CdL coalition provided a route for representation of business and Church interests that ameliorated some of the harsher aspects of the Bossi–Fini proposals. In terms of the numbers of migrants entering Italy then policy could be said to have failed, but if such outcomes are to be explained they must include consideration of the organization and structure of the political process that might be seen as generating success for some of the actors involved.

CONCLUSION

Instead of the sound of cannons (*il rombo dei cannoni*, as Bossi put it) Italian policies on immigration were characterized more by the shuffling sound of backtracking in intra-coalition negotiations. While Bossi–Fini did embody a notably illiberal approach to migration with its attempt to create guest worker-style recruitment and the framing of immigrant settlement as corrosive of social order, there was a huge increase in the legally resident immigrant population. The discovery of this gap between rhetoric and reality is nothing new. This contribution has, however, sought to develop insight into the ways in which party system and governmental variables play a key role in mediating the relationship between 'inputs' and 'outputs'. While the Lega Nord, FI and AN framed public discourse with a series of illiberal pronouncements on immigration, it was shown that the Ccd–Cdu was central to negotiations of Bossi–Fini. Meanwhile, the preoccupation of Berlusconi with other issues and Fini's approach to AN modernization meant that there was room for compromise. In particular, Church and business interests were brought to bear on discussions on a regularization that began with provisions for *colf* and *badanti* and were then extended to a more general regularization.

In terms of its general focus, this contribution has not been an argument for Italian exceptionalism. Rather, it has identified some specific aspects of Italian centre-right politics, and explored them by focusing on party system and coalition dynamics when the centre-right was in power between 2001 and 2006, to demonstrate how the case of Italy can provide useful insight into the general issue of the persistent gap between the rhetoric of control and the reality of continued immigration. It has shown that contradictions, paradoxes and ambiguities are functional elements of immigration politics (and of thorny social and political issues, more generally) and that talk, decision and action need not connect along one smooth continuum. Supposed policy failings must be related to the political process that generates them and to the pay-offs to political actors that occur within this process and that may well not be negative.

NOTES

1 Thanks to Federica Bicchi, Tony Messina, Luca Verzichelli and referees for help and comments. The usual disclaimer applies.
2 Or put another way that draws more directly from the literature on coalition government in Europe, the piece is interested in both the 'courtship' and 'marriage' stage of the coalition process (Müller and Strøm 2000).
3 The election to the Chamber of Deputies was fought on the basis of an electoral system that allocated 75 per cent of seats on a single-member plurality basis with a further 25 per cent allocated through a proportional representation top-up with a 4 per cent national threshold.

REFERENCES

Albertazzi, D. and McDonnell, D. (2005) 'The Lega Nord in the second Berlusconi government: in a league of its own?' West European Politics, 28(5): 952–72.
Allam, M. (2005) Vincere la paura: La mia vita contro il terrorismo islamico e l'incoscienza dell' Occidente, Milan: Mondadori.
Ballerini, A. and Benna, A. (2002) Il muro invisibile. Immigrazione e legge Bossi–Fini, Genoa: Fratelli Frilli Editori.
Bardi, L. (2007) 'Electoral change and its impact on the party system in Italy', West European Politics, 30(4): 711–32.
Bonifazi, C. (2007) L'immigrazione straniera in Italia, 2nd edn, Bologna: Il Mulino.
Brunsson, N. (1993) 'Ideas and actions: justification and hypocrisy as alternatives to control', Accounting, Organizations and Society, 18(6): 489–506.
Brunsson, N. (2002) The Organization of Hypocrisy: Talk, Decisions and Actions in Organizations, 2nd edn. Chichester: Wiley.
Calavita, K. (2004) 'Italy: economic realities, political fictions and policy failures', in Cornelius, W., Tsuda, T., Martin, P. and Hollifield, J. (eds), Controlling Immigration: A Global Perspective, 2nd edn, Stanford, CA: Stanford University Press.
Castles, S. (2004a) 'The factors that make and unmake migration policies', International Migration Review, 38(3): 852–84.
Castles, S. (2004b) 'Why migration policies fail?,' Ethnic and Racial Studies, 27(2): 205–27.
Colombo, A. and Sciortino, G. (2003) 'La legge Bossi–Fini: estremismi gridati, moderazioni implicite e frutti avvelenati', in Blondel, J. and Segatti, P. (eds) Politica in Italia 2003, Bologna: Il Mulino.

Cornelius, W., Martin, P. and Hollifield, J. (eds) (1994) *Controlling Immigration: A Global Perspective*, Stanford, CA: Stanford University Press.

Cornelius, W., Tsuda, T., Martin, P. and Hollifield, J. (eds) (2004) *Controlling Immigration: A Global Perspective*, 2nd edn, Stanford, CA: Stanford University Press.

Cotta, M. and Verzichelli, L. (2007) *Political Institutions in Italy*, Oxford: Oxford University Press.

Diamanti, I. (1996) *Il Male del Nord: Lega, Localismo, Secessione*, Roma: Donzelli.

Diamanti, I. (2003) *Bianco, Rosso, Verde...e Azzurro: Mappe e Colori dell'Italia Politica*, Bologna: Il Mulino.

Diamanti, I. (2007) 'The Italian centre-right and centre-left: between parties and "the party"' *West European Politics*, 30(4): 733–62.

Dyson, K. and Featherstone, K. (1996) 'Italy and EMU as a "Vincolo Esterno": empowering the technocrats, transforming the state', *South European Society and Politics*, 1(2): 272–99.

Einaudi, L. (2007) *Le Politiche dell'Immigrazione in Italia dall'Unità a Oggi*, Rome: Laterza.

Fallaci, O. (2002) *La Rabbia e l'Orgoglio*, Milan: Rizzoli.

Fella, S. and Ruzza, C. (2006) 'Changing political opportunities and the nature of the Italian right', *Journal of Southern Europe and the Balkans*, 8(2): 179–200.

Freeman, G. (1995) 'Modes of immigration politics in liberal democratic societies', *International Migration Review*, 29(4): 881–913.

Geddes, A. (2003) *The Politics of Migration and Immigration in Europe*, London: Sage.

Geddes, A. (2006) 'Europe's border relationships and international migration relations', *Journal of Common Market Studies*, 43(4): 787–806.

Geddes, A. (2008) *Immigration and European Integration: Beyond Fortress Europe?*, 2nd edn, Manchester: Manchester University Press.

Ginsborg, P. (2004) *Silvio Berlusconi: Television, Power, Patrimony*, London: Verso.

Gottmann, J. (1971) *The Significance of Territory*, Charlottesville: University of Virginia Press.

Ignazi, P. (1994) *Post fascisti? Dal Movimento sociale italiano ad Alleanza nazionale*, Bologna: Il Mulino.

Ignazi, P. (2002) *L'estrema destra in Italia*, Bologna: Il Mulino.

Ignazi, P. (2003) 'Italy', *European Journal of Political Research Political Data Yearbook*, 42: 7–8.

ISTAT (2006) *La popolazione straniera residente in Italia*, Rome: ISTAT.

Livi Bacci, M. (2002) 'Immigrazione: nuova legge ma quale politica?' *Il Mulino*, 51(5): 903–8.

Messina, A. (2007) *The Logics and Politics of Post-WWII Migration to Western Europe*, Cambridge: Cambridge University Press.

Meyer, J. and Rowan, B. (1977) 'Institutionalized organization: formal structure as myth and ceremony', *American Journal of Sociology*, 83(2): 340–63.

Müller, W. and Strøm, K., (eds) (2000) *Coalition Governments in Western Europe*, Oxford: Oxford University Press.

Newell, J. (2002) *The Italian General Election of 2001: Berlusconi's Victory*, Manchester: Manchester University Press.

Pasquino, G. (2007) 'The five faces of Silvio Berlusconi: the knight of anti-politics:', *Modern Italy*, 12(1): 39–54.

Poli, E. (2001) *Forza Italia: strutture, leadership e radicamento territoriale*, Bologna: Il Mulino.

Pugliese, E. (2006) *L'Italia: tra migrazioni internazionale e migrazioni interne*, Bologna: Il Mulino.

Quaglia, L. and Radaelli, C. (2007) 'Italian politics and the European Union: a tale of two research designs', *West European Politics*, 30(4): 924–43.

Reyneri, E. (1998) 'The role of the underground economy in irregular migration to Italy', *Journal of Ethnic and Migration Studies*, 24(2): 313–31.

Sartori, G. (2005) *Parties and Party Systems: A Framework for Analysis*, Colchester, Essex: ECPR Press.

Sciortino, G. (1999) 'Planning in the dark: the evolution of Italian immigration control', in Brochmann, G. and Hammar, T. (eds), *Mechanisms of Immigration Control: A Comparative Analysis of European Regulation Policies*, Oxford: Berg.

Tambini, D. (2001) *Nationalism in Italian Politics: The Stories of the Northern League 1980–2000*, London: Routledge.

Zincone, G. (2006) 'The making of policies: immigration and immigrants in Italy', *Journal of Ethnic and Migration Studies*, 32(3): 347–75.

Zolberg, A. (1987) 'Wanted but not welcome: alien labor in Western development', in Alonso, W. (ed.) *Population in an Interacting World*, Cambridge, MA: Harvard University Press.

Going different ways? Right-wing parties and the immigrant issue in Denmark and Sweden

Christoffer Green-Pedersen and Pontus Odmalm

INTRODUCTION

There are several reasons why Sweden and Denmark would approach questions relating to immigration and integration in a similar fashion. For a long time, both countries were (or at least perceived themselves to be) relatively homogeneous nation-states in terms of ethnicity. Both countries also have large, universal welfare states combined with a highly regulated labour market that limits job opportunities for low-skilled workers. During the 1970s and 1980s, there were also many similarities in terms of migration and migrant policy, which was based on a broad, cross-party consensus. However, by the early 1990s, the two countries started to diverge significantly as both Danish policy and the rhetoric surrounding it became notably more restrictive compared to Sweden, especially with regard to immigration.

The main argument of this contribution suggests that the explanation for this divergence should be sought in the differing positions of centre-right parties in the two countries. The more restrictionist position of the Danish centre-right parties has been central in turning immigration and integration into a highly salient and contested policy issue which has also contributed to significant policy changes. Elements of this development can also be found in Sweden, but the changes in the position of the Swedish right and subsequent policy changes have generally gone in a different direction from Denmark. In addition, the diverging positions of centre-right parties can be explained by looking at the coalition incentives of the centre-right parties in the two countries. As we go on to show, these differences relate to differences in the composition and strength of the right-wing blocs in the two countries. The Danish centre-right parties have traditionally been much stronger electorally than their Swedish counterparts, yet, as a coalition bloc, they are significantly less stable. Consequently, the Danish centre-right has had to rely on, and sometimes co-operate with, radical right-wing parties which has placed the two dominant right-wing parties in Denmark – the Liberals (Venstre) and the Conservatives – in a different strategic position from their Swedish counterparts, the Liberal Party (Folkpartiet) and especially the Conservatives (Moderaterna). The main argument of this article thus strongly supports Bale's contention that understanding the policy position of centre right-wing parties is crucial to understanding both the development of immigration and integration policy and the rhetoric surrounding it (Bale 2008).

The argument is constructed in several steps. We start by presenting the composition and strength of the right-wing blocs in the two countries. The difference between the two countries in this regard is a key factor in understanding the development in immigration politics[1] in the two countries. We also lay out the similarities in the societal context with regard to immigration and proceed to describe the similarities between the two countries until the early 1990s. We then turn to an analysis of how the centre-right parties and their positions have shaped both policy and rhetoric with regard to immigration politics in the two countries during the 1990s, causing the divergence between the two countries.

THE NATURE OF POLITICAL COMPETITION IN SCANDINAVIA

In the Scandinavian context, political contestation has traditionally revolved around competition between the bourgeois parties on the right, or the bourgeois bloc, and the strong Social Democratic parties on the left.[2] However, in both countries, the more centrist of the right-wing parties – the Social Liberals in Denmark and the Centre Party in Sweden – have often supported the Social Democrats.

In Denmark, the major right-wing parties are the Liberals, a former agrarian party which has developed into a mainstream right-wing party, and the Conservatives, which is a traditional conservative party with an upper-class background. In practical politics it has often been difficult to distinguish between the two parties, though there has been a tendency for the larger of the two to be more centrist while the smaller has had a more pronounced right-wing profile. The third traditional right-wing party is the Social Liberal Party, which is a centre-right party, coincidentally also with an agrarian history. The Social Liberals have, however, been more left-wing when it comes to certain non-economic issues such as defence policy. Since 1973, radical right-wing parties have also been represented in the Danish parliament. The Progress Party held seats until the 2001 election, while the Danish People's Party, which broke away from the Progress Party in 1995, emerged as the major radical right-wing party in the 1998 election.[3]

In Sweden, the bourgeois bloc has historically contained the traditional Conservative Party (Moderaterna), the traditional Agrarian Centre Party (Centerpartiet), and the Liberals (Folkpartiet).[4] In the 1991 election, the Christian Democrats gained representation for the first time which increased the bourgeois bloc to four parties. From 1991 to 1994, the radical right-wing party, New Democracy (Ny Demokrati), was represented in the Swedish parliament, but otherwise Sweden has had no radical right-wing party at the national level.

The difference in representation of radical right-wing parties is an obvious point that distinguishes the two countries. However, two further differences are worth mentioning. The first is that the right-wing bloc has always been stronger in Denmark. With the exception of a few shorter periods, the bourgeois bloc in Denmark has controlled the majority in the Danish parliament. On the occasions where the Social Democrats have led governments, this has been primarily due to the Social Liberals 'defecting' from the bourgeois camp. In Sweden, bourgeois majorities have been the exception to the rule and have always been followed by Social Democratic majorities. The second difference is that the point of gravity in the Danish right-wing bloc has always been towards the two sister parties, the Liberals and the Conservatives, which have been much stronger than the Social Liberals. In Sweden, the more centrist of the centre-right parties (the Liberals and the Centre Party) have most of the time been equal to the Conservatives in strength (Arter 1999). In the 1990s, these differences constituted different strategic contexts for the right-wing parties with regard to the immigration issue. These background settings thus help to explain why Danish and Swedish immigration politics began to diverge in the 1990s.

THE SOCIETAL CONTEXT

The two countries share many societal similarities which suggests strong similarities in the way that centre-right parties would respond to, and position themselves on, immigration and integration issues. First, the two have been relatively homogeneous in terms of ethnicity,[5] partly owing to the lack of a colonial past and partly owing to being late starters as countries of immigration. Second, both countries have highly developed welfare systems which provide generous and tax-financed benefits based on the principle of universalism with access to benefits without prior labour market participation. This welfare state is combined with a labour market where high minimum wages were meant to crowd out low-paid jobs in the private service sector which, in other countries, are exactly the type of jobs that would be open to low-skilled immigrants. This combination of high minimum wages, generous social benefits and high barriers of entry to the labour market has in many cases led to migrants ending up with low labour market participation and high dependency on social benefits. Thus low-skilled immigration can be expected to add to, rather than alleviate, financial problems in universal welfare states like Denmark and Sweden (Nannestad 2004). One noticeable difference, however, is the different share of immigrants in the population. In Denmark, the share of the population with a foreign background is 6.2 per cent where the similar figure for Sweden is 10.9 per cent (Green-Pedersen and Krogstrup, forthcoming). Finally, in terms of public opinion, there are many similarities between the two countries. In both countries, public opinion provides right-wing parties with an incentive to promote a restrictionist approach since it would be in line with the majority of the electorate (cf. Green-Pedersen and Krogstrup, forthcoming).

IMMIGRATION POLITICS AND POLICY IN THE 1970s AND 1980s – EXPECTED SIMILARITIES

Since the 1970s, migration flows to Denmark and Sweden have consisted primarily of asylum-seekers and family reunification (Freeman 1992; Gaasholt and Togeby 1995). This was due to an official stop on labour migrant recruitment introduced in both countries in the early 1970s. The broad consensus in both countries on halting labour immigration was a consequence of the regulated labour market and the strong influence exercised by the trade unions. The strong opposition to further migration from the trade unions, especially in Sweden, related to the privileged employment position that labour migrants enjoyed compared to other countries. This included the same social and economic rights as native workers which was said to be undermined by further, unregulated, labour migration (Geddes 2003).

The ease with which immigration policy was altered in Sweden can be attributed to the strong corporatist arrangements prevailing at the time, i.e. the close relationship between the state, trade unions and employer federations and the emphasis on full employment. The famous Swedish model for integration (Soininen 1999) was put into effect in the mid-1970s, having been preceded by an extensive government inquiry. This investigation proposed a new direction for the social, political and cultural status of migrants which, by international standards, was of a generous nature. The new guidelines put immigrants in a privileged position in terms of having access to rights and entitlements on a par with Swedish nationals (Borevi 2002). Although much praise has been given to the Swedish multicultural model (Castles and Miller 2003), it was also subject to significant criticism and debate by scholars and political actors in Sweden (Pred 2000; Ålund and Schierup 1991). The reasons for this can be summarized as follows: (a) perceived failure of multicultural policies; (b) increased socio-economic exclusion of foreign-born residents and their descendants; and (c) stigmatization and stereotyping. However, issues relating to immigration and integration were, up until the 1990s, characterized by a remarkable degree of cross-party consensus, explained in part by the strength of the Social Democrats, relatively low levels of immigration and high levels of labour market participation.

In Denmark, it was not until the early 1980s that immigration became a political issue at all (Hamburger 1989). A key turning point came in 1983 when a broad majority in parliament, with the exception of the radical right-wing Progress Party, passed a new, and in many ways, more liberal immigration law. The opportunities for family unification were strengthened, asylum-seekers achieved more rights, and expulsion of foreigners became more difficult (Brøcker 1990). In many ways, the debate on this more liberal immigration law, which had been prepared by an expert commission, continued along the lines of the 1970s discourse, but critical voices from the right-wing parties had become stronger. The Progress Party had strongly opposed existing policies since its entry into parliament in 1973 and also launched a number of xenophobic campaigns. More remarkable perhaps was the declaration by the Conservative Minister of Justice, Mr Erik Ninn Hansen, that the law would threaten Danish nationality. This declaration provoked strong reactions from the left-wing opposition (Jensen 2000; Brøcker 1990).

At the same time as the new law was implemented, an increasing number of refugees from the Middle East started to arrive in Denmark. This sparked a public debate where politicians from both the Conservatives and Liberals followed the critical immigration line introduced by the Minister of Justice (Jensen 2000). The new position included a revision of the law which tightened the conditions for asylum in Denmark (Brøcker 1990). In the end, the government managed to get its proposal passed in parliament relying on support from the Social Democrats, but without the support of the Social Liberals. After that, the issue more or less disappeared from the party political agenda during the remainder of the bourgeois minority government (Green-Pedersen and Krogstrup, forthcoming).

The debate in the mid-1980s showed that politicians from both the Liberals and the Conservatives wanted their parties to change direction towards tighter immigration controls and an integration policy that was more demanding for immigrants. Nevertheless, the broad party consensus around immigration politics survived. The reason for this was the special character of Danish coalition politics during this period. A parliamentary majority, including the Social Liberals, but not the government parties, existed in this period with regard to non-economic issues, especially foreign policy, justice and the environment (Damgaard and Svensson 1989). A more restrictionist position by the Liberals and Conservatives was thus a political dead-end because it would have sharpened the already existing conflict with the Social Liberals and could have threatened government survival.

Although comparatively more prominent in Denmark, immigration could by the end of the 1980s still be considered to be a minor political issue and the right-wing parties in both countries were still part of the broad national consensus on the issue. Policies in both countries had, however, moved somewhat in a more restrictionist direction and the consensus had showed signs of cracking in Denmark.

THE 1990s: GOING DIFFERENT WAYS?

Compared to Denmark, Sweden was in this respect lagging behind. Immigration became a hot and contested political issue 'only' in 1991 when the surprise success of the populist party, New Democracy, moved immigration up the agenda. Although New Democracy's success, as a party, was short-lived, the effects of its restrictive stance on immigration can today be found in mainstream politics. The repercussions of its proposed policy changes were present in subsequent elections as well as in the turn away from explicit multiculturalism in recent years. A telling example is the issue of language competency for naturalization. In 1992, New Democracy proposed that knowledge of Swedish should be a requirement for migrants wishing to become Swedish citizens. Their proposal was unsuccessful at the time, having been blocked by both left- and right-wing parties (Sveriges Riksdag 25/11/1992). However, in 1997 the Conservatives presented a very similar proposal which was subsequently picked up by the Liberal Party in their election campaign in 2002. The absorption of radical right policies and the mainstreaming of these are in Swedish politics symptomatic of how immigration and integration have gone from being a general welfare state concern, characterized by cross-party consensus, to being an issue used as a way of distinguishing and profiling parties.

This development had already gone one step further in Denmark where the incentives for making immigration a political issue had increased in the early 1990s and more particularly following the change of government in 1993. The Social Liberals now entered a coalition with the Social Democrats, the Christian Democrats and the Centre Democrats, the former having governed with the Liberals and Conservatives from 1982 to 1988. This new constellation put the parties in a very different situation compared to the 1980s, when they were in government. They now had no reason to avoid confrontation with the Social Liberals. Further, their major chance of getting back into government was to win a majority together with the Progress Party which diminished the need for the parties to distance themselves from the xenophobic rhetoric of the latter.

From 1993, the Danish Conservatives, and especially the Liberals, started to change their policy positions quite dramatically with regard to both immigration and integration. The first sign of this came in 1994 during a debate on how to deal with Bosnian asylum-seekers. The government, supported by the left-wing parties, wanted to allow the Bosnians to be granted refugee status. On the other hand, the right-wing opposition proposed temporary residence permits which meant repatriation to Bosnia once the war was over. The government was able to pass its proposal in parliament, but the debate showed that the right-wing parties had changed course, and thus abandoned the consensus around the immigration issue (Jensen 2000). However, in 1995, the Progress Party was splintered and the Danish People's Party emerged with the very popular leader, Pia Kjærsgaard. As mentioned above, the Progress Party had made immigration one of their key issues. The Danish People's Party focused almost exclusively on immigration and furthermore appeared as a much more reliable party, both in the eyes of the electorate and as a coalition partner, compared to the Progress Party which had constantly been plagued by internal disagreements and its eccentric leader, Mogens Glistrup. Finally, the Danish People's Party was also very keen to distance itself from any neo-Nazi groups and connections (Rydgren 2005a). The populist right became significantly stronger after the Danish People's Party had established itself in the Danish party system at the 1998 election when it won 7.4 per cent of the vote.

The pattern of confrontation between the government and the right-wing opposition was sharpened further after the 1998 election. The Liberals, under their former leader, Uffe Ellemann Jensen, had been reluctant to focus on immigration issues, but the new leader, Anders Fogh Rasmussen, realized that immigration could become a central point in the strategy of the Liberals to win government power. (Green-Pedersen and Krogstrup, forthcoming). Looking at the period from 1993 to 2001, the change in the position of, especially, the Liberals in Denmark is striking. In the party programme from 1995, they still focused on the right of immigrants to, for example, preserve their original culture (Venstre 1995), whereas in 2006 the focus is on what Danish society should demand from immigrants both culturally and economically (Venstre 2006). Another illuminating example was the question of the naturalization of immigrants. Until 1993, only the Progress Party had wanted to reopen the debate on this law, which had previously been passed in parliament without much controversy. However, from 1993, the Liberals and Conservatives also started to question the legislation (cf. Holm 2005: 93–113).

Developments in Sweden were generally different though with some similarities to Denmark. Although immigration and integration had been reasonably important issues for the electorate since the 1980s, they had not been crucial in determining party choice (Rydgren 2002). The mainstream parties, and especially those on the centre-right, had furthermore been slow to respond to changes in voter preferences and had not actively pursued the more right-wing voters (Rydgren 2005b). However, a turning point regarding the salience of immigration questions in Swedish politics and the stability of cross-party consensus on these issues came in the 1994 election. As in Denmark, the war in the Balkans had led to a dramatic increase in asylum applications which coincided with the Swedish economy's attempt to recover from the recession. These events prompted the election campaign to be dominated by questions of Sweden's commitment to refugee reception and, especially, the societal costs related to this type of migration. The change in issue preference can partly be attributed to the influence of New Democracy in shaping the agenda during the early 1990s and to the aggressive fashion in which they had pursued these issues.

The question of whether to restrict asylum and refugee migration was a key element in the election campaign as well as in the political debate in 1994. Relatively less attention was paid to issues of racism, discrimination and socio-economic exclusion (Boréus 2006). Why parties avoided addressing these issues is puzzling since, as Rydgren (2004b) points out, during the economic recession of the 1990s, Sweden had one of the highest levels of unemployment amongst non-European migrants within the Organisation for Economic Co-operation and Development.

Following on from the increased political hostility towards immigration and the perceived failure of the multicultural project, an expert committee was set up to formulate a new direction for Swedish integration policy. *The politics of integration* presented in September 1997 put forward some new guidelines for what had previously been considered 'the politics of immigrants'. A distinguishing feature of these policies was a move away from the corporatist orientation of previous policies that considered 'immigrants' to be yet another type of social grouping in a similar vein to 'labourers' or 'employers'. Instead, the new policy would focus more on the individual and his or her needs. Linguistically this change could be seen in the emphasis on 'integration' as opposed to 'immigrants' and a focus on providing equality of opportunities (Göransson 2005).

This new deal also prompted the birth of the Swedish Integration Board (Integrationsverket IV) which had the overall responsibility for ensuring that the visions and goals of Sweden's integration policies have an impact in different areas of society. An indication that immigration, yet again, was to be a hot political issue came prior to the 1998 election when a former employee of the Swedish Board of Immigration, Kenneth Sandberg, spoke out about the 'disastrous situation' that Sweden was in after decades of 'mass immigration' which generated intense media coverage. The relatively open climate that had emerged, which allowed commentators to speak out in a covertly racist language, can again be attributed to the influence that New Democracy and its populist rhetoric had in the early 1990s (Rydgren 2005a). Although this new policy direction by and large corresponded to key centre-right ideas of individualism and equal opportunities, the Conservative Party responded to the (primarily Social Democratic) policy by issuing a distinctly more radical proposal in time for the 1998 election. The rhetoric of the far-right had been absorbed and mainstreamed into the Conservative's Party manifesto of 1997, *Land for Hoppfulla* (Land of the Hopeful). This was one of the first manifestos by a mainstream party to directly address 'the problems of immigration' and the Conservatives had picked up on anti-immigrant sentiments among the electorate as well as the support for radical right parties. However, the manifesto was heavily criticized for legitimizing this type of far-right discourse, seeing that the manifesto implicitly blamed immigrants for their high levels of welfare dependency and their 'failure' to integrate. Less publicized but just as controversial, was the Conservative proposal to re-open the borders for labour migration in order to remedy skill shortages in certain sectors.

This new fertile political environment also allowed the populist and right-wing Sweden Democrats to re-mobilize. After shedding their connections with neo-Nazi and other far-right groups they increased their electoral support and eventually gained seats in eight localities (Ekman and Larsson 2001). Their success can be explained by how the debate on asylum and refugees had shifted towards criticizing the Social Democrats' spending on settled refugees and whether the various integration projects were producing any beneficial results.

In Denmark, the period up until 2001 saw a constant battle between the bourgeois opposition – the Liberals and the Conservatives – and the centre-left government. By accepting some tightening of immigration and asylum rules and some tougher integration measures, the government tried to close down the issue as a major point of political conflict. However, the bourgeois opposition was very successful at turning immigration into a crucial – if not the dominant – issue in the 2001 election campaign. The politicization of the issue was thus a major reason for the bourgeois victory and move into government in 2001 (Andersen 2003). The election in 2001 allowed the Conservatives and the Liberals to form a coalition which could rule with support from the Danish People's Party. The need to avoid open conflict with the Social Liberals, which had constrained the two parties in the 1980s, was no longer present and the policy measures which the two parties had advocated in opposition could now be implemented. The policy measures related to both immigration and integration issues. With regard to immigration, the rules on family unification were tightened significantly, making them much tougher than in other European countries (Tænketanken 2004). Family unification before the age of 24 became virtually impossible and married couples had to document a closer connection to Denmark than to the homeland of the person not already living in Denmark. With regard to integration, the central idea had been that labour market participation was the best way to integrate immigrants. In terms of policy instruments, the focus had been on securing economic incentives for immigrants to take a job which corresponded with the more general transformations of Danish labour market policy. However, the Danish system provided fairly generous social assistance in which the actual net gain from working, compared to receiving social benefits, could sometimes be quite limited. A central measure was the introduction of a special level of social assistance for non-EU migrants which was considerably below the normal level and was intended to serve as an incentive for immigrants to accept low-paid jobs. These policy measures can be seen as the culmination of the Danish right's transformation of immigration and integration policy which took place after the change of government in 1993 and which brought the parties fairly close to the position of the Danish People's Party.

Although questions of immigration and integration had been prominent in previous Swedish elections, the 2002 election was significant for how the centre-right chose to utilize immigration and integration as a profiling tool. Ljunggren (2003) points to two particular circumstances that enabled immigration to become one of the key election issues. First, as a way of pre-empting the Sweden Democrats from monopolizing the issue. The Sweden Democrats had closely monitored the success of the Danish People's Party and adopted a number of their tactics and policies which caused concern for the mainstream parties. Second, immigration, and especially criticism of the ruling Social Democratic bloc for incompetence in this area, served as an effective tool for profiling the centre-right parties. It also provided opportunities for the Liberal Party to put forward the issue of language tests as a requirement for naturalization. Although the proposal came under heavy fire from Social Democrats, relying on the rhetoric of equality and solidarity, it nevertheless corresponded, in parts, to the new integration directives from 1997. A key component of these policies suggested that integration should be the responsibility of the entire population, not just the receiving society. This indicated a significant shift towards the right when emphasizing the duties and responsibilities that migrants had and should adhere to if they wanted to integrate successfully. Although heavily criticized for being populist and fishing for the far-right vote, the Liberal Party was not opposed to Sweden's asylum and refugee policy as such, and was also in favour of a more flexible immigration system which allowed for future labour migration (Bale 2003).

The open attitude towards labour immigration was a continuation of what the Conservatives had already suggested in their 1997 manifesto and set the centre-right bloc apart from the left and the trade union view that labour migration should continue to be restricted. The centre-right also took the opportunity to further criticize the left in general, and the Social Democrats in particular, for having pursued a politics of integration which in many ways had 'failed'. A particular point was made regarding the high levels of unemployment, overrepresentation in criminal statistics and poor performance in schools by migrants and their descendants (Boréus 2006). Similarly, the revamped and sanitized Sweden Democrats exploited immigration as a profiling tool and focused their campaign on emphasizing the perceived differences between 'Swedes' and 'immigrants', using what for them was the novel approach of stressing the cultural clashes to which migration, and especially Islamic migration, gave rise to rather than using the traditional far-right discourse of race (Ares and Diaz 2006).

The relative success that the Sweden Democrats had in the 2006 election can be traced back to how salient integration and immigration issues were for the mainstream parties. In contrast to previous elections, immigration and integration issues were not as prominent in the 2006 election. Although immigration, and especially integration, figured frequently in public debate, these issues were somewhat overshadowed by the unexpected agreement reached by the centre-right alliance ('Alliance for Sweden') on a number of policies (growth, education, foreign policy, the welfare state, the labour market and justice), thus making them a serious contender for government (Aylott and Bolin 2007). Furthermore, the Conservatives had learned from the 1998 election and adjusted their rhetoric to once again frame integration in a general and ideologically-compatible language. Consequently, immigration and integration slipped down the priority list.

The Alliance parties' manifestos were indicative of these changes, with immigration and integration policies being vaguely formulated and appearing towards the end of the party manifestos. The proposed solutions to 'integration failures' did, by and large, correspond to the ideological positioning of the parties. The Conservatives' manifesto, for example, suggested that integration is a matter best dealt with by the labour market and consequently the barriers to participation in this area were to be removed (www.moderaterna.se), a view which was supported by the Centre Party (www.centerpartiet.se). In a similar vein, the Liberal Party identified unequal access to the labour market as a key problem but went one step further by also emphasizing that migrants have duties as well as rights (www.folkpartiet.se).[6] The lack of a clear cross-party strategy on how to confront far-right opponents, in combination with immigration and integration issues receiving a low priority, possibly played in favour of the Sweden Democrats, who managed to carve out a clear party profile in the 2006 election (Aylott and Brolin 2007). However, the shift in government structure in the 2006 election also marked a number of significant changes in terms of the Swedish approach to immigration and integration. Nyamko Sabuni, a Liberal Party member, was appointed as minister for integration and gender equality. Sabuni established herself as an important figure in the integration debate by quickly implementing the closing down of the Swedish Integration Board, a plan that had been hatched by the Alliance in the years running up to the 2006 election. The significance of this act should not be overlooked since it marks a clear disengagement from the Swedish model. Nevertheless, it was passed with remarkably little debate and controversy, although the Social Democrats and the Left Party criticized the decision for not being properly thought through. Further changes included emphasizing the importance of Swedish language education, combating discrimination and providing equal opportunities in the labour market.

CONCLUSION

The development of immigration politics in Denmark and Sweden since the 1990s shows a surprising degree of divergence given the similarities in societal context. In Denmark, the considerable changes in a more restrictive direction, which resulted from the politicization of the issue after the change of government in 1993, remain in place even though political attention to the immigration issue has cooled down somewhat since 2001. In fact, a new party consensus around these restrictive changes has emerged in Denmark as the Social Democrats have largely accepted them in an attempt to downplay the role of the immigration issue in Danish politics (see Bale *et al.* 2007).

The Swedish centre-right parties have not made a move in a restrictionist direction to anything like the same extent. For example, the Danish decision to restrict the immigration of dependants by raising the age limit for family reunification to 24 was viewed with scepticism in Sweden and there was no equivalent policy position by the Swedish right. The furthest move in a restrictionist direction was represented by the Conservative position up to the 1998 election, but even that contained a suggestion to re-open the borders for labour immigration. Such a liberal element is not found in the positions of Danish right-wing parties in the 1990s. Furthermore, the Swedish Conservatives more or less gave up this partial move in a Danish direction before the 2006 election to secure the coherence of the 'Alliance' with the centre-right parties.

It is important, however, not to misinterpret this lack of movement as an indication of Swedish immigration politics today being largely similar to that of the 1980s. Sweden has in fact moved away from cross-party consensus on integration to a somewhat more polarized situation between the centre-right and the left blocs. Consequently, the Swedish model of integration has undergone extensive restructuring. However, the disagreement between the left and right in Sweden revolves mainly around whether the welfare state or the market is the most effective tool for reducing socio-economic exclusion. It is much less about the right wanting a more restrictionist immigration policy than in Denmark.

The argument of this paper suggests that the difference in right-wing positions in the 1990s, and the differences in immigration politics to which this led, should be explained by the differences in coalition politics of the right-wing bloc. In Denmark, the change of side of the Social Liberals in 1993 which led to a change of government implied that the major parties of the right – the Liberals and Conservatives – now had no incentive to avoid confrontation with the Social Liberals over the immigration issue. This was what had kept them from turning in a more restrictionist direction in the 1980s. During the 1990s, the two parties turned steadily more restrictionist as part of a very successful strategy to politicize the issue. This politicization, which also involved co-operation with the radical right, led to a much more restrictionist policy in Denmark with regard to both immigration and integration (Green-Pedersen and Krogstrup, forthcoming).

In Sweden, a similar move by the Conservatives would have been, and continues to be, dangerous because it would damage the right-wing bloc's chances of presenting itself as a united alternative to the Social Democrats. The U-turn of the Swedish Conservatives in the direction of the traditional consensus around immigration politics before the 2006 election illustrates exactly this. The U-turn was necessary to establish the right-wing 'Alliance', which in the end won power. The increased polarization between the left and right on integration policies fits well with the coalition politics of the right because it corresponds with the classic class cleavage which has been the main divider in Swedish society.

The experiences in Sweden and Denmark clearly show that analysing the position of the centre-right is crucial for understanding immigration politics and thus clearly confirms the central argument of this volume. Further, by stressing the importance of the centre-right, and not just the radical right, this contribution also argues that the tendency of the literature to emphasize radical right-wing parties with regard to immigration and integration is problematic (Bale 2008). At the very least, the role of radical right-wing parties has to be seen in connection with the question of coalition politics of the entire right-wing bloc (Bale 2003). Radical right-wing parties have played a much stronger role in Danish politics but, as presented above, this difference only became important as part of Danish coalition politics during the 1990s. The presence of the Progress Party and its xenophobic rhetoric during the 1980s did not cause a break with the overall party consensus and thus a divergence from the Swedish situation. That break and that divergence only happened after 1993 when the coalition incentives of the centre-right in Denmark changed.

ACKNOWLEDGEMENTS

The authors would like to thank the editor, the referees and the participants at the University of Cambridge workshop for useful comments on this article.

NOTES

1 To make presentation easier, immigration politics in the following refers to both immigration and integration policies.
2 A more detailed introduction to the right-wing parties in Scandinavia and their development can be found in Arter (1999).
3 In 1973, two other small centre right-wing parties, the Centre Democrats and the Christian People's Party, also gained representation, which they have lost in recent years.
4 It is worth noting that the Swedish Liberals are much more of a centrist party than the Liberals in Denmark and as such are in many ways more similar to the Danish Social Liberals.
5 Although both countries have had linguistic minorities for centuries (Finnish and Saami communities in Sweden and the small German minority in southern Denmark), they have been subject to strong processes of assimilation over the years and have only recently been recognized as national minorities.
6 In comparison, the Social Democrats also pointed to the importance of the labour market but phrased this in traditional social democratic language of equality and inclusion (www.socialdemokraterna.se). The Left Party's manifesto, on the other hand, only mentioned immigration and integration indirectly when pointing out that it favoured a generous interpretation of the right to asylum. The Green Party's manifesto contained a vague paragraph on the benefits of a multicultural society but this is, on the other hand, complemented by a very detailed list of policy proposals on their webpage. The Greens were also, somewhat surprisingly perhaps, in favour of free immigration (www.mp.se) as well as a generous asylum and refugee policy.

REFERENCES

Ålund, A. and Schierup, C.-U. (1991) *Paradoxes of Multiculturalism*, Aldershot: Avebury.

Andersen, J.G. (2003) 'The Danish general election 2001', *Electoral Studies* 22(1): 186–93.
Ares, A. and Diaz, J.A. (2006) *Populism and Xenophobia: Sweden in Europe*, Norrkoping: Integrationsverket.
Arter, D. (1999) *Scandinavian Politics Today*, Manchester: Manchester University Press.
Aylott, N. and Bolin, N. (2007) 'Towards a two-party system? The Swedish parliamentary election of September 2006', *West European Politics* 30(3): 621–33.
Bale, T. (2003) 'Cinderella and her ugly sisters: the mainstream and extreme right in Europe's bipolarising party systems', *West European Politics* 26(3): 67–90.
Bale, T. (2008) 'Turning round the telescope. Centre-right parties and immigration and integration policy in Europe', *Journal of European Public Policy* 15(3): 315–30.
Bale, T., Green-Pedersen, C., Krouwel, A., Luther, K.R. and Sitter, N. (2007) 'If you can't beat them, join them? Exploring the European centre-left's turn against migration and multiculturalism: a four-country case study'. Unpublished MS.
Boréus, K. (2006) *Diskrimineringens retorik: en studie av svenska valrörelser 1988–2002*, Stockholm: Fritzes.
Borevi, K. (2002) *The Welfare State in a Multicultural Society*, Uppsala: Acta Universitatis Upsaliensis.
Brøcker, A. (1990) 'Udlændingelovgivningi Danmark 1983–1986: Faktorer i den politiske beslutningsproces', *Politica* 22(3): 332–45.
Castles, S. and Miller, M. (2003) *The Age of Migration*, Basingstoke: Palgrave.
Damgaard, E. and Svensson, P. (1989). 'Who governs? Parties and policies in Denmark', *European Journal of Political Research* 17(6): 731–45.
Ekman, M. and Larsson, S. (2001) *Sverigedemokraterna – den nationella rörelsen*, Stockholm: Ordfront Forlag.
Freeman, G. (1992) 'Migration policy and politics in the receiving states', *International Migration Review* 26(4): 1144–67.
Gaasholt, Ø. and Togeby, L. (1995) *I syv sind. Danskernes holdning til flygtninge og indvandrere*, Aarhus: Politica.
Geddes, A. (2003) *The Politics of Migration and Immigration in Europe*, London: Sage.
Göransson, A. (2005) 'Utländsk bakgrund – en tillgång eller hinder på vägen mot makt?', in A. Göransson (ed.), *Makten och Mångfalden*, Stockholm: Fritzes, pp. 7–41.
Green-Pedersen, C. and Krogstrup, J. (forthcoming) 'Immigration as a political issue in Denmark and Sweden. How party competition shapes political agendas', *European Journal of Political Research*.
Hamburger, C. (ed.) (1989) *Assimilation eller integration?*, Aarhus: Politica.
Holm, L. (2005) *Folketinget og Udlændingepolitikken*, Ålborg: Akademiet for Migrationsstudier i Danmark.
Jensen, B. (2000) *De fremmede i dansk avisdebat*, København: Spektrum.
Ljunggren, S. (2003) *I slutet av borjan – recension av de politiska partiernas integrationspolitiska program*, Norrköping: Integrationsverket.
Nannestad, P. (2004) 'Immigration as a challenge to the Danish welfare state', *European Journal of Political Economy* 20(3): 755–67.
Pred, A. (2000) *Even in Sweden: Racisms, Racialized Spaces, and the Popular Geographical Imagination*, Berkeley: University of California Press.
Rydgren, J. (2002) *Radical Right Populism in Sweden: Still a Failure, But For How Long?*, Stockholm: Department of Sociology, Stockholm University.
Rydgren, J. (2004) 'Mechanisms of exclusion: ethnic discrimination in the Swedish labour market', *Journal of Ethnic and Migration Studies* 30(4): 697–716.
Rydgren, J. (2005a) *Fran skattemissnoje till etnisk nationalism: hogerpopulism och parlamentarisk hogerextremism i Sverige*, Stockholm: Studenliteratur.

Rydgren, J. (2005b) 'Is extreme right-wing populism contagious? Explaining the emergence of a new party family', *European Journal of Political Research* 44(3): 413–37.

Soininen, M. (1999) 'The "Swedish model" as an institutional framework for immigrant membership rights', *Journal of Ethnic and Migration Studies* 25(4): 685–702.

Sveriges Riksdag, 25/11/1992, *Votering 58*, Stockholm: Riksdagsbiblioteket.

Tænketanken om udfordringer for integrationsindsaten i Danmark (2004) *Udlændingepolitikken i Danmark og udvalgte lande*, Copenhagen: Ministry of Refugees, Immigration and Integration Affairs.

Venstre (1995) *Mennesket frem for systemet, Principprogram for Venstre*.

On-line sources

Conservatives, http://www.moderat.se/material/pdffiler/moderat_11799.pdf, accessed 01-03-2007.

Centre Party, http://www.centerpartiet.se/templates2/Page.aspx?id=33691, accessed on 01-03-2007.

Green Party, http://www.mp.se/templates/Mct_77.aspx?number=326&avdnr=5, accessed 01-03-2007.

Left Party, http//www.vansterpartict.se/images/stories/media/dokument/rapporter/valplattform2006.pdf, accessed 01-03-2007.

Liberal Party, http://www.folkpartiet.se/FPTemplates/ImportantArea____20410.aspx, accessed 01-03-2007.

Social Democrats, http://www.socialdemokraterna.se/upload/Central/dokument/pdf/Socialdemokraternasvalmanifest2006.pdf, accessed 01-03-2007.

Venstre 2006. *Fremtid i frihed og fællesskab, Venstre principprogram* http://www.venstre.dk/index.php?id=3775.

Nicolas Sarkozy and the politics of French immigration policy

Sally Marthaler

Nicolas Sarkozy's first administration, formed in May 2007 following his election to the French presidency as the candidate of the centre-right Union for a Popular Movement (UMP), included a new Ministry of Immigration, Integration, National Identity and Co-Development. The ministry had been one of Sarkozy's key manifesto pledges and it maintained the momentum in migration policy-making that had begun with his appointment as Minister of the Interior at the start of Chirac's second presidential term of office in 2002. However, its creation was highly controversial since it made explicit what had hitherto been an implicit association between migrants and French national identity (Hargreaves 1995: 151). Its nationalist and xenophobic overtones drew criticism and it was attacked not only by the opposition Socialist Party (PS) and migrants' associations but also by the Christian democratic Union for French Democracy (UDF) and the Catholic Church. Nonetheless, the new ministry had the backing of 72 per cent of the French public (90 per cent on the right and 50 per cent on the left).[1]

Taking the shift in French immigration policy initiated by Nicolas Sarkozy as its starting point, this contribution has four aims. First, it sets out the background to recent developments in immigration policy-making in France. Second, it explores the way in which Sarkozy has repositioned the UMP, the dominant centre-right party of which he has been president since 2004, on immigration and examines how recent discourse and action diverge from earlier centre-right handling of the issue. Third, it seeks to explain why this evolution has taken place by identifying the forces shaping and constraining the conduct and stance of Sarkozy and his party. In particular, it analyses the extent to which changes in immigration policy are a function of political competition or a response to public opinion. Finally, it evaluates the effectiveness of the centre-right's handling of the immigration issue, both in political and social terms.

I. THE TERMS OF THE IMMIGRATION DEBATE IN FRANCE

France's immigrant population

According to the most recent census figures (Insee 2006), there are currently 4.9 million migrants in France, representing 8.1 per cent of the mainland population. This figure does not include those of immigrant origin who were born in France and have French nationality. Because no data have hitherto been collected in France on ethnicity, it is impossible to know the precise size of the ethnic minority population (Geddes and Guiraudon 2004: 339). Estimates of illegal immigrants (*sans-papiers*) vary between 200,000 and 500,000.

Today, 60 per cent of immigrants in France are of non-European origin, compared with 51 per cent in 1999 and 43 per cent in 1975 (Mayer 2007a: 1). Since the suspension of labour migration from non-European Community (EC) countries in 1974, the main source of immigration into France has been family reunification. In 2005, 70 per cent of migrants entered the country for this purpose and only 7 per cent for work. About 70 per cent of French immigrants come from former colonies in North and West Africa and the largest migrant community is from the Maghreb, especially Algeria and Morocco. There is also a growing Turkish community, producing a significant Muslim community of over 4 million (Wihtol de Wenden 2005: 153) making up around 7 per cent of the population, the largest percentage of Muslims in any European Union (EU) member state.

What was initially a simple question of economics in terms of a cheap and flexible workforce has, since 1974, been transformed into an issue with social, political and cultural as well as economic dimensions. If, as Schain (2004: 2) puts it, 'we presume that public policy is generally a response to a perceived problem', then in France the 'problem' is the perceived threat represented by migrants to French employment, law and order, and national identity. According to Fetzer,

Immigration politics in France appears to turn just as much on whether the country's culture will remain primarily Catholic and European as on whether most native-born French workers will be able to find jobs. In other words, in the French mind Maghrebi immigrants represent at least as much of a threat to France's dominant culture as Muslims as they do to the French labour market as low-wage, relatively unskilled employees.

(Fetzer 2000: 122)

The French republican tradition, with its emphasis on equality, universalism and secularism, has had an important influence on the development of the French model of integration, which has prioritized the assimilation of migrants (Hollifield 1994). According to this tradition, minorities or ethnic communities are not officially recognized and differences in language or culture, including religion, are confined to the private sphere. The perception that migrants, particularly Muslim migrants, are no longer assimilable has been a predominant issue in the immigration debate since the mid-1980s (Geddes 2003: 69).

The politicization of the immigration issue

The politicization of immigration in France is associated primarily with the rise of the far-right National Front (FN), formed in 1972. However, the FN had little electoral success in its first decade, winning less than 1 per cent of the vote in national elections, and it was not until the early 1980s that immigration became the subject of public concern and debate (DeLey 1983: 201), partly as a result of the Communist Party (PC) highlighting the issue in the 1981 presidential elections when it presented migrants as a threat to the French working class. The FN first became a significant political player and began to dominate the debate on immigration after a series of electoral successes in the early 1980s in local and European elections before breaking through at a national level in the 1986 parliamentary elections, contested under a new (and temporary) system of Proportional Representation (PR), when the party won 35 seats in the National Assembly. Parliamentary representation allowed the FN a claim to legitimacy. Between 1986 and the 2007 presidential election Le Pen and his party consistently won between 10 per cent and 15 per cent of the national vote, achieving their best result in the cataclysmic first round of the 2002 presidential elections when Le Pen polled 17 per cent, eliminating the PS candidate Lionel Jospin before being defeated by Chirac in the second-round run-off.

The FN programme and discourse on immigration incorporates xenophobic and discriminatory rhetoric portraying non-European immigrants as a threat to French national identity, living off state handouts, fuelling crime and creating a climate of insecurity and even subversion. The party is vehemently opposed to multiculturalism and its policy of 'national preference' would give priority to French nationals in housing, social security benefits and employment. Its other proposals include zero immigration, the expulsion of illegal immigrants, French control of national borders and the reform of French nationality laws to replace *jus soli* with *jus sanguinis*. A new anti-immigration party, the Movement for France (MPF), was founded in 1994 by Philippe de Villiers with a programme also constructed on hostility towards migrants and using similarly inflammatory rhetoric. However, de Villiers has sought to differentiate himself from Le Pen by emphasizing religious difference and in particular the 'creeping Islamization' of France, which he links with terrorism.

The presence of the far-right has had a profound effect on the French political space. The political configuration which emerged during the 1980s and 1990s has been described as an evolution from bipolarization to 'tripartition' (Grunberg and Schweisguth 2003) because of the strong and persistent presence of the far-right alongside the moderate right and left. While the centre-right has an ideological advantage over the centre-left on the issues of migration and insecurity, the electoral success of the FN has confronted it with a dilemma: whether to try to undercut the FN's electoral appeal by making concessions to its nationalist and xenophobic immigration policy, to seek strategic agreements with Le Pen, or to ignore him and his party. Each of these alternatives carries the risk of helping to legitimate the FN and thus strengthen its electoral appeal but each has been resorted to at different times.

After a 'conciliatory phase' when formal and informal links were developed between the mainstream and far-right during the 1980s, the centre-right Rally for the Republic (RPR) (which merged into the UMP in 2002) and UDF chose to refuse any electoral alliance with the FN (Ivaldi and Swyngedouw 2005: 1). Instead, their strategy was to compete with the far-right in discourse and policy terms while placing a *cordon sanitaire* around Le Pen and his party. Thus, the discourse of the centre-right on immigration has been characterized by 'significant exclusionary features' (van der Valk 2003: 310). Not unlike the far-right, it has linked migrants with rising crime levels, fraud and abuse of the welfare state as well as cultural decline, generating a climate of suspicion towards immigrants which 'clearly has a function to justify harsh measures to restrict immigration without risking being accused of repressive policies' (van der Valk 2003: 339).

In an effort to win back voters lost to the FN in the early 1980s, the RPR and UDF made a commitment in their joint 1986 manifesto to tighten up French nationality and asylum laws, although once in government the proposed legislation was withdrawn in the face of fierce opposition. The policy changes were not finally made until 1993 when they were included in the laws introduced by the hardline Minister of the Interior, Charles Pasqua, which were supplemented in 1995 by the Debré law on illegal immigration. At the same time, the centre-right continued to promote the traditional assimilationist model for long-established legal migrants (van der Valk 2003: 310).

The immigration issue was virtually ignored by the moderate parties of both left and right during the 1993 parliamentary, 1994 European and 1995 presidential elections. In part this may be accounted for by their reluctance to draw attention to an issue which the FN 'owned' or to risk inflaming tensions which were becoming increasingly visible in the early 1990s with confrontations between youths and riot police in the run-down suburbs (*banlieues*) and the shooting by the police of a second-generation immigrant, Khaled Kelkal, after the 1995 Paris metro bombings attributed to the Armed Islamic Group (GIA). As Benson (2002: 6) points out, by the early 1990s, media coverage of such incidents was becoming more sensationalist and playing a more significant role in shaping public political debate. In addition, while there was a consensus among the mainstream parties on many aspects of immigration policy such as the need to balance immigration control and integration, each of them also had internal divisions which they did not want to advertise. The FN's message in the 1995 presidential election, on the other hand, was unequivocal: sending 2 million immigrants home would cancel out France's 2 million unemployed.

In their 1997 joint manifesto, the RPR and UDF declared their attachment to the republican values of 'tolerance, brotherhood, responsibility and patriotism' but the only explicit reference made to immigration was in terms of combating illegal immigration and illegal work. Other measures that would facilitate the integration of the immigrant population were included in more general objectives of equal opportunities and social support for the disadvantaged. In contrast, the Socialists set out specific proposals to repeal the repressive Pasqua–Debré laws, re-establish *jus soli* and guarantee the right to asylum. Yet the reforms introduced after their victory in the 1997 parliamentary elections were far more modest than their manifesto pledges and led to a rift within the left-wing coalition (*gauche plurielle*). However, as Boswell (2003: 21) observes, 'calls for more restrictive measures appeared to have died down by the end of the 1990s; migration and asylum were no longer a central topic of party political debate.'

The declining salience of immigration during this period may be attributed to social, economic and political factors. The victory of a multi-ethnic (*black-blanc-beur*) French football team in the World Cup in July 1998 helped to create a mood of greater tolerance and optimism, to which falling unemployment in the late 1990s contributed. Also in 1998, the far-right was weakened after divisions within the FN resulted in a split and Bruno Mégret formed the National Republican Movement (MNR). Ethnic tensions resurfaced after the September 11 attacks. In October 2001 a football match between France and Algeria was disrupted when ethnic-minority spectators booed the national anthem and invaded the pitch. Despite this reversal, the 2002 UMP manifesto once again made no explicit reference to integration, which was subsumed under measures to strengthen social cohesion. The only specific migration policy objective given was the fight against illegal immigration. The Socialists did not propose any major policy on immigration or integration other than the introduction of voting rights for foreigners in local elections.

II. THE EVOLUTION OF THE CENTRE-RIGHT POSITION ON IMMIGRATION AND INTEGRATION SINCE 2002

The impact of the 2002 French presidential election

The crushing rebuke delivered to the mainstream parties in the 2002 presidential election when Le Pen won 16.9 per cent of the first-round vote suggested that their strategy towards the far-right had failed. Nonetheless, Le Pen's success cannot simply be explained by his stance on immigration. The fragmentation of the left-wing vote, the high level of abstention and the rise of a generalized protest vote all played a role. And in 2002 immigration was the most salient election issue for only 14 per cent of the electorate as a whole.[2] However, crucially, it was the primary concern of 46 per cent of Le Pen supporters.[3] Furthermore, during the 2002 presidential election, immigration was increasingly reframed as a question of law and order, a major preoccupation for 58 per cent of far-right voters.[4] These two issues had become closely interlinked in the public consciousness as a result of the episodes of urban violence in the *banlieues* during the 1990s.

The outcome of the 2002 presidential election indicated that the immigration policy of both the centre-left and centre-right was perceived by key sections of the electorate as being too lax, and addressing this issue became a major focus of Chirac's second presidency. Sarkozy was appointed Minister of the Interior and rapidly won high public approval for his actions. Sixty per cent of respondents in a 2002 poll[5] expressed confidence in his policy on fighting insecurity (44 per cent on the centre-left, 88 per cent on the centre-right and 53 per cent on the far-right), while only 21 per cent considered it too repressive. Sixty-three per cent had confidence in his action on controlling illegal immigration (55 per cent on the centre-left, 77 per cent on the centre-right and 61 per cent on far-right) and 50 per cent for his action on improving integration (40 per cent on the centre-left, 70 per cent on the centre-right, 43 per cent on the far-right). Over the next four years during his two periods at the Ministry of the Interior (May 2002 to March 2004 and May 2005 to March 2007), Sarkozy introduced two major pieces of legislation covering immigration control, nationality and integration.

The 2003 *Loi Sarkozy*

The first of Sarkozy's laws (Law 2003-1119 of 26 November 2003 on immigration control, the residence of aliens in France and nationality) adopted a two-pronged approach, offsetting more restrictive measures on immigration control with provisions to improve integration. The new law had two key objectives: first, to restrict illegal immigration, fixing a target of 25,000 deportations in 2006 (compared with 10,000 in 2002) and, second, to reduce the number of asylum-seekers. The justification for more repressive immigration control was that this would facilitate the integration of immigrants already settled in France.

The shift in centre-right policy under Sarkozy towards a tougher and more radical approach appears to have been driven by party political as well as public policy considerations. In the aftermath of the 2002 presidential election, he was prepared to turn what had hitherto been a threat to the centre-right into an opportunity by adopting a more hardline position to compete with Le Pen on his territory. This involved two principal risks: potentially alienating the more centrist section of the centre-right electorate and helping to legitimate the far-right programme. However, it also presented Sarkozy with an opportunity, primarily but not solely, in electoral terms.

In electoral terms, the opportunity was clear. In the 2002 presidential election, the far-right (Le Pen and the MNR candidate, Bruno Mégret) had won 5.5 million votes, appealing strongly to a section of the electorate for whom immigration and insecurity were the major issues, including a significant section of the working class. Philippe de Villiers' electorate was of less interest since the MPF had polled only 0.8 per cent in the 2002 parliamentary elections.

Sarkozy's strategy was to win back far-right voters by directly addressing their concerns. Evidently, he did not believe that Le Pen's defeat in the second round of the 2002 presidential election had neutralized his or his party's political influence, and his judgement on this is supported by opinion polls which, as late as 2006,[6] showed a 24 per cent public approval rating for Le Pen's position on immigration, identical to the figure for 1988 and 1998. Not only has support been consistent over the last two decades but there has been a growing acceptance of Le Pen's ideas, which only 34 per cent found unacceptable in 2006 compared with 48 per cent in 1997. Similarly, over a third felt that the far-right was close to the concerns of the French and enriched political debate, particularly on immigration and law and order.

These are minorities of the electorate but nonetheless significant minorities and a failure of the mainstream parties to respond to the public concerns that they represent would risk a further withdrawal of support in future elections. It seems then that in part at least a political calculation lay behind Sarkozy's decision to make a rightward shift in UMP policy and discourse. This also reflected Sarkozy's readiness to challenge taboos, an early and glaring example of which was his willingness to participate in television debates with Le Pen in 2002 and 2003. Chirac had refused to have any encounter with the FN leader, saying 'Faced with intolerance and hate, there can be no dealings, compromise or debate'.[7] Sarkozy has apparently been less inhibited by such scruples and openly declared his intention of reaching out to FN voters. In one interview he candidly admitted that he was prepared to seek them out 'one by one', adding that 'If the FN has made headway, it's because we haven't done our job. By refusing to talk about some of the subjects which Le Pen has taken ownership of, we have driven part of our electorate to despair'.[8] Not only was he prepared to take up some of Le Pen's themes, but he talked about them in straightforward, often 'politically incorrect' language quite different from the 'code language' and circumlocutions to which he attributed the exasperation of a section of the French electorate. This new strategy went down particularly well with far-right voters.[9]

Yet Sarkozy balanced his tough stance on immigration and law and order with proposals for an integration policy which would be considered un-republican by many at the political centre, supporting positive discrimination and foreigners' right to vote in local elections, a position that put him at odds with Chirac and the majority of the UMP. He also proposed the financing of mosques in France and supported the creation of the French Muslim Council (*Conseil français du culte musulman* or CFCM) in 2003 which gave Islam an official voice in France. In contrast to this apparent openness to multiculturalism, Chirac maintained an assimilationist, secularist stance.

These more progressive positions also gave ammunition to the far-right, who accused Sarkozy of promoting 'foreign preference' and speaking a 'double language'. Why he supported these policies, whether out of conviction (as the son of an immigrant), to appeal to the ethnic minority vote or to wrong-foot his rivals, is unclear, and ultimately he backtracked on them during the 2007 presidential election campaign. In any case, it was his new harder-line stance on immigration control and law and order that was popular with the public rather than his position on integration and multiculturalism.

Soon after the adoption of the 2003 law, the government embarked on a new reform of the Code for the Entry and Residence of Foreigners and the Right of Asylum (CESEDA) (Masquet 2006: 45) which resulted in the second *Loi Sarkozy* in 2006. Whereas the 2003 law had prioritized the fight against illegal immigration, this one was aimed at better adapting immigration to France's capacity to receive immigrants and to the country's economic needs. In June 2005, at a UMP conference entitled 'Selective Immigration for Successful Integration', Sarkozy stated his objective of reversing the proportion of family immigration to labour immigration. Having won the leadership of the UMP in November 2004, his control of the party gave him a new platform and mandate to pursue this tougher line.

However, the fact that new legislation was being proposed before the provisions of the 2003 Act had been fully implemented begged the question as to why they had not been included in the first bill. The timing of the announcement, soon after the victory of the 'No' vote in the referendum on the EU constitutional treaty on 29 May 2005, was significant. Illegal immigration had been one of the main concerns of 'No' voters and urgently needed to be addressed. In the aftermath of the referendum, de Villepin had replaced Raffarin as prime minister and Sarkozy, replacing de Villepin, had returned to the Ministry of the Interior for a second period.

One of the first actions of the new prime minister was to announce the setting up of an inter-ministerial committee on immigration control to co-ordinate the actions of the ministries of the interior, social affairs and foreign affairs. On 11 July 2005, Sarkozy announced the main measures to be included in a second bill, saying that he wanted to 'profoundly transform immigration policy in France'. He made a commitment to increase the rate of expulsions of illegal immigrants by 50 per cent because 'France can only remain generous if those who are here in violation of our rights and our laws are returned home.' Sarkozy also declared his intention 'to put an end to all forms of procedural abuse, particularly in the case of marriages of convenience, state health care and asylum-seeking.'[10]

It is likely that electorally expedient motives also underlay this new package of reforms. Sarkozy's presidential ambitions were well known and in the run-up to the 2007 presidential election further legislation on immigration would reinforce his image as a hardline, proactive politician. On a visit to one of the largely immigrant Parisian suburbs in June 2005, he talked of cleaning up the area with an industrial hose (*nettoyer au Kärcher*), sparking off a heated controversy. The riots which broke out in the *banlieues* in autumn 2005, triggered by the deaths of two young immigrants who were fleeing the police, were interpreted by some as a failure of integration policy. However, they presented Sarkozy with an opportunity to talk tough in language which would resonate with FN supporters. His reference to youths in another troubled suburb in October 2005, as *racailles* (rabble), provoked the hostility of young immigrants in these sensitive areas but over two-thirds of the public approved of his handling of the riots.[11]

Sarkozy also faced competition within the UMP for the presidential nomination from Dominique de Villepin, Chirac's preferred candidate. In October 2005 Sarkozy, who had been in first place in the popularity ratings since 2002, fell one point behind de Villepin. His rivalry with the prime minister was marked by public disagreements about immigration quotas, positive discrimination and the right to vote. On the latter point, President Chirac indirectly rebuked his Minister of the Interior by 'clarifying' the French position,[12] which differed from Sarkozy's. 'In the French republican conception of voting, the right to vote is linked to citizenship. We have an integration policy which rejects multiculturalism.' At this point, Sarkozy began to veer away from the rhetoric of 'generosity' towards that of 'firmness'.

The 2006 *Loi Sarkozy*

The second *Loi Sarkozy* (Law 2006-911 of 24 July 2006 on immigration and integration) was enacted in the wake of the 2005 riots and less than a year before the 2007 presidential elections. Setting out his rationale for the new legislation, Sarkozy remarked that 'In France, immigration retains negative connotations because it is not adequately regulated and not sufficiently linked to our economic needs, and because it is not accompanied by an ambitious integration policy'.[13] The primary emphasis now was therefore on 'selective' immigration (*immigration choisie*) rather than 'imposed' immigration (*immigration subie*). 'Imposed' immigration included family reunification and asylum-seekers, which made up the vast majority of immigration into France, and 'selective' immigration would be tailored to France's economic requirements, with the introduction of a renewable three-year residence permit called a 'skills and talents' permit (*carte de compétences et talents*) for highly qualified non-EU workers. Initial plans to introduce a quota system for immigrants with professional skills proved too controversial and were abandoned.

Sarkozy asserted that, in those countries where selective immigration is practised, xenophobia and the far-right are weaker than in France. Thus, 'selective immigration is a defence against racism'[14] and would also reduce the incidence of 'squats, ghettos and rioting'. The government also needed to react to the breakdown of the integration system which produced the paradoxical situation where 'the children and grandchildren of the first generation of immigrants feel less French than their parents and grandparents'.[15] At the same time, the 2006 law abolished the *de facto* regularization of illegal immigrants after ten years' residence on French territory: henceforth each immigrant would have to make an individual case for remaining in France. According to the provisions of the 2006 law, foreigners would only be allowed into the country if they could prove that they had sufficient financial means to support family members and their eligibility for welfare benefits would be greatly reduced. New workers would have to sign a 'Reception and Integration Contract' (*Contrat d'accueil et d'intégration*) in which they make a commitment to learn French and to respect French values.

The 2007 presidential election

In the period leading up to the 2007 presidential election, Sarkozy's discourse hardened once again. Speaking to the UMP in 2006, he said 'If there are people who are not comfortable in France, they should feel free to leave a country which they do not love'.[16] This contained echoes of the slogan first used by Le Pen in the 1980s, 'Love France or leave it' (*La France, aimez-la ou quittez-la*) and later taken up by Philippe de Villiers. In the same speech Sarkozy said that the need for 'order, authority and firmness' in French society had never been greater and stated explicitly his desire to appeal to the working class and to former Communist Party supporters. Here, Sarkozy was competing not only with the far-right but with the Socialist candidate, Ségolène Royal.

Socialist policy on immigration as set out in Royal's '100 propositions' was more conciliatory than Sarkozy's but essentially there was little to distinguish their positions. She pledged to reinstate the regularization of illegal immigrants who had been resident in France for ten years, but still on a case-by-case basis rather than automatically, and she would give voting rights in local elections to those who had lived in France for five years. Instead of 'selective' immigration, Royal proposed 'shared' immigration (*immigration partagée*) with greater emphasis on co-development with sender countries. She was vehemently opposed to the proposed new immigration ministry, condemning the implication that immigrants were a threat to national identity, but also called for French citizens to be more patriotic. She counterbalanced respect for family reunification with a policy of firmness towards illegal immigration, which represented a potential economic threat to the PS's traditional working-class electorate, saying 'We cannot, any more than our neighbours, simply open up our borders without creating intolerable economic and social imbalances, in particular a strong downward pressure on pay.'[17]

In the televised debate between Sarkozy and Royal between the two rounds of the 2007 presidential election, the question of immigration was relegated to the closing minutes and was confined to the regularization of illegal immigrants, with both candidates agreeing that there would be no 'amnesty' or automatic right but each case would be considered individually, although Royal stressed her concern that the *sans-papiers* were not being treated humanely. This underlines the predicament of Royal and the Socialists on immigration: the need to appeal both to the concerns of their more progressive middle-class electorate about human rights and to those of their traditional working-class voters about the impact of immigration on employment and wages. It is perhaps with an eye on the more conservative working-class vote that Sarkozy changed tack on the questions of foreigners' right to vote (which did not appear in the 2007 manifesto) and watered down his proposals for positive discrimination. Perhaps most significant was his backtracking on some of his earlier statements on multiculturalism as he reverted to a more assimilationist approach.

Sarkozy's offensive seemed to pay off. Le Pen's showing in the first round of the 2007 presidential election was significantly down on 2002, falling to 10.4 per cent from 16.9 per cent, his worst result in a presidential election since the FN's first decade and a million votes less than he had won in 2002. Polls showed that 38 per cent of Le Pen's 2002 electorate voted for Sarkozy in the first round compared with 53 per cent for Le Pen and that his support among the working-class electorate had almost halved from 26 per cent in 2002 to 15 per cent in 2007.[18] Sarkozy's strategy had worked on the left too, with 56 per cent feeling closer to him on immigration and only 32 per cent to Royal.[19]

The results of the presidential election appeared to validate Sarkozy's decision to target the far-right electorate, and in the subsequent legislative elections 30 per cent of those who had voted FN in the first round were prepared to vote for a UMP candidate in the second. After the presidential and parliamentary elections, Sarkozy immediately introduced the legislation he had promised. A new bill on immigration control, integration and asylum was presented to the National Assembly by the new immigration minister, Brice Hortefeux, in July 2007. It completed its passage through parliament in October, despite vociferous opposition to a controversial amendment to the bill which proposed that DNA tests should be carried out on those seeking to join family members living in France. This was attacked not only by the PS but also drew criticism from within Sarkozy's own party and government, notably from Fadela Amara, Minister for Urban Policy, who described DNA testing as 'disgusting', and his Foreign Affairs Minister, former socialist Bernard Kouchner. However, a majority of the public approved of DNA testing.[20]

III. PUBLIC ATTITUDES TOWARDS THE ISSUES OF IMMIGRATION AND INTEGRATION IN FRANCE

Sarkozy's tougher discourse and action on migration issues appear, then, to have won back for the centre-right a section of the French electorate, particularly on the far-right and among the working class, but how accurately does it reflect the concerns of the public as a whole and how effective are the new measures judged to be? The main measure of trends in attitudes towards immigration in France is

Table 1 Percentage agreeing that there are too many immigrants in France, 1984–2007

1984	*1988*	*1990*	*1995*	*1997*	*2002*	*2003*	*2005*	*2005*	*2006*	*2007*
58	65	68	73	59	60	59	56	63	59	56

Sources: FNES (1988, 1995, 1997, 2002); Mayer (2007b: 432); otherwise Sofres.

a question asking whether people consider that there are 'too many immigrants' in France which has been regularly included in French national election surveys (FNES)[21] and opinion polls since the 1980s. Between 1984 and 2007 the view of a majority of the French public was that there were too many foreigners in France (see Table 1) with a peak of 73 per cent in 1995.

There are clear partisan differences in attitudes, with negative views on the number of immigrants being more prevalent on the right, particularly the far-right, than the left (see Table 2). According to Mayer (2007b: 432), in 2007 90 per cent of Le Pen voters thought there were too many immigrants in France. Yet a growing section of the electorate as a whole rejects the principle of national preference which lies at the heart of the FN doctrine, with the proportion thinking that 'priority should be given to a French person over an illegal immigrant' halving from over 40 per cent in 1991 to around 20 per cent in 2006.[22] Similarly, the sense of 'no longer feeling at home' in France is experienced by a minority and is also declining,[23] as is the fear that immigration might lead to a loss of national identity.[24] This would suggest that Sarkozy's emphasis on national identity is designed to appeal to a small but electorally significant section of the French electorate.

On questions of immigration control, however, most of the measures proposed in the 2007 bill meet with the approval of a large majority of the public, particularly on the right and the far-right (see Table 3). While the most discriminatory aspect of the proposed legislation, the application of quotas, clearly disquiets supporters of the centre-left, there is little difference in levels of approval between the centre-right and the far-right. In other words, in pursuing these policies, Sarkozy is appealing to both right-wing electorates, not simply to Le Pen's supporters. The main disagreement is over the regularization of illegal immigrants (where a majority of far-right voters are

Table 2 Percentage of Le Pen voters agreeing that there are too many immigrants in France, 1988–2007

	1988	*1995*	*2002*	*2007*
FN voters	95	97	97	90
All voters	65	74	65	56

Source: Mayer (2007b: 432).

Table 3 French public attitudes towards immigration control

% in favour of	All	Vote in 1st round 2007 presidential election		
		Royal	Sarkozy	Le Pen
immigration quotas	74	45	95	97
case-by-case regularization of illegal immigrants	70	66	73	30
limiting family reunification to those who can speak French	74	64	85	90
limiting family reunification to those earning at least the minimum wage (SMIC)	69	49	81	85
immigration quotas based on occupation	60	35	82	82
immigration quotas based on nationality	49	25	67	80

Source: OpinionWay poll, 17 September 2007.

against any regularization at all) and over nationality-based quotas, of which the far-right strongly approve.

A large majority of the public are positive about the likely effectiveness of these measures in terms of immigration control, notably on the centre- and far-right, but expectations about their impact on integration are more muted, with centre-left voters displaying considerable scepticism (see Table 4).

These conflicting views about models of integration are illustrated by Tiberj (2007: 1), who identifies three types of attitude in France: 'multiculturalists' (10 per cent), 'republicans' (36 per cent) and 'assimilationists' (46 per cent). Republicans and multiculturalists, who together represent around half the population, attribute the failings of integration to French society rather than to migrants and are in favour of policies to reduce inequality and discrimination. In contrast, assimilationists tend to blame migrants themselves for their lack of integration

Table 4 French public attitudes towards the 2007 immigration bill

It will be a good thing for	All	Vote in 1st round 2007 presidential election		
		Royal	Sarkozy	Le Pen
combating illegal immigration	75	52	92	99
combating illegal work	73	51	92	98
integrating immigrants	57	35	78	52

Source: OpinionWay poll, 11 October 2007.

and are doubtful about the extent to which they want to become French. Thus, a perceived failure of 'selective' immigration to address this issue is likely to produce different responses. While the left might be able to make a convincing case for a more 'inclusive' approach, with greater emphasis on positive discrimination in employment and housing and an extension of the right to vote in local elections, the right-wing electorate might ascribe the failure of integration to the migrant population, leading to demands for a more restrictive and assimilationist approach, which would risk mobilizing the PS and dividing the UMP.

CONCLUSION

The immigration policy of the French centre-right, driven largely by Nicolas Sarkozy, has been highly successful in electoral terms. His strategy towards Le Pen has succeeded where all others have failed. By targeting a section of the electorate, albeit a fairly narrow one, for whom immigration is a key issue, the UMP has substantially strengthened its support base. Yet the far-right was clearly not the only factor driving Sarkozy. His hardline approach also enabled him to compete more effectively with his presidential rivals both within his own party and in the PS. Most significantly, his discourse and action have consistently met with the approval of a broad section of French public opinion. But by deliberately highlighting the immigration question, Sarkozy has also raised expectations about results. The question now is whether he can meet these expectations and whether his claims that selective immigration will lead to successful integration can be substantiated.

Persistent public concerns about the effects of unsuccessful integration as evidenced, for example, by urban unrest would suggest that underlying factors, such as the economic, social or political marginalization of ethnic minorities, are not being adequately addressed. The proposal to authorize the collection of ethnic data contained in the 2007 immigration bill should lead to more accurate analysis of levels of discrimination and integration but these measures are offset by stricter targets for illegal immigration, family reunification, deportations and the voluntary return of migrants. The inclusion in Sarkozy's new administration of politicians from an immigrant background sends a positive message to the ethnic communities but the new president once again broke the *cordon sanitaire* around the FN by inviting Le Pen to the Elysée Palace to brief him (in his capacity as an MEP) in advance of the EU summit in June 2007. Confusing signals are being transmitted. While these apparent contradictions might be seen as reflecting the ambivalence and divisions within the French electorate, a more coherent response will be required if France is to resolve the complex issues confronting a multicultural polity and to achieve the fundamental objective of social cohesion.

NOTES

1 TNS-Sofres, 18–19 May 2007.
2 Louis Harris, 5–6 May 2002.
3 Ipsos, 21 April 2002.
4 Sofres, 21 April 2002.
5 Ipsos, 29–30 November 2002.
6 TNS-Sofres, 6–7 December 2006.
7 *Libération*, 24 April 2004.
8 *Parisien-Aujourd'hui en France*, 29 March 2006.
9 *Le Monde*, 1 October 2005.
10 Speaking at the UMP conference 'Une immigration choisie, une immigration réussie', 9 June 2005.
11 Ipsos, 12 November 2005.
12 *Le Monde*, 27 October 2005.
13 Sarkozy's New Year wishes to the press, 12 January 2006.
14 Interview in *Le Monde*, 28 April 2006.
15 Quoted from his 2006 book, *Témoignage*.
16 Addressing the UMP, 22 April 2006.
17 In a letter to the association *France Terre d'asile*, 8 February 2007.
18 LH2, 23 April 2007.
19 TNS-Sofres, 26–27 April 2007.
20 56 per cent according to an OpinionWay poll, 11 October 2007.
21 Access to the FNES datasets was provided by the Banque de Données Socio-Politiques (BDSP) at IEP Grenoble.
22 TNS-Sofres, 6–7 December 2006.
23 *Eurobarometer* 65, French special report, Spring 2006.
24 FNES and Sofres.

REFERENCES

Benson, R. (2002) 'The political/literary model of French journalism: change and continuity in immigration news coverage, 1973–1991', *Journal of European Area Studies* 10(1): 49–68.
Boswell, C. (2003) 'European migration policies in flux: changing patterns of inclusion and exclusion', *Chatham House Papers*, Oxford: Blackwell.
DeLey, M. (1983) 'French immigration policy since May 1981', *International Migration Review* 17(2): 196–11.
Fetzer, J. (2000) *Public Attitudes toward Immigration in the United States, France and Germany*, Cambridge: Cambridge University Press.
Geddes, A. (2003) 'France: still the one and indivisible republic?', in A. Geddes, *The Politics of Migration and Immigration in Europe*, London: Sage, pp. 52–78.
Geddes, A. and Guiraudon, V. (2004) 'The emergence of a European Union policy paradigm amidst contrasting national models: Britain, France and EU anti-discrimination policy', *West European Politics* 27(2): 334–53.
Grunberg, G. and Schweisguth, E. (2003) 'La tripartition de l'espace politique', in P. Perrineau and C. Ysmal (eds), *Le Vote de tous les refus. Les élections presidentielle et législatives de 2002*, Paris: Presses de Sciences Po, pp. 341–62.
Hargreaves, A. (1995) *Immigration, Race and Ethnicity in Contemporary France*, London: Routledge.

Hollifield, J.F. (1994) 'Immigration and republicanism in France: the hidden consensus', in W. Cornelius, P. Martin and J. Hollifield (eds), *Controlling Immigration: A Global Perspective*, Stanford, CA: Stanford University Press, pp.143–75.

Insee (2006) 'Enquêtes annuelles de recensement 2004 et 2005', *Insee première* no. 1098 August; http://www.insee.fr/fr/ffc/ipweb/ip1098/ip1098.pdf

Ivaldi, G. and Swyngedouw, M. (2005) 'Comparing the extreme right in Belgium and France'; http://halshs.archives-ouvertes.fr/halshs-00090333/en/

Masquet, B. (ed.) (2006) *Politique de l'immigration*, Regards sur l'actualité no. 326, Paris: La documentation française.

Mayer, N. (2007a) 'Diversité, ethnocentrisme et votes'; http://www.cevipof.msh-paris.fr/bpf/analyses/analys0.htm

Mayer, N. (2007b) 'L'électorat Le Pen aspiré par Nicolas Sarkozy', *Revue française de science politique* 57(3–4): 429–45.

Schain, M.A. (2004) 'Politics, immigration and multiculturalism in France and the United States'; http://www.ceri-sciencespo.com/archive/march04/artms.pdf

Tiberj, V. (2007) 'La France de la diversité, la France face à la diversité: représentations et réalités'; http://www.cevipof.msh-paris.fr/bpf/analyses/Tiberj_diversite.pdf

Van der Valk, I. (2003) 'Right-wing parliamentary discourse on immigration in France', *Discourse and Society* 14(3): 309–48.

Wihtol de Wenden, C. (2005) 'Les grandes tendances de la politique française d'immigration', *Migrations Société* 17(101): 27–38.

A double-edged sword! The Dutch centre-right and the 'foreigners issue'

Kees van Kersbergen and André Krouwel

INTRODUCTION

How do the Dutch centre-right parties, the Christen Democratisch Appèl (Christian Democratic Appeal, CDA, Christian democrats) and the Volkspartij voor Vrijheid en Democratie (People's Party for Freedom and Democracy, VVD, conservative liberals), cope with the issues of migration, asylum-seekers, integration, multiculturalism and European integration? The centre-right parties in the Netherlands have come under pressure with regard to their stance on these issues. Centre-right pro-Europeanism and pro-multiculturalism have been abandoned for more typically right-wing and hard-line positions on these issues. The parties now favour more restrictive laws on immigration and asylum-seekers that seem more consonant with their ideological position. Moreover, after the referendum on the European Constitutional Treaty both the CDA and the VVD adopted less Euro-enthusiastic stances.

In this contribution we explore the effects of the immigration-related issues on the internal cohesion of the parties in terms of factionalism and the struggle for party leadership. In addition, we analyse the reasons for the centre-right's shift towards the more hard-line and restrictive immigration policies. Historically, issues such as immigration, asylum and European integration should be electorally advantageous to centre-right parties, since voters on the right often favour tougher law and order policies and more nationalistic and Eurosceptical policies. Particularly when issues of immigration can be connected to right-wing core issues of law and order, centre-right parties have a strategic advantage over the left. Both Dutch centre-right parties seem to operate, as elsewhere (see Bale 2008), on the assumption that the politicization of issues related to nationalism, especially the so-called 'foreigners issue', will win them votes. Our argument, however, is that these parties have also moved in this direction under pressure from populist political entrepreneurs who successfully mobilized voters and resources on this issue, most obviously Pim Fortuyn (the leader of the Lijst Pim Fortuyn, LPF, who was assassinated in 2002) and Geert Wilders (who left the VVD in 2004 and founded his own Partij voor de Vrijheid (Party for Freedom, PVV) in 2006).

Our central thesis is that the politicization of immigration issues is a double-edged sword for centre-right parties. On the one hand, centre-right parties can benefit electorally from these issues because they are the traditional owners of law and order as well as nationalist issues. In addition, centre-right core voters traditionally favour the direction in which policies have changed in recent years. On the other hand, hard-line right-wing stances on immigration and multiculturalism can, at the same time, go against core centre-right values like economic liberalism and – at least for the Christian democrats – compassion with and charity for the poor and weak. Adopting too harsh a profile on law and order, the nationalism and foreigners run the risk of ripping the centre-right apart.

We highlight the recent tensions that have emerged within the CDA and the VVD around these issues. Hardest hit seems to be the VVD as the conservative liberals have experienced a successful breakaway party (Wilders' PVV) and a severe internal conflict between the more libertarian wing (in favour of economic liberalism, personal freedoms and multiculturalism) and a more conservative faction (in favour of a more Eurosceptical and nationalistic stance, more stringent immigration and asylum policies and a more monocultural outlook). This internal conflict within the VVD has been raging ever since Frits Bolkestein left as party leader in 1998 and it has only partly been suppressed by the need for cohesion while in government up until 2006. When after serious electoral losses in the 2006 elections the party ended up in opposition, the internal tensions around immigration culminated in a dramatic struggle over party leadership between the popular ex-minister Rita Verdonk (the voice of the nationalistic, anti-immigration and monocultural faction of the party) and the current party leader Mark Rutte (a libertarian). This tension resulted in another split from the party, when Verdonk was expelled from the VVD parliamentary group and subsequently founded her own anti-immigration party (Trots op Nederland – Proud of the Netherlands) in October 2007.

Within the CDA discontent with the much tougher party line on immigration has not culminated in a crisis of party leadership, but emerged at the grass-roots level, where CDA members and representatives have voiced opposition to the harsher party line on immigration, integration of minorities and multiculturalism.

The tougher line on immigration within the centre-right has been a slow and gradual process that began in the 1990s (Joppke 2007). But it was accelerated when in 2002 a populist party, LPF, won 17 per cent of the popular vote on the basis of an anti-immigrant platform. Despite the fact that the ensuing centre-right coalition of LPF, CDA and VVD collapsed within 90 days owing to internal tensions within the new populist party, the centre-right has maintained a stricter position on immigration and related issues.

We first describe how, over the last decade or so, a new political agenda of non-material and cultural issues emerged and, next, show how the epicentre of political competition has shifted from economic or left–right issues to non-material issues such as national identity, immigration, asylum, law and order, and the future of European integration. Now, the traditional wisdom that Dutch party competition primarily focuses on the left–right divide (i.e. socioeconomic issues of redistribution, income, government intervention in the economy and the welfare state) is being challenged. A second, non-material dimension has become more salient. This dimension includes: (a) ideas on the format of the democratic system, where libertarian and pluralist views conflict with traditional and conservative ideas of a more moral and authoritative state; and (b) cosmopolitan visions of citizenship versus (ethnic) nationalistic and monocultural identities. The issue of European integration – particularly since the referendum on the Constitutional Treaty – has increased the saliency of this non-material dimension. As a result, we see the development of an unprecedented polarization precisely around the complex 'foreigners issue' in the Dutch political system. This polarization is visible in that all major parties of the centre-right (and of the centre-left as well) now face strong and radical competitors. Why and how this new political agenda has emerged is the topic of the next section.

THE EMERGENCE OF A NEW POLITICAL AGENDA

For reasons explored below, the issue of immigration and asylum became far more salient during the 1990s than it had been previously. The transformation of the issue structure culminated in the enormous electoral success of Fortuyn's LPF at the national elections of May 2002 and of the PVV led by Geert Wilders, which came from nowhere to win 5.9 per cent in November 2006. Apparently, an increasing number of voters are discontented with how the established parties of the centre-right and centre-left handle issues of immigration, the European

Union (EU), asylum and multiculturalism. As a consequence, the two major forces in Dutch politics, Christian democracy and social democracy, have been unable to stop the downward trend in popular support since the 1960s (Christian democrats) and late 1970s (social democrats). The trend is clearly down for the representatives of these party families, the CDA and the Partij van de Arbeid (PvdA). See Figure 1.

Conversely, the VVD – representing the third current in Dutch politics, conservative liberalism – has seen important electoral gains throughout the 1990s. The VVD, in particular under the leadership of Bolkestein (1990–98), was the first to put the 'foreigners issue' on the political agenda in the early 1990s, long before the emergence of Fortuyn. The VVD was aware of the widespread dissatisfaction among the electorate with policies dealing with (labour) immigration and European integration and had consciously politicized the issue for electoral gain. In the eyes of an increasing number of voters, problems of labour immigration from new European democracies, unemployment, social security, housing, health care, the integration of political refugees and immigrants into Dutch society, crime and

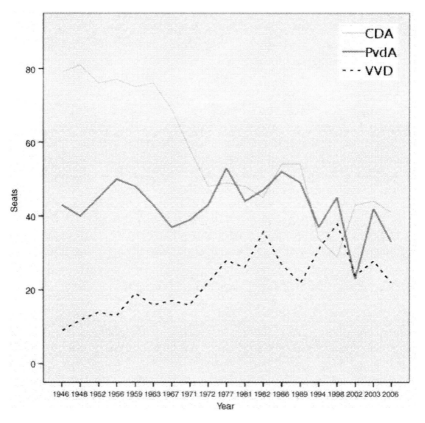

Figure 1 Seats held by largest three parties (CDA, PvdA, VVD)

slow economic growth were all connected in a 'multicultural drama' that threatened the Dutch way of life (Scheffer 2000).

While the Netherlands had been a country of relative political stability and social peace – according to *The Economist*, the Netherlands coped better than other countries with the economic crisis of the 1980s – this was soon to be changed. Because of its comprehensive welfare state and corporatist policy process, Dutch citizens were relatively well sheltered from the rapidly transforming world economy and the problems generated by this. However, during the 1990s – in a period of relatively high economic growth – citizens slowly began to notice the market-oriented neo-liberal and activation-oriented 'third way', social democratic transformation of the welfare state (Green-Pedersen *et al.* 2001) and the privatization of many public utilities. Also, the structural transformation of the labour market – where job security declined rapidly and competition from outside (Asia) and inside (immigrants) increased – became noticeable. Life in the Netherlands became much less secure than it had been in the 1980s. These structural changes have also transformed the political outlook of the Dutch electorate and the party attachment of voters. Dutch election studies (see particularly Thomassen *et al.* 2000) show that there has been a strong electoral base favouring more immigration control, yet that these voters were not being mobilized by any of the major parties until Bolkestein's VVD started tapping into this potential electorate. Bolkestein, however, was unable to fully pursue the much tougher line on immigration that large numbers of voters wanted as he also needed to keep on board both the libertarian wing and a business community that saw immigration as a supply of cheap labour. In addition, from 1994 until 2001 the VVD governed in a historically unique coalition with the social democrats, who traditionally have had a large immigrant voting base and were reluctant to introduce overly stringent immigration policies that, moreover, would have been at odds with the internationalist and solidaristic traditions of the party. Bolkestein was thus constrained in how far he could move the VVD in an anti-immigration, Euro-critical and monocultural direction by both intra- and inter-party considerations. The latter applied not just to the PvdA but also to the VVD's traditional coalition partner, the CDA – a staunch defender of both further European integration and multiculturalism, the latter fitting very well the pillarization model of integration that Christian democrats historically cherished and that had helped to stabilize segmented Dutch society. Given all this, the VVD could not cater to the entire anti-immigrant vote.

There was, therefore, a considerable political space left for any political populist entrepreneur to pick up that vote, particularly since the electorate had become much less structured along the lines of class and religion. Since the 1960s, an increasing number of voters had started to choose on the basis of individual preferences rather than automatically following the logic of group membership (Catholics voting for the Catholic party, secular workers for social democracy, the secular middle class for the conservative liberals, the Protestants for one of the Protestants parties, etc.). Election studies since the late 1960s consistently show that Dutch voters increasingly had multiple party-identification and could easily cast their vote for several parties within the left- or right-wing of the political spectrum (e.g. van der Eijk and Niemöller 1983). Even those with a strong attachment to one party often identify too with other parties within the same ideological bloc. When asked about the likelihood that they would vote for a specific party, 25 per cent of Dutch voters in 2003 and 2006 gave two or more parties a nine or ten (on a ten-point scale). Moreover, 20 per cent of the electorate gave none of the parties a score above eight (Irwin 2006: 10–11). This shows that the majority of Dutch voters are comfortable with switching from one party to another and are also available for new competitors within the same ideological bloc. Hence, the number of voters who change party has steadily increased, particularly in the last decade. As can be seen in Figure 2, electoral changes during the 1960s and 1970s were moderate compared to the recent period. Since the 1990s we see a strong increase in electoral volatility, measured as the number of seats that change party per election. Up until the elections of 1989, a change of 20 seats was considered to be a landslide, thereafter overall volatility has rapidly increased. Between 1994 and 2006 the number of seats changing party passed 30, with a record high in 2002 when almost a third of all parliamentary seats changed party (46 seats).

Clearly, Dutch voters switch between parties with increasing ease, yet one needs to bear in mind that most of the volatility is within-bloc volatility.

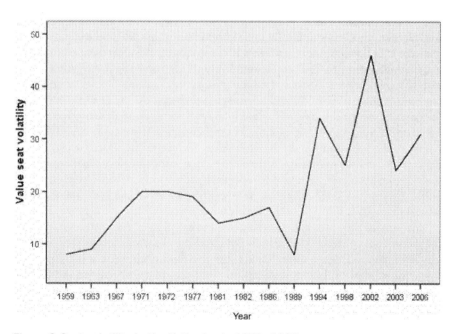

Figure 2 Seat volatility in the Netherlands 1959–2006

The balance of power between the left and the right has been relatively stable, even in recent decades. There is relatively little movement across the left and right divide and at election time most voters choose between parties of the left bloc (Socialist Party (SP), GreenLeft and PvdA) or between parties of the centre-right (VVD, CDA and one of the radical populist right parties). Nevertheless, those voters who move in and out of the electorate also have to be taken into account. Between 20 and 25 per cent of the Dutch electorate does not show up at the polls, yet, as Pim Fortuyn and his LPF showed, these voters can be mobilized, in populist fashion, on issues of immigration and the multicultural society.

Everywhere populist leaders have tried to tap into the xenophobic potential among the electorate and to employ it against migration and the multicultural society. Populism also appealed to those dissatisfied with wider issues, such as the representativeness of democratic institutions and the poor performance of the political élite, all producing a growth of political cynicism. In the Netherlands, this emerged as a populist revolt against the closed nature of the still pillarized political system. The populist attack aimed particularly at the consociational political culture, including the system's consensus-seeking logic, the sticky decision-making process in politics and economics (corporatism), élites too keen on compromise, the unrepresentative political class, and the perceived underperformance of public services.

Crucially important for the position and role of the centre-right in Dutch politics was that the latent xenophobia in Dutch society surfaced in the form of a frontal assault on political correctness, i.e. the moral pressure exerted on citizens not to speak negatively about any aspect related to migration. Since the revolt, Fortuyn's notorious adage 'I say what I think and I do what I say' has opened up a whole new, previously suppressed, political space in Dutch public debate. In 1997, Hans Janmaat, the leader of an insignificant extreme right-wing party, was convicted on the grounds of 'inciting' race discrimination after promising publicly to 'abolish the multicultural society as soon as we have the opportunity and the power'. Post Fortuyn – who himself wanted to remove the anti-discrimination article 1 from the Dutch constitution, called Islam a retarded culture, and promised that once in power he would close Dutch borders to Islamic migrants – people who use similar or even stronger terms than Janmaat do not have to fear criminal prosecution. Clearly, the nature of public debate has shifted considerably and the political space on the right has been increased.

But it was not just the widening of such a space that mattered. Just as important was Fortuyn's ability – by speaking out loudly and proudly in a way that chimed with voters who were tired of what they saw as political correctness (Van Holsteyn *et al.* 2003) – to roll together migration, asylum-seekers, the multicultural society and criminality into a powerful amalgam: the 'foreigners issue' (see Van Kersbergen and Krouwel 2003; Van Kersbergen, forthcoming). Fortuyn managed to present separate issues of labour migration (employment, social security, health care, housing), political refugees and socioeconomic and cultural integration of migrants as essentially one single problem. In his political campaign this single 'foreigners issue' was subsequently coupled to issues of law and order (criminality, insecurity, inner-city decline), the threat of Islam to Dutch culture, the erosion of social cohesion, and the malfunctioning of political parties.

The impact of the 'foreigners issue' was boosted by the 9/11 terrorist attacks in the US, Pim Fortuyn's own actions and campaign, and the electoral success of populist movements at the local level (March 2002). Opinion research shows that 17 per cent of the supporters of the populist party Leefbaar Nederland (at that time Fortuyn still led that party before he founded his own list) favoured a stricter policy towards asylum-seekers in October 2001. Only five months later, 52 per cent of LPF voters favoured harsher policies (Van Praag 2003: 107). 'Fortuyn succeeded in forging an electoral coalition of various population groups that came together because of their shared political cynicism and their views on public security and the multicultural society' (Van Praag 2003: 113; our translation). Clearly, populists not only bank on discontent but also generate it (Van Kersbergen and Krouwel 2003; Krouwel and Abts 2007; Van der Brug 2003).

CHANGING IMMIGRATION AND INTEGRATION POLICY OF THE CENTRE-RIGHT

Mobilization and polarization – and also the political space – around issues of immigration, asylum and multiculturalism increased, then, between 1998 and 2002, particularly in the last months of 2001 and early 2002, with the attack on the World Trade Center in New York, the rise of Pim Fortuyn in the local elections of March 2002, the subsequent murder of Fortuyn and the instability of the party he left behind. Subsequently the space has been widened – or at least maintained – by Wilders' PVV. And each of the Netherlands' centre-right parties has, in its own way, tried to invade and occupy some of that space.

The CDA, in particular, showed considerable flexibility in changing its policy positions and adapting to the new situation, especially given that such a trans-formation did not come as 'naturally' as it did to, say, the VVD which had already dipped its toe in the water in the 1990s. Having been locked up in opposition for eight years – problematic for a party that had been in govern-ment since 1918 – the CDA immediately seized the opportunity to push forward a new agenda of 're-establishing the norms and values of society'. During the 1980s and 1990s the CDA had de-emphasized its Christian identity in order to link into the dominant neo-liberal trend. Now, however, the party reinvented itself with a new moral agenda and was eager to shift party competition to non-material issues (see Van Kersbergen, forthcoming).

In the two years following the Fortuyn revolt, both centre-right parties – CDA and VVD – rewrote their policy on immigration, integration of minorities and the multicultural society (CDA 2004; VVD 2004). Both policies show many similarities, but certain differences are crucial. The CDA policy – summarized as 'integration begins with active citizenship' – contains an ideological message, whereas the VVD policy shows a formal, legalistic and bureaucratic approach to the integration of non-western immigrants. The CDA advocates that integration can only be achieved when policies tap into the belief system – norms and values – of citizens and thus opts for a long-term policy rather than quick fixes of certain laws. Through better access to education and the labour market, young (second-generation) immigrants must be integrated into mainstream society.

Although both parties use the term individual responsibility, they clearly start from different ideological positions. Based on Christian democratic principles, the CDA emphasizes an individual's responsibility to take an active role in society. The VVD, on the other hand, advocates a more legalistic policy of obligations and duties for immigrants. The conservative liberals emphasize the superiority of western civilization, its core value of freedom and the rule of law ('rechtsstaat'). The liberals denounce multiculturalism for its elements of western 'self-hate'. They argue that immigrants come here precisely to enjoy western liberal achievements and should thus know, and adhere to, the rules and laws of the land and adapt to the dominant norms. In terms of norms that underpin immigration and integration policies, both centre-right parties emphasize democratic freedoms, the equality of men and women, the state monopoly of violence and the need for tolerance. While both parties argue that education is key to the solution of problems of integration, the CDA defends the constitutional right to found schools on a religious basis, whereas the VVD advocates policies that would promote people from different backgrounds going to the same school. Thus, the CDA strongly focuses on freedom of religion, does not object to Islamic schools, and emphasizes the value of self-organization in religious institutions. According to the CDA, religion should not be limited to the private sphere. In order to avoid social apartheid and segregation, the VVD sees the need for stricter control and legislation for Islamic schools and argues that integration can only be achieved when immigrants also function outside their own group. The VVD does not rule out the need to limit the freedom of parents to choose a school for their children and objects to the role and high visibility of the Islamic religion in the public domain.

Despite its liberal origin, the VVD finds it necessary to curb individuals' choice of partner via conditions relating to income and labour market participation. Rita Verdonk, who was minister for integration for the VVD in the Balkenende II and III governments (2003–07), even introduced compulsory Dutch language and culture tests for non-Dutch prospective brides and grooms. Both parties want to abolish arranged marriages, ban domestic violence and advocate policies that would lead to the emancipation of women within minority groups.

Christian democratic party leader Jan Peter Balkenende made a speech in 2002 in which he explained the change of direction of his party with respect to the integration of migrants. He emphasized that society could not thrive unless migrants accepted the basic values of Dutch culture. Newcomers were said to be obliged to learn Dutch norms and values and to live according to them. The right to start a family had to be made dependent on the obligation of migrants to integrate. This involved, among other things, learning the Dutch language, history and culture. In the same speech, he announced a farewell to multiculturalism.

THE FOREIGNERS ISSUE AND THE SHIFT IN POLITICAL COMPETITION

Balkenende's speech, like Fortuyn's interventions, had resonance because, in the Netherlands, the 'foreigners issue' seems to be related to a deeper social cleavage that separates two groups. On the one side, we find a group of people enjoying a reasonable measure of protection, who are neither insecure nor anxious. They see the market as an opportunity for progress, they view the unification of Europe as a success, they live alongside rather than inside the multicultural society, they have a strong, individualized lifestyle and are not interested in the neighbourhood as a centre for solidarity and social control. They feel perfectly safe and secure and their individual prosperity gives them the means to avoid contact with the deteriorating public domains and services. They usually cope well with bureaucracy and feel competent in their dealings with the various branches of government. They view the established parties as legitimate and necessary organizations for shaping the democratic process, but consider them entirely irrelevant in terms of their personal lifestyles.

On the other side of the divide, we find the people who fear the future and feel threatened by the market, the enlargement of the EU (Polish migrant workers, Turkey) and European integration (the extra inflation caused by the euro), continuing immigration and the multicultural society, the collapse of the social infrastructure, the loss of the tradition of helping your neighbours and solidarity networks in working-class areas, the internationalization of the economy, the inadequate safety of the public domain and the deterioration of public services. They really do live in the midst of the multicultural society and have experienced enormous change in the social relations that used to constitute such an important part of their lives. This group of people have lost all confidence in the traditional political parties, because they do not see them as organizations that represent their interests or even have a feel for their needs and worries, but as part of the failing state machinery. Political parties are part of the establishment and the cause of their anxiety. Government is perceived as the opponent or enemy. In the eyes of this frightened, insecure part of the electorate, all their problems are directly linked to the arrival of foreigners. The presence of foreigners has allowed globalization to become a concrete reality, and all the associated dangers (the disappearance of low-skilled jobs, the undermining of national identity) have been personified (see Van Kersbergen and Krouwel 2003; Krouwel and Abts 2007).

During the post-war period, Dutch political competition was primarily oriented towards economic issues such as employment, taxation, wages and the development of the welfare state. During the 1990s, the centre of gravity of political competition shifted to a different dimension, one of a cultural and non-material nature. This non-material dimension is not new; in fact, it is the oldest political dimension in the Netherlands and dates back to the cleavage between 'preciezen' (orthodox Calvinists) and 'rekkelijken' (the libertarian, permissive bourgeoisie) in the sixteenth century. Even in the 1970s the cleavage between religious and non-religious voters appeared to be as fundamental as the socioeconomic left–right dimension (Bronner and De Hoog 1981). Kleinnijenhuis and Pennings (2001) found that in the 1990s, based on issue positions for individual parties in their respective party programmes, a second dimension labelled orthodox–permissive was salient, in addition to the socioeconomic left–right dimension. Kriesi et al. (2006) also found that, although the left–right divide has remained salient in the Netherlands, another dimension has become visible, dividing those who favour cultural liberalism from those who favour restrictive immigration policies. A non-material dimension has always been present, but it has become more salient and complex in the last decade.

To summarize the complex multidimensionality of this non-economic dimension, we will use the labels coined by Marks et al. (2006), GAL–TAN. On this dimension a Green, Alternative and Libertarian (GAL) position faces a Traditional, Authoritarian and Nationalistic (TAN) outlook in life.

To show the structure of party competition on this dimension, we plotted – on the basis of the party programmes of the 2006 elections – all relevant Dutch parties in a two-dimensional space: the traditional left–right dimension and the cultural, non-material GAL–TAN dimension. We took the 36 most salient issues on the party platforms and positioned the parties on a five-point Likert scale on each of the issues (see Kleinnijenhuis and Krouwel 2007). All issues have been assigned to either of the two axes, based on an assessment as to which dimension an issue belongs as well as with respect to the question as to which side of a dimension a specific issue position belongs. The results are shown in Figure 3. The political landscape of 2006 shows that (moderate) left-wing and progressive or Green–Alternative–Libertarian parties face competition from centre-right conservative or Traditional–Authoritarian–Nationalistic parties. The parties, apart from Democrats 66 and the Christian Union are aligned along a diagonal, leaving the right-progressive and left-conservative quadrant almost void.

Clearly visible along the diagonal is the centrist position of the CDA, albeit somewhat towards the right-wing and conservative pole of the spectrum. The Christian democrats have traditionally occupied this centre ground (Krouwel 1999; Van Kersbergen and Krouwel 2006). The VVD has a clear right-wing profile but occupies an almost neutral profile on the GAL–TAN axis. This position is the result of a very liberal pamphlet – in the form of a newspaper – that served as the party manifesto for the VVD in 2006. It allowed the EU accession of

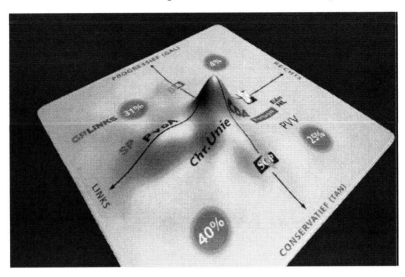

Figure 3 The Dutch political landscape 2006 (36 salient issues)
Notes: On the x-axis parties are positioned along the left–right dimension and on the y-axis along the non-material GAL–TAN dimension on the basis of 36 salient issues. GRLINKS = Green Left; SP = Socialist Party; PvdA = Partij van de Arbeid, social democrats; D66 = Democrats 66, liberals; CDA = Christen Democratisch Appel, Christian democrats; Chr. Unie = ChristenUnie, orthodox Protestants; VVD = Partij voor Vrijheid en Democratie, conservative liberals; and three populist radical right parties: Fortuyn = Lijst Pim Fortuyn, EenNL and PVV, Partij voor de Vrijheid.

Turkey and did not address the immigrant issue, despite the VVD's strong profile on this issue during its last term in office. To avoid the risk of an internal battle between libertarians and conservatives, the VVD downgraded its traditional profile, as shaped by its former leader Frits Bolkestein to a point where the party was unrecognizable on the non-material GAL–TAN dimension. Notwithstanding this, the VVD's position on the immigrant issue played an important role in the media. The former minister of immigration for the VVD, Rita Verdonk, staged a fierce and personal campaign on the issue. Despite losing the internal election for the party leadership, Verdonk had become number two on the party list and eventually achieved a unique result in Dutch political history: she received a larger number of preferential votes than the number one on the list, party leader Mark Rutte. This lack of profile in the official party line versus the strong profile of Rita Verdonk on the immigration issue consistently led to internal rivalry and tensions, up to the point where the VVD split in October 2007, when Rita Verdonk founded her own party.

That immigration was the defining issue in the elections can also be seen in Figure 3 where three radical-populist political groupings were just waiting to sweep up the voters who favoured tougher anti-immigration policies and a more negative stance towards European integration. In particular, the PVV of Wilders, who campaigned to 'stop the tsunami of Muslims', banked on its radical anti-immigration position and is close to the TAN-pole of the political spectrum. With the VVD looking divided, the PVV of Wilders – a former VVD member of parliament himself who left the party in 2004 – could easily distinguish his party from the VVD with pronounced stances on immigration, asylum, the integration of minorities and the EU.

If we look at the distribution of voters in the two-dimensional left–right and GAL–TAN political spectrum (see Figure 3), we see great potential for competition on both the left and the right. With an increasing number of voters not strongly attached to a party, and strong challenger parties for all the major political forces in the Netherlands, competition is fierce. More importantly, on the left and the right issue ownership (a potential benefit in the struggle) is fundamentally challenged: the SP challenges the PvdA's ownership of the welfare state and redistribution; and first Fortuyn, later Wilders, challenge the VVD's and – to a lesser extent – the CDA's ownership of law and order and security issues, including the 'foreigners issue'.

As the placement of parties based on their 2006 platform was also offered to the electorate in the form of a party profiling website (www.kieskompas.nl) where voters could test their 'distance' from all the parties, we have obtained data on policy preferences for almost 1.7 million respondents. Since the data were collected by self-reporting and do not constitute a random sample of Dutch voters with known background characteristics, we have to be cautious in our interpretation. However, the sheer number of respondents and the fact that the data were obtained without the interference of an interviewer make us sufficiently confident to report some aggregate analyses. Again, the assumption is that party competition is structured along the left–right or material dimension and the non-material dimension of GAL–TAN.

Factor analysis (data available from the authors upon request) indicates that the extracted factors do not entirely confirm the existence of a bipolar left–right dimension and a bipolar GAL–TAN dimension, but they do indicate a pattern of factors largely coherent with the assumed main dimensions of political competition in the Netherlands (see also Kleinnijenhuis and Krouwel 2007). Indeed, the GAL–TAN dimension is theoretically a cluster of a green–environmental dimension, plus a dimension where cosmopolitan attitudes face a nationalistic stance and a third dimension which refers to a more libertarian and democratic view of the state versus a more moral and authoritarian view of state action. Our analysis does indeed unearth a pattern of factor loadings which indicates two orthogonal dimensions representing the left–right axis. However, the GAL–TAN dimension does not emerge as a coherent GAL-group of issues versus a consistent TAN-group of issues, but rather as a separate Green-Alternative group and a Traditional-Authoritarian group. The libertarian dimension seems to be a relatively unique set of positions, appearing as a separate L-cluster of issues. More importantly, issues related to nationalism seem to be highly associated with traditional right-wing issues in the most predominant first factor. In fact, this clustering of nationalistic and traditional right-wing issues and its predominance clearly demonstrate what has occurred in Dutch politics during the 1990s. Nationalistic and anti-immigration issues have become very closely aligned with traditional socioeconomic right-wing issues for many voters. Indeed, this cluster of issues, which we coined the 'foreigners issue', has become increasingly important in determining party choice for larger groups of voters.

This latter finding may not come as a complete surprise, since the Christian democrats have a long tradition of representing both rightist and paternalistic-nationalistic (colonial) policies. In fact, paternalism and (implicit) nationalism were quite common in Dutch history (see Woltjer 1992: 167; Voorhoeve 1979; Andeweg and Irwin 2005: 206). Nevertheless, for the VVD the clustering of rightist and paternalistic-nationalistic issues has been both an opportunity and a nightmare. Since the libertarian dimension with strong loadings on economically liberal issues is orthogonal to nationalism, it is hard to satisfy both types of voters at once. This means that the core electorate of the VVD – an uneasy coalition of libertarians and conservatives – is increasingly difficult to rally behind a coherent political programme. However, the findings reveal a similar nightmare for left-wing parties as we find that a leftist–populist dimension is completely orthogonal to the traditional leftist side of the left–right axis, which boils down to favouring transfers by the government of wealth from the rich to the poor. The left–populist dimension, on the other hand, consists of viewpoints that all kinds of services and goods should be free for all (e.g. housing, school books, day care centres, social benefits) and that everybody should have the right to be included in various kinds of decision-making (e.g. referenda, elected mayor).

What these data show is that – despite the relatively stable blocs of left-wing voters and right-wing voters – all traditional parties will increasingly face difficulties in maintaining the social coalitions that make up their core electorates. The CDA will increasingly feel the tension over adopting a more neo-liberal, right-wing and nationalistic position in order to attract part of the right-wing vote, while at the same time appealing to a large section of their core electorate that favours more socioeconomic redistribution. The Christian Union already flirts with this discontented electorate and is making strong inroads among former CDA voters. For now, there is one structural obstacle as the orthodox Protestant Christian Union needs time to make a credible appeal to southern Catholics who have traditionally voted for the CDA. For the core electorate of the VVD these structural obstacles to any vote losses seem absent. Large sections of the right-wing electorate seem willing to support candidates (like Verdonk) and parties (first LPF and now PVV) that favour highly restrictive immigration policies, adopt a nationalistic and Eurosceptic stance in combination with traditional right-wing socioeconomic policies. Rita Verdonk, with her movement Proud of the Netherlands, seems to adopt precisely such a political agenda.

CONCLUSION

The Dutch party-political game is still characterized by overall bloc stability, but it seems that the centre of gravity of the centre-right bloc has moved to the right, while the centre of gravity of the left bloc has moved to the left. In other words, where Dutch politics was characterized for a long time by a logic that produced governments that governed from the centre (Gladdish 1991), it seems that the 'foreigners issue' makes this logic much more difficult to follow as it restructures party competition. The parties on the centre-right have to adapt to the trans-formation of political competition that involves a shift from traditional left–right competition on socioeconomic issues to competition on the non-material issues around immigration and multiculturalism.

Wansink's (2004) study of Dutch politics since 2001 concludes that the populist uprising in the Netherlands has brought the political system, which was overly focused on élite cartel consensus-building in the centre, much more in line with the normal European pattern of competitive electoral élite politics. Reacting to Wansink, Andeweg and Irwin identified two options:

> One is the fragmentation of proportional systems that leads to an impasse, the fear of Weimar. The other is to find some means to co-operate. This would be to fall back on the traditions of consensus government that have held the country together for so long, and have served it so well. It therefore seems likely that the influence of '2002' will be relatively short-lived and that the Netherlands will return to its own type of 'normality'.
>
> (Andeweg and Irwin 2005: 234–5)

It is probably still too early to tell, but our data seem to indicate that the recent development of the competitive space in the Netherlands makes fragmen-tation just as likely an outcome as a return to Dutch idiosyncratic normality.

Our main finding, then, is that both the CDA and the VVD are struggling to politicize the 'foreigners issue' (and the dissatisfaction in society that one finds behind this issue) in a manner that can benefit them electorally, particularly with regard to their main rivals who compete with types of answers that lure substan-tial numbers of voters away from the centre-right to the extreme and populist right. The manner in which nationalist issues (such as immigration and multi-culturalism) are associated with traditional right-wing socioeconomic issues among large sections of the (right-wing) electorate also necessitates the centre-left forging new policy mixes and social coalitions. It seems that the CDA is, so far, more successful than the VVD in the struggle for the centre. The VVD has more difficulty in finding a winning electoral strategy. If the party only takes a libertarian direction and follows the line of economic liberalism, it risks losing the right-wing vote to its populist challengers. It has therefore tried to be both nationalistic and libertarian. This, however, is unappealing to many voters and has led to a continual and potentially destructive fight between the libertarian wing and the anti-immigration, nationalistic faction of the party. The solution to this dilemma, if found, will largely determine the stance that the VVD takes on the 'foreigners issue'. It will affect the other parties' prospects in electoral competition, and ultimately it will influence Dutch immigration and integration policy.

ACKNOWLEDGEMENTS

Kees van Kersbergen wishes to thank the University of Konstanz's Centre of Excellence 'Cultural Foundations of Integration', and especially its Institute for Advanced study, for their generous hospitality and support.

REFERENCES

Andeweg, R.B. and Irwin, G.A. (2005) *Governance and Politics in the Netherlands*, 2nd edn, Basingstoke: Palgrave Macmillan.

Bale, T. (2008) 'Turning round the telescope. Centre-parties and immigration and integration policy in Europe', *Journal of European Public Policy* 15(3): 315–30.

Balkenende, J.P. (2002) 'Multiculturele samenleving is voor mij geen doel', *NRC Handelsblad*, 25 January 2002.

Bronner, F. and De Hoog, R. (1981) 'Choice models and voting behaviour: the case of the Dutch electorate', *Public Choice* 37(3): 531–46.

CDA (2004) *Nederland Integratieland; echte integratie begint bij actief burgerschap*, Den Haag: CDA.

Gladdish, K. (1991) *Governing from the Centre. Politics and Policy-making in the Netherlands*, London: Hurst/The Hague: SDU.

Green-Pedersen, C., van Kersbergen, K. and Hemerijck, A. (2001) 'Neo-liberalism, the "third way" or what? Recent social democratic welfare policies in Denmark and the Netherlands', *Journal of European Public Policy* 8(2): 307–25.

Irwin, G. (2006) *Bandwagon Without a Band*, Leiden: Universiteit Leiden.

Joppke, C. (2007) 'Transformation of immigration integration. Civic integration and antidiscrimination in the Netherlands, France and Germany', *World Politics* 59(2): 243–73.

Kleinnijenhuis, J. and Krouwel, A. (2007) 'The nature and influence of party profiling websites'. Paper for the Politicologenetmaal 2007, Antwerpen, Belgium, 31 May–1 June.

Kleinnijenhuis, J. and Pennings, P. (2001) 'Measurement of party positions on the basis of party programmes, media coverage and voter perceptions', in M. Laver (ed.), *Estimating the Policy Positions of Political Actors*, London: Routledge, pp. 162–82.

Kriesi, H., Grande, E., Lachat, R., Dolezal, M., Bornschier, S. and Frey, T. (2006) 'Globalization and the transformation of the national political space: six European countries compared', *European Journal of Political Research* 45(6): 921–56.

Krouwel, A.P.M. (1999) 'The catch-all party in Western Europe 1945–1990: a study in arrested development'. Ph.D. thesis, Amsterdam: Vrije Universiteit Amsterdam.

Krouwel, A. and Abts, K. (2007) 'Varieties of euroscepticism and populist mobilization: transforming attitudes from mild euroscepticism to harsh eurocynicism', *Acta Politica* 42(2/3): 252–70.

Marks, G., Hooghe, L., Nelson, M. and Edwards, E. (2006) 'Party competition and European integration in the East and West. Different structure, same causality', *Comparative Political Studies* 39(2): 155–75.

Scheffer, P. (2000) 'Het multiculturele drama', *NRC Handelsblad*, 29 januari.

Thomassen, J.J.A., Aarts, K. and Kolk, H.v.d. (2000) *Politieke veranderingen in Nederland 1971–1998: kiezers en de smalle marges van de politiek*, Den Haag: Sdu.

Van der Brug, W. (2003) 'How the LPF fuelled discontent: empirical tests of explanations of LPF support', *Acta Politica* 38(1): 89–106.

Van der Eijk, C. and Niemöller, B. (1983) *Electoral Change in the Netherlands: Empirical Results and Methods of Measurement*, Amsterdam: CT Press.

Van Holsteyn, J., Irwin, G.A. and den Ridder, J.M. (2003) 'In the eye of the beholder: the perception of the List Pim Fortuyn and the parliamentary elections of May 2002', *Acta Politica* 38(1): 69–87.

Van Kersbergen, K. (forthcoming) 'The Christian democratic phoenix and modern unsecular politics', *Party Politics*.

Van Kersbergen, K. and Krouwel, A. (2003) 'De buitenlanderskwestie in de politiek in Europa', in H. Pellikaan and M. Trappenburg (eds), *Politiek in de multiculturele samenleving*, Meppel: Boom, pp. 188–218.

Van Kersbergen, K. and Krouwel, A. (2006) 'De veranderende beleidsfilosofie van het CDA van-Balkenende', in F. Becker, W. van Hennekeler and M. Hurenkamp (eds), *Vier jaar Balkenende, WBS Jaarboek 2006*, Amsterdam: Mets en Schilt-WBS, pp. 38–53.

Van Praag, P. (2003) 'De LPF-kiezer: rechts, cynisch of modaal?', *DNPP Jaarboek 2001*, Groningen: DNPP, pp. 96–116.

Voorhoeve, J.J.C. (1979) *Peace, Profits and Principles: A Study of Dutch Foreign Policy*, The Hague: M. Nijhoff.

VVD (2004) *Integratie van niet-westerse migranten in Nederland*, Den Haag: VVD.

Wansink, H. (2004) *De erfenis van Fortuyn: De Nederlandse democratie na de opstand van de kiezers*, Amsterdam: Meulenhoff.

Woltjer, J.J. (1992) *Recent verleden: de geschiedenis van Nederland in de twintigste eeuw*, Amsterdam: Balans.

Towards consensus? Centre-right parties and immigration policy in the UK and Ireland

Julie Smith

Since the 1990s both Ireland and the United Kingdom (UK) have seen significant migratory pressures. Concerns were initially raised in each country about the numbers of asylum-seekers, although citizens in both countries appeared quite sanguine about people coming to live and work in their country. Nevertheless, immigration has often been one of the most salient issues in the British political debate. It has been less high-profile in Ireland, although many social concerns linked to immigration, especially relating to pressures on public services and English-language teaching, have been on the Irish political agenda. In contrast to most continental European states, the UK and Ireland have not seen the emergence of effective far-right parties. Thus, it has been left to mainstream parties to respond to concerns about immigration control and immigrant integration. In fact, centre-right and centre-left have appeared to converge: they may vie for a tougher rhetorical stance but there is little evidence that the centre-right parties currently in opposition in the UK or

Ireland would behave very differently from the ruling parties if they were to take office. Contemporary debates often seem to be just that – wars of words high-lighting rhetorical differences rather than signalling a genuine intention to implement distinctive policies.

This article looks at the difficulty the centre-right has had in carving out a distinctive voice on immigration in these two moderate polities. It begins by establishing a basis for comparison, then goes on to look at the changing pat-terns of immigration in the UK and Ireland and how political parties have tackled issues of control, and assesses the extent to which there is a distinct centre-right stance in either country. In neither case, it argues, is the agenda being set by parties of the far-right, although in the UK the more hostile moves do appear to reflect public opinion as expressed in opinion polls and the media. By contrast, the Irish media are more liberal while, with only a decade's experience as a country of immigration, Irish citizens appear quite san-guine about immigration, perhaps a result of the fact that to date they have only experienced migratory pressures during a prolonged period of economic success. It concludes that, in both countries, immigration has essentially become a valence issue rather than a position issue: the main parties agree on the broad policy parameters and compete only on the detail of policy and implementation. While the British Conservatives have traditionally been seen as 'strong' on immigration, the reality is that the mainstream parties have espoused broadly similar policies in practice over the last 40 years, even if their rhetoric has dif-fered (Favell 1998: 331). Gradually, a similar situation appears to be emerging in Ireland, where Labour and Fine Gael seek to critique the ruling Fianna Fáil party less on its immigration policies so much as on its competence in implementing them.

IRELAND AND THE UK AS CASES FOR COMPARISON

Britain has long been a country of immigration, facing complex patterns of immigration, emigration, and transit migration.[1] In the last decade, as a result of international crises, European Union (EU) membership and economic success, Ireland – always more ethnically homogeneous than the UK – also became a country of immigration (Kenny 2007; Fanning et al. 2007: 10). The UK and Ireland have a shared but not common history and decisions taken in Dublin reflect the geographical proximity and political connections of the two states, which share a common travel area. Despite their disparities of size, differing experiences of migration and, until the recent past, the tempes-tuous nature of Anglo-Irish relations, the two countries have several similarities that make a comparison of their responses to globalization and immigration of particular interest for a special issue on parties of the centre-right: their moderate politics and lack of far-right populist parties; late membership of the EU, which has impacted on the politics of both countries, albeit in different ways; and their decisions to allow free movement of workers from the eight Central and East European (A8) countries that joined the Union in 2004.

First, both countries have moderate politics, with relatively few significant political parties (though in each the number of parties has gradually increased over the last quarter of a century) and both lack a strong far-right presence (Garner 2007; Geddes 2003: 30; Farrell 1999: pp. 46–7). Both the UK and Ireland differ from the continental mainstream in not having a Christian Democrat (CD) party. The British Conservatives are essentially pragmatic, centre-right vote-maximizers and have, since the late 1970s, espoused a more neo-liberal approach than most CD parties, rejecting the corporatist model that evolved in many continental European states. Unlike many European Liberal parties, the UK Liberal Democrats are distinctly centre-left on both social *and* economic policies, so there is no obvious competition to the Conservatives on the centre-right in the UK. Small far-right parties, the National Front and later the British National Party (BNP), have challenged mainstream parties on immigration issues but have had only limited political success. While not in the far-right tradition seen elsewhere in Europe, the anti-EU UK Independence Party (UKIP) has, since the late 1990s, sought to take ground from the Conservatives, both on the issue of EU membership and, since 2004, also on immigration.

The Irish party system is unique in Western Europe, owing more to questions of nationalism and relations with the UK than to traditional socio-economic cleavages, and it is not easy to characterize the Irish parties along the left–right spectrum. The two largest parties, Fianna Fáil (FF) and Fine Gael (FG), both have origins in the Sinn Féin movement which campaigned for Irish independence: FG is descended from those who supported the 1921 Anglo-Irish Treaty, while FF came from the anti-Treaty faction, while the small liberal Progressive Democrats (PDs) broke away from FF in part over Anglo-Irish relations. Irish parties have inevitably adopted a range of social and economic policies that enable us to give some indication of where they might fit on the left–right spectrum and FF, FG and the PDs can all be considered to at least some extent to be centre-right. Indeed, Garner argues that in the 1980s 'around 80 per cent of Irish voters supported centre-right parties, compared to the European average of 40 per cent' (Garner 2007: 112–13). However, whereas FF may be considered centre-right on social issues and has a nationalist tendency, it has been more left-wing on economic policies, at least until it took office with the PDs in 1997.

Second, the UK and Ireland both joined the EU in 1973, essentially for economic reasons, though Ireland's decision to enter, predicated as it was on Britain's, proved to be far more popular. Whereas the UK immediately questioned membership, the Irish profited enormously from membership, both directly from the common agricultural policy and structural funds and indirectly from its status as an EU member. In recent years the Irish economy has enjoyed phenomenal growth (CSO 2007: 144), which has resulted in a dramatic downturn in unemployment (down from 15 per cent to below 5 per cent in a decade; PDs 2005; Pogatchnik 2007), and reversed its traditional position as a country of emigration.[2]

Third, Ireland and the UK both took the unusual decision (along with Sweden) to allow immediate free movement of workers from the Central and East European states that entered the EU on 1 May 2004. Whereas most states feared competition from cheap labour from Central Europe, both the UK and Ireland recognized the economic benefits that could accrue at a time when their levels of unemployment were low and, in the British case at least, there were skills shortages (see Boswell *et al.* 2005). When Romania and Bulgaria joined the Union on 1 January 2007 the two countries again acted in tandem, this time both placing much tighter constraints on would-be migrants from these two countries. While it can be argued that 'immigration' from other EU member states does not really count as immigration in the traditional sense, since EU citizens have certain rights in other EU states *qua* EU citizens, the ramifications on labour markets and on public opinion of the arrival of hundreds of thousands of migrants suggest that this factor must be taken into consideration in assessing how British and Irish parties of the centre-right have responded to the challenges of globalization, immigration and Europe.

IDENTIFYING THE CENTRE-RIGHT IN THE UK AND IRELAND

For decades the UK had a two-party system divided primarily along class lines, with a centre-right Conservative Party attracting predominantly middle-class voters, as well as a substantial minority of working-class voters. This situation has gradually changed as a result of both social and partisan de-alignment, creating more opportunities for the party to maximize votes. It is essentially pragmatic rather than values-based and, while it was traditionally associated with the Church of England, there is no clerical (or religious) element to its policies; indeed, like Ireland, the UK does not have the sort of lay/clerical cleavage that developed in many continental European states. The Conservatives have evolved considerably over the years as they have sought electoral success, but remain essentially centre-right with a commitment to the market and to individuals. Paradoxically, it has been the Labour Party that has vied with the Conservatives on some traditionally right-wing issues, including crime and immigration, owing in part to the attitudes of many of their own supporters, who were socially conservative.

There are two parties to the right of the Conservatives – UKIP, whose *raison d'être* is to oppose British membership of the EU, and the far-right BNP. The BNP have won seats on various councils, notably in racially divided towns in the North-West and in East London, giving rise to the view that they pick up support that would otherwise have gone to Labour and therefore pose less of a threat to the Conservatives than might be imagined (Green 2007a). The Conservatives also face electoral competition from UKIP, which has arguably contributed to the strengthening of the Tories' Eurosceptic tendencies as they seek to stem the flow of support to a party that performed well at the

Conservatives' expense in the 2004 European Parliament elections, securing 12 seats (see Bale 2006). The Conservatives, like the other mainstream British parties, have been reluctant to support moves towards European-level decisions on asylum and immigration, although on this there is little to distinguish them from many mainstream EU parties (Geddes 2003: 31; Favell 1998: 328–33).[3] Under leader Nigel Farage, UKIP began to adopt an anti-immigration stance from 2004 onwards, taking the unusual (and in the EU context illegal) stance of refusing further immigration from within the Union at its annual conference in 2007.

Fianna Fáil is perhaps the Irish party most similar to the Conservatives in being a pragmatic vote-maximizing party, although it is essentially a catch-all populist, nationalist party, and its economic policies are normally more expansionary than the Conservatives'. Moreover, it draws its support more broadly from the working and middle classes, and, unlike the Conservatives, has strong and long-standing links with the trade unions. In addition, Ireland typically has coalition government and FF tends both to be in the governing coalition (though never with FG) and to adapt to whichever party it is in government with. Thus the coalition with the PDs from 1997 to 2007 pursued a very liberal economic policy. FF is nationalist in outlook, as its membership of the Union for a Europe of the Nations in the European Parliament would imply, although its decision to join a nationalist grouping stems partly from the fact that FG was a member of the European People's Party (EPP), which might in some ways be FF's more natural home on many policy issues.

Fine Gael, which refers to itself as 'a party of the progressive centre' (Fine Gael, no date), perhaps approximates best to the conventional view of a centre-right party. It typically wins support from the educated middle classes and has been more willing than other parties to take a liberal stance on social issues, including contraception and divorce, despite being a member of the EPP, which was a predominantly Christian Democratic grouping when FG joined in the 1970s. The PDs fit into the liberal mainstream in Europe, being full members of the European Liberal Democrat and Reform Party, and espousing both social and economic liberal policies during their ten years in office. The PDs performed very badly in the 2007 general election, retaining only two seats in the Dáil and their future seemed limited at the time of writing. However, the significance of their role in government in the previous decade renders their policies of interest.

PARTY POLITICS AND IMMIGRATION IN THE UK – 1960s TO EARLY 1990s

For centuries, the UK has been the recipient of significant migrant flows, including groups of refugees and those who intended to emigrate to the New World but then stopped in British ports and decided to remain, with Irish immigrants always among the most numerous. In the aftermath of the Second World War, the UK, like several other European states, benefited from considerable, albeit unplanned, inward migration, particularly from the New Commonwealth, including the Caribbean, India and Pakistan, and later Bangladesh (Geddes 2003: 33).

The Conservatives sought to limit Commonwealth immigration from the early 1960s, with the Commonwealth Immigrants Act (1962); Labour was initially critical, seeing 'the legislation as a betrayal of the Commonwealth and as a concession to racism' (Geddes 2003: 34), but swiftly adopted similar policies themselves, squeezed as they were in marginal seats (Geddes 2003: 34). Thereafter it would be difficult to see much practical difference in immigration policy between Labour and the Conservatives, even if the rhetoric was distinctive.[4] For Geddes (2003: 36), 'an outline of an immigration policy consensus can be seen resting on two pillars: tight restriction of black and Asian immigration coupled with anti-discrimination legislation introduced in three "race relations" acts of 1965, 1968 and 1976.'

Immigration hit the headlines in the UK in 1968 when Conservative Shadow Secretary of State for Defence Enoch Powell advocated curbing migration in his now infamous 'rivers of blood speech' (Powell 1968). His reward was to be sacked from the Tory front bench by Edward Heath, who denied that the Conservatives endorsed restrictive immigration policies.[5] Yet it would be Heath himself who introduced restrictive legislation in 1971, only to be forced to admit a large influx of Ugandan Asians fleeing Amin's regime. Then, barely a decade after Powell's pronouncements, the new Conservative leader, Margaret Thatcher, articulated similar concerns, albeit in more coded language (see Bale 2008: note 3), arguing primarily that it was necessary to discuss immigration openly: failure to do so was likely to send people to the extremes (at that time the National Front), while (as Labour ministers had themselves made clear in the 1960s) curbing immigration would be the way to enhance race relations. Whether or not Thatcher's willingness to address the issue was a factor in the demise of the far-right National Front in the 1970s, her intervention, and her government's reforms of the early 1980s, boosted the Conservatives' reputation for being tough on immigration. Notwithstanding the fact that Labour has often introduced restrictive legislation when in office, opinion polls have consistently shown that the Tories are more trusted in this area.

While Powell and Thatcher may well have tapped into latent popular concerns about immigration, hostility to immigration potentially sits badly with Conservative values and policies, particularly the neo-liberal approach espoused by the Thatcherite right in the 1980s: free trade, after all, would logically entail free movement of workers. Possibly one was a cover for the other: Boswell (2003: 16) argues that the Conservatives' approach was 'an attempt to mitigate the destabilizing impact of neo-liberal reforms with a nationalist rhetoric which promised to guard citizens against external threats ... [inter alia] through protecting Britain from an influx of New Commonwealth immigrants or asylum-seekers'. Equally, the Conservatives' vote-maximizing approach means that internal policy coherence matters rather less to them than to more ideological parties; tapping into populist sentiment over immigration would certainly have been a way to win support from certain sections of the traditional working class and hence attractive to the Conservatives, especially the party's more populist wing (Geddes 2003: 33).

THE UK AND IRELAND – NEW MAGNETS FOR MIGRANTS

Restrictive immigration legislation notwithstanding, from the early 1990s, the UK began to receive significant numbers of migrants, including a large influx of asylum-seekers, typically fleeing war in the Balkans, as well as large numbers of voluntary migrants, seeking to live and work or study in the West, whether permanently or temporarily, as well as family members of earlier migrants via family reunion schemes.[6] It also attracted a number of illegal immigrants, some of whom arrived clandestinely, others of whom tried to claim asylum, recognizing that their chances of being admitted as economic migrants would be slim. When the EU expanded in 2004, the UK was willing to welcome workers from new member states – clearly migrants, albeit with more legal rights than extra-EU third-country nationals – indicating an acceptance of labour migration on the part of the government.

The collapse of Yugoslavia also led to large numbers of asylum-seekers arriving in Ireland while, from 1997, a sustained period of growth in the country saw significant inward economic migration. This involved return migration as well as net inward migration from third countries, notably from the new member states of the EU, but including, for example, Chinese students and Nigerians (Hughes and Quinn 2004). As Ireland moved into a period of economic growth and full employment from the late 1990s (Hughes and Quinn 2004: 6), it was well placed to benefit from economic immigration as significant numbers of Central Europeans, predominantly Poles, arrived between 2004 and 2007, contributing over 10 per cent of the workforce in Ireland.[7]

BRITISH CONCERNS OVER IMMIGRATION

British citizens have been broadly favourable towards immigrants whom they feel make a contribution to the economy (Boswell *et al.* 2005). Coupled with a belief that migrant workers from A8 states, particularly Poland, are hard-working, this ensured that there was relatively little public opposition to the large inflows of Central and East European (CEE) workers after 1 May 2004. The fact that CEE nationals were not eligible for welfare benefits further contributed to the general acceptance of migration, not least because they were frequently willing to undertake jobs that British workers would not. Nevertheless, the sheer numbers of migrants – 500,000 compared with the 13,000 the government initially predicted – led to some concerns, contributing to the government's decision not to open up the labour market to Bulgarians and Romanians when their countries joined the EU on 1 January 2007. By contrast,

British voters tend to be less comfortable with asylum-seekers who do not contribute to the economy, even though many are highly skilled.

The impact of immigration has been subject to heated debate and differing interpretations in the UK, as demonstrated by two papers published in autumn 2007. The first, official, report from the Home Office and Department of Work and Pensions argued forcefully that immigration contributed to growth as well as having a positive impact on tax returns and helping with the UK's pensions crisis (Home Office 2007a: 8–11). Yet, the following day, a report from the government's Migration Impacts Forum outlined a series of concerns articulated by the UK regions, including the impact of migrants on the education system, particularly language teaching, and on the health service and policing in certain parts of the country (Home Office Border and Immigration Agency 2007).[8] This followed the frustrations voiced by the chief of police in the county of Cambridgeshire in September 2007, who argued that immigration was putting considerable additional pressure on her forces and necessitated more resources (BBC News 2007).

The British print media have been willing to discuss questions of immigration and asylum, with some, notably the *Daily Express*, raising the issue in especially negative terms over a long period of time. Moreover, journalists have been willing to criticize the political élites for not discussing immigration more, not least since it is an issue of high political salience for the voters. Writing in the *Daily Mail*, Stephen Glover asserted:

> Ever since New Labour won the election in 1997, there has been a lively debate about immigration in this country, and it has not made a blind bit of difference ... A few politicians have spoken up, but their warnings have not been heeded – or, if they have, nothing has changed. The Tories have picked up the issue and then dropped it. At the moment they are wondering whether to pick it up again.
>
> (Glover 2007)

CENTRE-RIGHT RESPONSES TO MIGRATORY PRESSURES – THE UK

Glover had a point. Under Michael Howard, the Conservatives did address the issue of immigration, adopting a clearly restrictive position; once he ceased to be leader the party's approach shifted considerably. In 2004, a Commission led by Tory Member of the European Parliament (MEP) Timothy Kirkhope published its report, *Building a Fair Immigration System*. While this report did not reject immigration entirely, it criticized the extent of low-skilled immigration, asserting, 'The business community may benefit from cheap labour, especially in the short term, but low-paid, low-skilled British workers, many of whom are British-born from settled immigrant communities, lose out from fresh immigration' (Kirkhope 2004: 8). This highlighted a lack of coherence in Conservative policies: cheap labour as a factor of production would normally be welcomed by economic liberals. The report recommended tightening up various procedures, including the rights to sponsor spouses entering the country and, in response to the Labour government's 1998 decision to end exit checks, to increasing checks on people entering and leaving the country (Kirkhope 2004 20–1). In a move to reduce 'health tourism', which the report claimed put pressure on the National Health Service, the Commission called for medical examinations for people coming to live in the UK for more than six months (Kirkhope 2004: 29).

During the 2005 general election, the Conservatives put immigration at the forefront of their campaign ('...it's not racist, as some people claim, to talk about controlling immigration': Howard 2005a). Howard made a great play about his own immigrant origins and said he accepted that immigration had benefited the country (Howard 2005a). Nevertheless, he went on to assert that immigration needed to be controlled, thereby deliberately distinguishing himself and his party from Labour and the Liberal Democrats, whom he asserted 'believe[s] that immigration should be unlimited' (Howard 2005b), a reference to the fact that Home Secretary David Blunkett was on record as saying that there was no obvious upper limit on immigration (Happold *et al.* 2003). Specifically, the Conservatives called for border controls to be improved, an 'Australian-style points system for work permits' that would 'give priority to people with the skills Britain needs', with Parliament to set annual limits on immigration (Conservatives 2005: 19).

More controversially, Howard called for a 'quota' for asylum-seekers, claiming, 'Our communities cannot absorb newcomers at today's pace.' Such a policy would have breached the UK's commitments under the Geneva Convention on Refugees, but the party seemed sanguine about this. Adopting an anti-EU slant on the issue, the manifesto pledged to 'take back powers from Brussels to ensure national control of asylum policy, withdraw from the 1951 Geneva Convention, and work for modernized international agreements on migration' (Conservatives 2005: 19).

The Tories rethought their policy on asylum when David Cameron succeeded Howard as party leader. Although Cameron had been the architect of the 2005 manifesto, he appointed the left-leaning Damian Green as his shadow immigration spokesman and the party reversed its policy on quotas for asylum-seekers. The thrust of Conservative critiques now turned to the government's management of the immigration system as well as the impact of immigration on public services, which seemed both more moderate and to be in line with citizens' concerns (see, for example, Davis and Green 2006). Responding to police concerns over the pressures that migrants were putting on their service, Shadow Home Secretary David Davis asserted that 'Labour's open door approach to immigration failed to consider, let alone cater for, the impact of this influx on housing and public services' (quoted in Attewill 2007). Blaming the government for its failure to anticipate the impacts of immigration, Shadow Immigration Minister Damian Green argued, 'Every new piece of evidence shows how damaging the government's failure to control immigration has been. They have ignored the fact that uncontrolled movements of people can cause strains on society, as well as bringing economic benefits' (Harper and Leapman 2007).

Conservative criticism of the government's supposedly incompetent management of immigration, rather than attacks on immigration *per se*, was to become the norm for the Conservatives under David Cameron. In the summer of 2007 a few words by Cameron in response to a TV interview saw some leap to the conclusion that the Conservatives were reverting to the so-called 'core vote' strategy of 2005, not least since immigration, alongside tax and Europe, were key issues on which the Tories' views appeared to coincide with those of the voters. Damian Green, however, was quick to reject this idea, arguing that 'Having a firm immigration policy is a way of contributing to better community cohesion in this country' (Green 2007b). Reversion, after all, would alienate potential voters whom the Tories were hoping to woo back from the Liberal Democrats. Emulating that party's position, however, was most certainly not on the cards. When the Liberal Democrats adopted a policy to regularize irregular migrants who had been in the country for more than ten years (Liberal Democrats 2007) Green, immediately accused the party of 'living in a fantasy world' (BBC 2007).

The fact that Labour's response to the Liberal Democrat idea mirrored that of the Conservatives, however, was illustrative of the limited scope for the Conservatives to articulate a distinctive voice without moving to the political extremes. In 2006, the government pledged to strengthen borders, with Home Secretary John Reid and Minister for Nationality, Citizenship and Immigration Liam Byrne asserting, 'We will put in place an effective approach to managing the identity of foreign nationals to help secure our borders, manage migration, cut illegal working and shut down fraudulent access to benefits and services' (Home Office 2006: 2). Then in 2007, the government appeared to adopt the very policy Michael Howard had espoused in 2005 when it decided to increase border controls 'to screen people it wants to enter the UK and to deny entry to those it does not, even before they get here' (Home Office 2007c). Immigration Minister Byrne's comment at the launch of the strategy also seemed reminiscent of the Howard Tory Party's rhetoric: 'It is essential that we have a fair and effective migration system, trusted by the people as a whole and those who rely on it' (Home Office 2007c).

In 2007, Byrne announced that a points-based system would be introduced from 1 January 2008 as a way of curbing immigration from non-EU countries. Again, this policy was very similar to the Conservatives' position, reflecting a willingness on the part of the Labour Party to adopt restrictive policies in practice. Byrne argued that: 'In 12 months' time our immigration system will have changed out of all recognition. From next year, a points-based system, modelled on the success of Australia, will ensure that only people Britain needs can come to work and study' (Border and Immigration Agency 2007). Byrne also took the opportunity to assert that the government would deal with illegal immigration: 'We will attack the root cause of illegal journeys, which is illegal jobs, with big new fast-track fines for employers turning a blind eye or breaking the rules' (Border and Immigration Agency 2007).

The new Prime Minister, Gordon Brown, also turned his attention to the ramifications of immigration. Aware that many of the new jobs created during ten years of Labour government had gone to migrants and that unemployment was creeping up among the indigenous population, Brown announced to the Trades Union Congress that he would create 500,000 'British jobs for British workers' (Wintour 2007). Brown's populist turn led to criticisms from the Conservatives, who argued that this was the language of the National Front and that it was in any case illegal under EU law. Agreeing that Brown's proposals would be illegal under EU law, UKIP was quick to note that the significant migratory pressures in the UK came from CEE workers and that the Conservatives had been keen advocates of eastward expansion of the EU, highlighting an apparent inconsistency in Conservative policy (UKIP 2007).

RESPONSES TO MIGRATORY PRESSURES – IRELAND

The Irish have been broadly tolerant of immigration, not least because of their experiences as a country of emigration. Having been the beneficiaries of financial receipts from relatives who moved overseas during times of economic difficulty, they have been broadly willing to welcome economic migrants. However, like the UK and some other countries (see Thielemann 2006), Ireland does not allow asylum-seekers to work, thus each country left potential skills untapped and fuelled negative public reactions as voters perceived asylum-seekers to be receiving benefits for which they had not worked. This was compounded by ill-founded rumours suggesting, for instance, that asylum-seekers were given BMW cars. As the number of asylum-seekers dropped back again, it ceased to be a salient political issue in Ireland; indeed, there have been cases where asylum-seekers threatened with deportation received strong support from the communities into which they had settled.

The question of immigration acquired political salience temporarily in Ireland as concern arose that pregnant women were coming to Ireland to give birth in order that their offspring would acquire Irish citizenship and, hence, that they and their families would have the right to remain in the country. This led to Irish women being displaced from maternity hospitals in Dublin and eventually led to a referendum on a new Citizenship Law (Irish Nationality and Citizenship Act 2004), which, like the British changes four decades earlier, removed the automatic right of citizenship for those born in the state. The Act was passed with 80 per cent in favour, indicating the depth of feeling on the issue. While the mainstream parties all supported the law, Sinn Féin and the trade unions criticized the move as racist. Yet, once the Law was passed, immigration slipped down the agenda again. This may have had something to do with lack of media pressure. The Irish are generally concerned not to appear racist and the broadsheet newspapers in particular tend to be liberal-leaning (Collins 2007). Thus, they are unlikely to whip up anti-immigrant sentiment in the way that certain sections of the British media have been willing to do, although political élites and journalists are both aware of and, one might suppose, influenced by, the British debate (Collins 2007; Lenihan 2007).

POLITICAL REACTION TO IMMIGRATION IN IRELAND

In Ireland, all the political parties accepted the economic benefits of immigration, seemingly without hesitation. Thus FG Enterprise spokesman, Paul Coghlan: 'It is a simple fact that Ireland will need to import skills to ensure we remain a world-class player' (Coghlan 2005). In the case of the PDs, their neo-liberal economic approach fitted well with a positive view of economic immigration, though their manifesto pledges on immigration demon- strated the limits of their liberalism, asserting that 'No foreign national has an absolute right to come here' (Progressive Democrats 2007: 59). These responses reflect the strongly held view in Ireland that economic migrants work harder than the native population and that they contribute to curbing wage inflation (seen as a plus by business leaders), though there is some concern that migrant workers may displace native workers (Lenihan 2007; Manning 2007). This concern, however, is far more evident on the left of the political spectrum. Trade unions, for instance, have argued that Irish workers are being pushed out of jobs in favour of immigrants on lower wages. The case was picked up and supported by Pat Rabbitte, the leader of the Labour Party in Ireland until summer 2007, who asserted 'We had the outrageous scandal last week of Mr Ahern the Taoiseach doling out €4.3 million of taxpayers' money to a company, Irish Ferries, to displace Irish workers and to replace them with cheaper labour' (*Irish Times* 2007). Thus, when FG leader Enda Kenny brought up the issue of immigration in January 2007, Rabbitte was the first to congratulate him (Donohoe 2007).

Enda Kenny sought to bring immigration and integration to the forefront of the 2007 Irish general election (Kenny 2007). While his primary intention was to stimulate debate on this sensitive (and hence often ignored) issue, like Thatcher in the UK three decades earlier, his efforts led to criticism, in part because he referred to Ireland as having a Christian and Celtic history. In addition, Kenny, followed by other FG candidates, referred to various problems that they claimed were associated with immigration, in particular petty crime and driving offences (issues that were also raised in the UK debate), as well as the impact on the education system and public services. Housing, a key issue in the UK debate, featured rather less in Ireland, both because most immigrants rented and because the housing rental market was not as tight as in the UK. The situation could change as EU nationals gradually become eligible for social housing but was not a feature in 2007. Despite Kenny's attempts to stimulate debate, immigration did not feature significantly in the 2007 election, as parties could see little political advantage in politicizing the issue (Manning 2007). Moreover, as for the Conservatives in the UK, FG found there was little political space available as the governing parties' policies differed little in practice from those advocated by FG.

This was true in the context of rights for Bulgarian and Romanian nationals to work in Ireland following accession to the EU in January 2007. FG had raised concerns about opening Ireland's borders, arguing that 'before this accession takes place, the Government should announce the details of a transitional arrangement to restrict access to the Irish labour market for the citizens of these states' (Fine Gael 2006a). The party welcomed the FF/PD government's decision not to open the market immediately but noted that the decision had become inevitable once the British decision had been taken, owing to the common travel area (Fine Gael 2006b).

CONCLUSION

Immigration does not form a powerful political cleavage in the UK or Ireland. It is a salient political issue in the UK, arousing considerable interest and concerns among voters, but the mainstream player on the centre-right, the Conservative Party, has typically been cautious about playing overtly anti-immigration policies. The recent exception during Michael Howard's period as leader of the Conservative Party seemed to yield little political advantage and the policies of that brief era were quietly dropped by the new leadership after 2005 in favour of a consistent attack on the government's competence. The fact that the governing Labour Party was willing to tighten the immigration rules (if not practices) arguably left the Conservatives with little space on the political spectrum. A clear move to the right might win them a limited number of votes that would otherwise go to the BNP or UKIP but risks alienating many floating voters whom they are trying to woo back from the Liberal Democrats. Thus, the political advantage was seen to accrue to a more measured approach – to valence as opposed to position politics. By 2007, immigration was not a highly politicized issue in Ireland and hence centre-right parties there saw little potential advantage in breaching the liberal consensus on the issue. This in part reflected tolerance on the part of the indigenous population but also the fact that a prolonged period of growth minimized many of the social impacts of immigration. The outstanding question for Ireland is whether this positive approach will persist if or when the country falls on harder times.

ACKNOWLEDGEMENTS

I should like to thank Ted Hallett for his guidance and assistance in organizing interviews in Dublin and Meng-Hsuan Chou for research assistance, as well as Tim Bale and two reviewers for their comments. I should also like to thank all interviewees, including one not mentioned in the references, Philip Watt.

NOTES

1 For recent data on migratory flows, see Salt (2006).
2 In 2005, 70,000 people moved to Ireland and only 16,000 emigrated – a high point in the reversal of previous patterns (Quinn 2006: viii).
3 While it is true that most EU states have been reluctant to cede sovereignty in the areas of asylum and immigration, Britain and Ireland, along with Denmark, are the only states with opt-ins or opt-outs from these parts of the *acquis*. For the specific British and Irish opt-ins, see Peers (2007: Annex IV).
4 There are some notable differences, e.g. Labour abolished the Conservatives' 1980 'primary purpose' legislation, which had limited the scope for family reunification. However, the rules remained tight (Geddes 2003: 35).
5 The depth of discomfort provoked by Powell's speech was clear 40 years later when, in autumn 2007, a Tory parliamentary candidate was obliged to resign for implying that Powell might have been right.
6 For a discussion of types of migration, as well as statistics on the inflows, see Salt (2005).
7 The precise figures are difficult to substantiate since Ireland, like the UK, does not have exit checks at ports of departure. The most recent Irish census, conducted in 2006, suggests that there were 410,000 non-nationals usually resident in Ireland (Central Statistics Office Ireland 2007: 5).
8 Out of eight regions, five mentioned crime and education as problems, six health and seven housing as having been negatively impacted by immigration (Home Office Border and Immigration Agency 2007: 15).

REFERENCES

Attewill, F. (2007) 'Increased immigration boosts knife crime and drink-driving, police chief says', *Guardian Unlimited*, 19 September, available at http://society.guardian.co.uk/crimeandpunishment/story/0,,2172384,00.html, accessed on 21-10-07.

Bale, T. (2006) 'Between a soft and a hard place? The British Conservative Party and the need for a new "Eurorealism"', *Parliamentary Affairs* 59(3): 385–400.

Bale, T. (2008) 'Turning round the telescope. Centre-right parties and immigration and integration policy in Europe', *Journal of European Public Policy* 15(2): 315–30.

BBC (2007) 'Lib Dems back migrant "amnesty"', available at http://www.news.bbc.co.uk/1/hi/uk_politics/6999611.stm, accessed on 21-06-07.

BBC News (2007) 'Police chief fears migrant impact', available at http://newsvote.bbc.co.uk/mpapps/pagetools/print/news.bbc.co.uk/1/hi/uk/7001768.stm, accessed on 21-10-07.

Border and Immigration Agency (2007) 'Byrne heralds new balance in migration policy', available at http://www.indhomeoffice.gov.uk/aboutus/newsarchive/byrneheraldsnewbalance, accessed on 17-10-07.

Boswell, C. (2003) *European Migration Policies in Flux: Changing Patterns of Inclusion and Exclusion*, Oxford: Royal Institute of International Affairs and Blackwell Publishing.

Boswell, C., Chou, M.-H. and Smith, J. (2005) *Reconciling Demand for Labour Migration with Public Concerns about Immigration: Germany and the United Kingdom*, London and Berlin: Anglo-German Foundation.

Central Statistics Office (CSO) Ireland (2007) *Statistical Yearbook of Ireland 2007 Edition*, available at http://www.cso.ie/releasespublications/statistical_yearbook_ireland_2007.htm, accessed on 11-11-07.

Coghlan, P. (2005) 'Speech to Seanad Éireann on the rights of migrant workers', 13 April, available at http://www.finegael.ie/news/index.cfm/type/details/nkey/25810, accessed on 29-05-07.

Collins, S. (2007) Political Correspondent, *The Irish Times*, Dublin, interview, 4. October.

Conservatives (2005) *Conservative Election Manifesto 2005*.

Davis, D. and Green, D. (2006) *Controlling Economic Migration*, London: The Conservative Party.

Donohoe, M. (2007) 'Rabbitte praises Kenny speech on immigration', *The Irish Times*, available at http://www.ireland.com/newspaper/ireland/2007/0127/1169680751356_pf.html, accessed on 22-02-07.

Fanning, B., Shaw, J., O'Connell, J.-A. and Williams, M. (2007) *Irish Political Parties, Immigration and Integration in 2007*, Dublin: University College Dubin.

Farrell, D.M. (1999) 'Ireland: a party system transformed?', in D. Broughton and M. Donovan (eds), *Changing Party Systems in Western Europe*, London: Pinter, pp. 30–47.

Favell, A. (1998) 'Multicultural race relations in Britain: problems of interpretation and explanation', in C. Joppke (ed.), *Challenge to the Nation-State: Immigration in Western Europe and the United States*, Oxford: Oxford University Press, pp. 319–49.

Fine Gael (2006a) 'Government should introduce labour market restrictions before next EU enlargement – Fine Gael', available at http://www.finegael.ie/news/index.cfm/type/details/nkey/29369/pkey/653, accessed on 19-11-07.

Fine Gael (2006b) 'Bulgaria/Romania work permit decision the right move but Government had little choice – Allen', available at http://wwwfinegael.ie/news/index.cfm/type/details/nkey/29570/pkey/653, accessed on 19-11-07.

Fine Gael (no date) 'Our values', available at http://www.finegael.ie//page.cfm/area/information/page/OurValues/pkey/1084, accessed on 29-05-07.

Garner, S. (2007) 'Ireland and immigration: explaining the absence of the far right', *Patterns of Prejudice* 41(2): 109–30, available at http://dx.doi.org.10.1080/00313220701265486, accessed on 19-06-07.

Geddes, A. (2003) *The Politics of Migration and Immigration in Europe*, London: Sage.

Glover, S. (2007) 'If the BBC's worried about immigration, can we have an honest debate about it?', *The Daily Mail*, 19 September, available at http://www.dailymail.co.uk/pages/live/articles/columnists/columnists.html?in_page_id=1772&in_article_id=482776&in_author_id=244, accessed on 21-10-07.

Green, D. (MP) (2007a) Shadow Spokesman on Immigration, Wilton Park, interview, 16 June.

Green, D. (2007b) 'Green rejects "core shift" shift', *BBC News*, available at http://news.bbc.co.uk/1/hi/uk_politics/6970005.htm, accessed on 11-01-08.

Happold, T. *et al.* (2003) 'Blunkett: no UK immigration limit', *Guardian Unlimited*, 13 November, available at http://politics.guardian.co.uk/homeaffairs/story/0,11026,1084149,00.html, accessed on 19-11-07.

Harper, T. and Leapman, B. (2007) 'Foreigners "commit fifth of crime in London"', *Telegraph.co.uk*, 24 September, available at http://www.telegraph.co.uk/news/main.jhtml?xml=/news/2007/09/23/ncrime123.xml, accessed on 21-10-07.

Home Office (2006) *Borders, Immigration and Identity Action Plan – Using the National Identity Scheme to Strengthen Our Borders and Enforce Compliance within the UK*, London: Home Office.

Home Office (2007a) *The Economic and Fiscal Impact of Immigration: A Cross-Departmental Submission to the House of Lords Select Committee on Economic*

Affairs, London: Home Office in partnership with the Department of Work and Pensions.

Home Office (2007b) *Securing the UK Border – Our Vision and Strategy for the Future*, London: Home Office and Foreign and Commonwealth Office, March.

Home Office (2007c) 'Government to strengthen "off-shore" border', available at http://www.ind.homeoffice.gov.uk/aboutus/newsarchive/governmenttostrengthen offshore, accessed on 21-06-07.

Home Office Border and Immigration Agency (2007) 'Regional impacts – evidence from our regional consultation on the impacts of migration', available at http://www.ind.homeoffice.gov.uk/lawandpolicy/migrationimpactsforum/meeting17octo-ber/ accessed on 21-10-07.

Howard, M. (2005a) 'Firm but fair immigration controls', Speech at Conservative Campaign Headquarters, available at www.conservatives.com/tile.do?def=news.story.page&obj_id=119004&speeches=1#, accessed on 11-11-07.

Howard, M. (2005b) 'I believe we must limit immigration', advertisement in *The Sunday Telegraph*, 23 January.

Hughes, G. and Quinn, E. (2004) *The Impact of Immigration on Europe's Societies: Ireland*, Dublin: European Migration Network, available at http://www.esri.ie/pdf/BKMNEXT057_Impact%20of%20Immigration.pdf, accessed on 14-11-07.

Irish Times Editorial (2007) 'Celtic and Christian people', available at http://www.ireland.com/newspaper/opinion/2007/0126/1169680649362_pf.html, accessed on 22-02-07.

Kenny, E. (2007) 'Immigration must help to improve living standards', text of speech to special meeting of the Fine Gael parliamentary party and Dáil candidates reprinted in *The Irish Times*, available at http://www.ireland.com/newspaper/ireland/2007/0125/1169673791567_pf.html, accessed on 22-02-07.

Kirkhope, T. The Commission on Immigration (2004) *Building a Fair Immigration System*, available at http://www.conservatives.com/pdf/kirkhopecommission.pdf, accessed on 09-11-07.

Lenihan, C. (TD) (2007) Minister for Integration, Dublin, interview, 4 October.

Liberal Democrats (2007) 'Immigration in the 21st century', Policy Motion adopted at Party Conference on 18 September.

Manning, M. (2007) President, Irish Human Rights Commission, Dublin, interview, 4 October.

Peers, S. (2007) *Statewatch Analysis EU Reform Treaty Analysis No. 4: British and Irish Opt-outs from EU Justice and Home Affairs (JHA) Law*, available at http://www.statewatch.org/news/2007/aug/eu-reform-treaty-uk-ireland-opt-outs.pdf, accessed on 11-11-07.

Pogatchnik, S. (2007) 'Ireland's Ahern looks for party allies', *Seattle Post-intelligencer*, available at http://seattlepi.nwsource.com/national/1103AP_Ireland_Election.html, accessed on 30-05-07.

Powell, E. (1968) Speech to the Annual General Meeting of the West Midlands Area Conservative Political Centre, Birmingham, 20 April, available at ttp://theocciden-talquarterly.com/vol1no1/ep-rivers.html, accessed on 18-06-07.

Progressive Democrats (PDs) (2005) *What Have the PDs Ever Done for Me?*, available at http://www.progressivedemocrats.ie/events/10/, accessed on 29-05-07.

Progressive Democrats (2007) *From Good to Great: Continuing Ireland's Radical Trans-formation*, available at www.progressivedemocrats.ie, accessed on 20-10-07.

Quinn, E. (2006) 'Policy analysis report on asylum and migration: Ireland mid-2004 to 2005, Dublin: European Migration Network, available at http://www.esri.ie/pdf/BKMNEXT076.pdf, accessed on 14-11-07.

Salt, J. (2005) 'Types of migration in Europe: implications and policy outcomes'. Paper presented at European Population Conference 2005, on Demographic Challenges for Social Cohesion, available at http://www.geog.ucl.ac.uk/mru/docs/migration_types.pdf, accessed on 09-11-07.

Salt, J. (2006) 'International migration and the United Kingdom – report of the United Kingdom Sopemi Correspondent to the OECD, available at http://www.geog.ucl.ac.uk/mru/docs/Sop06_final_200207.pdf, accessed on 09-11-07.

Thielemann, E. (2006) 'The effectiveness of governments' attempts to control unwanted migration', in C. Parsons and T. Smeeding (eds), *Immigration and the Transformation of Europe*, Cambridge: Cambridge University Press.

United Kingdom Independence Party (2007) 'Tory "hypocrisy" on immigration', available at http://www.ukip.org/ukip/index2.php?option=com_content&task=view&id=273&Itemid=57, accessed on 19-11-07.

Wintour, P. (2007) 'Brown plans new migrant controls to get unskilled Britons back to work', *The Guardian*, 10 September.

Immigration and the transnational European centre-right: a common programmatic response?

Fraser Duncan and Steven Van Hecke

INTRODUCTION

Despite widespread academic recognition of the politicization of immigration in Europe, studies of immigration's impact on political parties – and vice-versa – have been thin on the ground. Party specialists have been predominantly drawn towards the far-right's mobilization around the issue while migration theorists have tended to downplay or overlook the central role of political parties in immigration control and immigrant integration policy. Yet 'policies are made by actors, not by institutions or economic trends' (Giugni and Passy 2006: 13) and greater attention to the preferences and behaviour of parties is needed. This is also true at the European level where, as more components of control and integration policy shift to the European Union (EU) with a greater role for the European Parliament (EP), the European Parliament party groups (EPGs) and the European party federations (EPFs) will increasingly acquire more importance in co-ordinating policy choices.

Exploring the nature of political parties at the European level is a more complex task than investigating national parties as it potentially involves analysing the behaviour of political actors in multiple national, transnational, inter-governmental and supranational institutions (see Hix and Lord's 'organigram' of parties in the EU, 1997). Our aim here, however, is more limited and we focus on exploring party manifestos at the transnational level. We do this by charting the positions on immigration taken by the major EPFs – the European People's Party (EPP), the European Liberal Democrat and Reform Party (ELDR), the Party of European Socialists (PES) and the European Federation of Green Parties (EFGP)[1] – and those of national party members of the EPGs at EP elections.

In the process, we assess the overall levels of programmatic congruence within transnational parties. In view of their limited organizational capacity, the problems of EPFs in developing coherent responses to policy problems are markedly more intense than their national counterparts. These difficulties are particularly acute in relation to issues connected to immigration. National variations in social, economic, cultural and geographic characteristics and very different migration histories present considerable obstacles to developing a common transnational platform. On the other hand, the slow move towards the communitarization of immigration policy in the EU should increase the incentives for transnational party co-operation. This contribution explores the tension between these two pressures by analysing the predictive power of national and transnational ideological variables in EP manifesto positions.

First, then, the marginal role accorded to political parties in the study of migration will be outlined, followed by the specific difficulties facing the European parties in formulating policy responses on immigration. The third section reviews previous attempts to measure transnational party positions on immigration while the fourth section charts the programmatic reaction of transnational parties to the heightened salience of border control and multi-culturalism. Against our initial expectations, the manifesto data provide evidence of a degree of intra-transnational party programmatic congruence on migratory issues. They also underline that different political logics underpin immigration control and migrant integration. The distinction made by Hammar (1985) between immigration control (i.e. border and aliens' control) and immigrant policy (i.e. the conditions provided for resident migrants) has been widely accepted within the study of immigration policy. Our study confirms Givens and Luedtke's earlier findings (2005) that this distinction is crucial in understanding party responses to immigration. Party differences between left and right are clearest on immigrant integration policy while control issues actually divide the centre-right, with Liberal parties diverging from their Christian Democratic and Conservative counterparts. Nonetheless, even though Christian Democratic and Conservative parties are generally more restrictionist and less multicultural than the other major party groups, there is little sign of an attempt to co-opt the hardline appeal of parties further to their right.

POLITICAL PARTIES AND IMMIGRATION

One distinct strand of research in the study of migration has concentrated on the nature of national immigration policies and the influences that shape and constrain them. As Bale (2008) observes, however, a notable omission from most accounts of immigration policy has been political parties. Despite parties' role in representing, aggregating and mobilizing the citizenry, partisan differences between left and right have not been adjudged to have much impact on immigration policy in liberal democracies. It has been suggested that immigration is a cross-cutting issue which defies easy integration into the existing left–right framework (see, for instance, the views of Members of the European Parliament (MEPs) in Lahav 2004) and much migration theory is based on the idea of a hidden consensus between mainstream left- and right-wing parties (Triadafilopoulos and Zaslove 2006).

Indeed, it has often been difficult to distinguish between the immigration policies pursued by left- and right-wing governments in western Europe. Governments regardless of partisan composition have often been fearful of public backlash. Successive British governments post-1945 have followed a similar restrictive logic (Spencer 1997), at least until the election of New Labour, and similar patterns can be discerned elsewhere (see Schain 1988 for a discussion of France). Immigration has proved troublesome for the internal ideological cohesion of parties of both the left and right. For left-wing parties, there is a tension between representing the interests of the native working class and wider concerns about social justice. For the centre-right, restrictiveness may accord with the belief in a strong state, but might also contradict liberal or Christian elements of their ideological heritage and the desire of employers to fill domestic labour market gaps.

Through statistical analysis of the effect of partisanship (together with issue salience, economic factors and the scale of immigrant inflows) on the restrictiveness of government policy, Givens and Luedtke (2005) found evidence confirming that the party in power was not a significant predictor of restrictive immigration control policies. Their study, however, also discovered that partisanship did have a significant and strong impact on the restrictiveness of integration laws towards resident immigrants. On the evidence of the policies pursued by European centre-left governments in the late 1990s, this seems plausible. A common theme of the German Red-Green, French *Gauche Plurielle* and Italian Olive Tree governments was a more liberal stance in relation to immigrants mixed with the maintenance of the tough control regulations introduced by earlier centre-right governments. Applying this to our study, we expect the distinctiveness of transnational centre-right immigration politics to emerge only in policies towards resident immigrants. Yet we also need to disaggregate the centre-right, something which Givens and Luedtke do not do. They discuss only 'Right governments' and there is no appreciation that the presence of Liberals within a centre-right coalition may alter policy aims. Therefore, we also explore the extent to which Liberal positions at the

European level resemble Christian Democrat and Conservative stances and whether they also follow the 'different political logics' of control and integration policies (Givens and Luedtke 2005: 2).

PROBLEMS OF TRANSNATIONAL PARTY CO-OPERATION ON IMMIGRATION

Givens and Luedtke's study indicates that ideology does impact on certain national immigration policy outputs. However, at the transnational level, reaching intra-party accord on immigration is far from an easy task and a number of obstacles potentially stand in the way of common policy stances. These can be separated into the difficulties generated by the Europeanization of immigration and the general weaknesses of EPFs.

The development of EU policy competence on immigration and asylum matters has been incremental (Geddes 2003). The development of the common market and drive towards freedom of movement led to greater national co-operation in this area, but the sluggish pace of Europeanization provided more confirmation of the vital link between state sovereignty and the control of borders and membership (Dauvergne 2004). Despite the attempts to lay out the foundations of a common immigration policy in the Amsterdam Treaty (1997) and European Council meetings in Tampere (1999), Seville (2002) and The Hague (2004), the reluctance of member states to grant power to the supranational bodies of the EU was obvious in the failure of the Commission's directive on conditions of admission and stay of third-country workers. Overall, there has been a general lack of progress in realizing the ambitious agenda set out in Tampere although the Reform Treaty would open up the prospect of more qualified majority voting on legislation surrounding legal migration.

In view of the protection of national immigration control by member states, the prospects of a coherent common stance being developed by transnational parties do not appear favourable. Furthermore, in formulating immigration policy, large disparities between member states on a wide range of critical background factors have to be reconciled. Not all states within the EU are equally attractive to would-be migrants as geography, language, existing migrant communities, colonial links, labour market dynamics and other socioeconomic factors all shape the net 'pull' of the receiving state (Geddes 2003), with recent EU enlargements adding considerably to the already existing diversity. Variations in migratory pressure and the existing size of the foreign population are marked across the EU. For instance, asylum applications in 2004 ranged from 50,545 in France to five in Latvia while the size of the foreign population in 2005 varied between 39 per cent of the total population in Luxembourg to 0.4 per cent in Slovakia.[2] Some member states are only now experiencing the transition from sending state to host state, but even amongst those EU states familiar with mass immigration there have been wide differences in attitudes towards permanent settlement, access to citizenship and expectations of assimilation.

For the transnational party federations, 'undoubtedly very weak institutions ... that suffer from the need to respect the specificities and objectives of their national components' (Bardi 2006: 13), these national differences are obviously problematic. The role of the EPFs in co-ordinating policy stances across different EU institutions has increasingly been recognized in EU treaties and they now qualify for direct financial support. The EPFs are also responsible for European election manifestos, setting out policy commitments shared by all member parties. These documents, though, play a marginal role in the actual EP elections. National parties also produce their own electoral programmes and national issues dominate EP campaigns. In any case, the construction of EPF manifestos has been a consistent source of difficulties as a result of ideological heterogeneity within the transnational parties (Hix and Lord 1997: 168–9). The positions of the EPFs have tended as a consequence towards a lowest common denominator approach.

Transnational party co-operation has been complicated by the fluidity in the membership of the EPFs and the EPGs. The growing power of the EP together with EU enlargements compelled the EPFs to prioritize alliance building over ideological purity. The EPP has accepted the Spanish People's Party (PP), Forza Italia, French Gaullists and a variety of parties from the new member states as members, in the process moving from an exclusively Christian Democratic party federation into a broader centre-right alliance encompassing Christian Democrats, Conservatives and Liberals. Since 1999, the party group has also been named the European People's Party-European Democrats (EPP-ED) in recognition of the distinct position of the British Conservatives, the Portuguese PP and the Czech Civic Democratic Party (ODS) as aligned non-members with considerable latitude to diverge from group policies. The ideological coherence of the ELDR party federation and its EPG has always been problematic in view of the split in European liberalism between free market orientated parties (e.g. the Dutch People's Party for Freedom and Democracy, VVD) and more social liberal parties (e.g. the British Liberal Democrats) (Sandström 2004: 174), but internal diversity has intensified recently. Enlargement in the 1990s brought the incorporation of parties (such as the Swedish and Finnish Centre Parties) lacking the integrationist enthusiasm of older ELDR member parties. Since 2004, ELDR MEPs have sat as part of the Alliance of Liberals and Democrats for Europe (ALDE) EP group along with the European Democratic Party (EDP) and a handful of independents and MEPs from other parties.

The enlargement of transnational parties and EPGs presents the risk of identity dilution. Existing studies of the role of parties in the EU, however, suggest that this is more likely to be the case for the EPFs than the EPGs. In contrast to the still limited institutional development of the transnational party federations, there are increasing signs of cohesion within the EPGs. Admittedly, national parties continue to wield considerable power through the selection of candidates and the determination of the party group destination of their MEPs is controlled by national parties. Nonetheless, national parties have largely avoided close supervision of their MEPs and national party interventions have been rare. The EPGs, too, are not without incentives and disciplinary powers to ensure that their interests prevail over national interests while policy influence is contingent upon group cohesion. Thus, numerous studies have demonstrated that the party groups are increasingly important in organizing political competition in the EP with the national background of MEPs decreasing in importance (e.g. Hix 2001).

ESTIMATING TRANSNATIONAL PARTY POSITIONS ON IMMIGRATION

As migratory matters are drawn into the EP's competence through the co-decision procedure, this tests the extent to which transnational party ideology transcends national priorities. As with national parties, a number of different methods of positioning EPGs have been developed, including élite interviews, expert surveys, manifesto analysis and behavioural measurements. In this section we review how these have been applied to immigration politics thus far, highlighting that, irrespective of methodological differences, a common failing is the lack of differentiation between immigration control and immigrant integration policy.

Lahav (2004; see also Lahav and Messina 2005) carried out surveys of MEP attitudes on migration in 1992–93 and again in 2003–04. Both surveys confirmed that membership of an EPG structured responses to immigration although we cover only the earlier survey as the later survey included different questions. Members of the Radical Left group, followed by their counterparts in the Socialist and Liberal groups in the EP,[3] were most likely to express a preference for more immigration while support for greater restrictions on immigration was by far strongest in the DR (European Right) Far Right group (see Table 1). Minority opinion within the EPP and ELDR also favoured lower immigration but the majority in both groups supported current levels of immigration. MEP responses to the question of immigrant rights provided further evidence of the adoption of common positions within the party groups (see Table 2). The vast majority of Green, Radical Left (European United Left/Nordic Green Left, EUL/NGL)

Table 1 MEP preferences of general immigration levels by party group (%) 1992–93

	GUE	SOC	ELDR	EPP-ED	DR	EP average
Increase	60	30	21	8	0	25
Same	40	56	50	59	17	51
Decrease	0	14	29	33	83	24

Source: Lahav (1997: 388).

Table 2 MEP support for extension of immigrant rights by party group (%) 1992–93

	Greens	GUE	SOC	ELDR	EPP-ED	DR	EP average
Increased immigrant rights	100	90	97	60	62	0	77

Source: Lahav (2004: 140).

and Socialist MEPs favoured greater rights for immigrants. Amongst Liberals and Christian Democrats/Conservatives, a majority backed greater rights but the more ambivalent position of these groups was evident in the considerably lower proportion supporting the extension of rights compared to the groups of the left.

Distinct party group stances on immigration also emerged from McElroy and Benoit's recent expert survey (2007) of the policy positions of the party groups in the EP. EP specialists were asked to locate the party groups on a 20-point scale on eight policy dimensions, including immigration, and on a general left–right scale just prior to the 2004 elections. On the immigration policy dimension, 1 represented a preference for 'policies designed to help asylum-seekers and immigrants integrate into European society' while 20 reflected a belief in 'policies designed to restrict access of asylum-seekers and immigrants to Europe' (2007: 22). Figure 1 shows the results of the survey. The EPP-ED group is located to the right of centre on the spectrum, roughly midway between the ELDR to the left and the Union for Europe of the Nations (UEN) and Europe of Democracies and Diversities (EDD) on the right. The ELDR's position is particularly interesting owing to its proximity to the PES and it is much closer to the Greens and EUL/NGL than to the EPP-ED.

The standard deviations across the expert scores are greater for immigration than for the left–right dimension, but are not high enough to cast doubt on the placements. More problematic is the nature of the question which fuses issues of border control ('access ... to Europe') with those of immigrant integration. This prevents comparison of partisan positions on the two separate dimensions of control and integration policies whilst also blurring the distinction between different types of integration policies (i.e. multicultural or assimilationist).

Further proof of a cohesive transnational party approach on migration-themed legislation in the EP can be found in Hix and Noury's (2007) study of 61 roll-call votes between 1999 and 2004. From the roll-call data, Hix and

Figure 1 Expert placement of EP party groups on immigration
Source: Adapted from McElroy and Benoit (2007).

Noury created an index ranging from 0 (consistently anti-immigration) to 100 (consistently pro-immigration) for all MEPs who had participated in at least a quarter of the votes. Figure 2 shows the mean score for the MEPs by political group. Again, a clear contrast can be seen between the party groups, with the most pro-immigration parties being the Radical Left and the Greens/European Free Alliance (G/EFA), followed by the Socialists and Liberals. However, the position of the EPP-ED stands out against the earlier studies. On the roll-call votes studied, its MEPs on average were even more hostile to liberal migration policies than non-attached, Eurosceptic (EDD) and nationalist (UEN) MEPs. One possible explanation for this is that it reflects the traditionally influential position of the German Christian Democratic Union (CDU), whose MEPs' restrictiveness is second only to that of the British Conservatives,[4] within the EPP-ED. The CDU were in opposition throughout the period covered by the study and had on occasion attempted to make political capital from opposition to the Red-Green government's liberal immigration and citizenship policy (see Cooper 2002).

The evidence from these different studies of transnational party positioning on immigration all point, then, to immigration slotting into existing ideological divisions. Party groups in the EP, according to MEP behaviour, experts and MEPs themselves, adopt distinct stances on migration issues that are determined more by ideology than by national interests. On the whole, the party positions depicted are consistent across different studies, with the EPP-ED's fairly extreme restrictiveness in the Hix and Noury data the only deviation. However, only Lahav analytically distinguished control and integration position, leaving us uncertain whether partisan differences apply to both dimensions of immigration policy. Moreover, the datasets measure only the EPGs, rather than the party federations outside the EP. While the EPGs are an important component of the transnational parties, the extra-parliamentary EPFs are equally interesting, providing a glimpse into the developing Europeanization of party politics. As the previous section made clear, the extant literature on EPGs and EPFs suggests that the increasing levels of party group cohesion inside the EP are not found outside it. Therefore, to measure the degree of positional congruence within

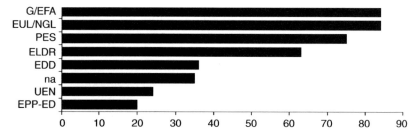

Figure 2 MEP migration scores by political group
Source: Hix and Noury (2007: 192).

transnational parties on both control and integration issues, we instead focus on election manifestos.

PROGRAMMATIC REACTION

Our analysis of the programmatic reaction of parties at the European level to the heightened salience of immigration is based on the dataset from the Euromanifestos Project (EMP).[5] The EMP developed as an application of the content analysis methodology of the Comparative Manifestos Project (CMP) (see Budge *et al.* 2001 for a full explanation of the CMP methodology) to EP elections, covering four EPFs (EPP, PES, ELDR, EFGP) and all national parties winning representation in the EP. The CMP coding frame was used but expanded to encompass an exclusively European policy domain (Domain 3.2: Political System of the European Union) and subcategories allowing for greater precision (e.g. splitting references to Freedom from those of Human Rights) and sensitivity to contextual variations.

In the following analysis, we chart the immigration control and migrant integration positions of the EPFs and national parties at EP elections. This allows us to compare the programmatic scores with the placements from the earlier studies and assess the degree of programmatic uniformity within EPGs. For the national parties, our analysis is largely confined to the 1999 and 2004 EP elections as, owing to greater EU enlargements and fewer unavailable documents, they provide greater numbers of cases and increase our confidence in our results. To minimize confusion over the frequent EPG name changes, we use the most recent of these throughout: namely, ALDE for the Liberal group, SOC for the Socialist group, Union for Europe of the Nations (UEN) for Nationalists, and Independence and Democracy (IND/DEM) for the Eurosceptic parties. Finally, it is important to note the different compositions of EPFs and affiliated EPGs: as mentioned earlier, the EPP and ELDR MEPs sit in the EPP-ED and ALDE groups respectively while Green MEPs have been allied with the regionalist European Free Alliance (EFA) parliamentarians since 1999. In each case, the incorporation in the EPG of parties outside the EPF might dilute the group's programmatic congruence.

In order to test Givens and Luedtke's argument that immigration control and immigrant integration entail different political logics, we developed two scales measuring policy positions on immigration control and immigrant integration following the standard methodology of scales based on quantitative manifesto analysis.[6] The former sums the percentage of each manifesto (as measured in quasi-sentences) devoted to liberal control policies and then subtracts this from the percentage of the programme focusing on restrictionism. The latter scale totals the percentage of the manifesto advocating multicultural policies and subtracts this figure from the percentage accorded to assimilationist policies (see Appendix). This allowed us to place the manifestos of transnational party federations (TPFs) and national parties at EP elections on scales where the minimum score is -100 (i.e. a manifesto wholly devoted to liberal/multicultural policies) and the maximum +100 (i.e. a manifesto entirely detailing restrictionist/assimilationist positions). Owing to the range of other issues covered in manifestos, however, all parties fall between −16.22 and 18.31 on the control axis and most between −37.5 and 33.33 on the integration axis.

Figure 3 illustrates the positions of the EPFs on both axes since 1989. The EPP's manifestos have regularly been the most restrictionist on the control axis. By contrast, the EFGP and, increasingly, the ELDR have adopted more liberal positions. Relative positions on integration are less consistent, but generally the PES and EFGP have adopted the most multicultural programmes with the EPP and ELDR less multicultural. Two major conclusions can be drawn from Figure 3. First, in line with Givens and Luedtke's findings, there is little to distinguish EPP positions on control from those of the PES. The consensus on control, however, has not extended to the ELDR which has instead been much closer to the stance of the Greens. Second, there is little sign of a universal movement to the right as immigration has risen in salience. Rather than attempt to co-opt far-right positions, the EPP in 1999 and 2004 moderated the strong restrictionism of 1994 while recent EFGP and ELDR manifestos have also been characterized by movement towards a more liberal control position. On integration issues, too, the ELDR and PES manifestos have become increasingly

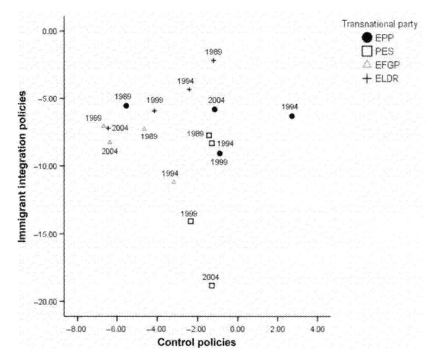

Figure 3 Transnational party placements on control and integration scales, 1989–2004

multicultural and there is no clear trend among the programmes of the EPP and EFGP.

We then applied our two dimensions of immigration policy to the national party manifestos produced for EP elections to test whether the EPF differences on control and integration policy were replicated by national parties at EP elections. As a test of the accuracy of our data, we first compared the party positions obtained from our dataset with those found in the expert survey carried out by McElroy and Benoit and Hix and Noury's measurement of party behaviour in the EP by computing party group means weighted by parliamentary seats on the two axes and correlating these figures with the expert and EP scores.

As Table 3 illustrates, significant positive correlations[7] are found between our two dimensions of programmatic competition, expert placements and MEP migration scores. The expert survey and the EP voting behaviour scores have the strongest association while migrant integration policy has the weakest correlation coefficient with each of the other measurements. This, though, need not be seen as a question mark against the validity of the programmatic placements. First, of the 61 votes comprising Hix and Noury's scale, 51 concern control issues. Therefore, their scale is more indicative of control positions than MEP attitudes towards migrant integration. Second, the disproportionate focus on control issues within the EP is also likely to influence experts' opinions on

Table 3 Correlations between manifesto scores, expert placements and MEP voting behaviour

		Expert placements	EP behaviour	Control policies	Immigrant integration policies
Expert placements	Pearson correlation	1	0.865**	0.786**	0.694**
	sig. (2-tailed)		0.000	0.001	0.006
	N	14	14	14	14
EP behaviour	Pearson correlation	0.865**	1	0.728**	0.652*
	sig. (2-tailed)	0.000		0.003	0.011
	N	14	14	14	14
Control policies	Pearson correlation	0.786**	0.728**	1	0.509
	sig. (2-tailed)	0.001	0.003		0.063
	N	14	14	14	14
Immigrant integration policies	Pearson correlation	0.694**	0.652*	0.509	1
	sig. (2-tailed)	0.006	0.011	0.063	
	N	14	14	14	14

** Correlation is significant at the 0.01 level (2-tailed).
* Correlation is significant at the 0.05 level (2-tailed).

party positions on immigration in view of the fact, as mentioned earlier, that McElroy and Benoit fuse questions of control with those of integration. Third, a certain divergence between programmatic stances and EP behaviour (and by extension expert judgements on party positioning) is to be expected. Parties do not always fulfil manifesto pledges and electoral programmes are, by their nature, prone to short-term fluctuations in response to events. More importantly, as was argued earlier, the capacity of EPGs to enforce intra-group discipline is far greater than the ability of the extra-parliamentary EPF to impose uniformity on its constituent member parties. Thus, the programmatic differences between the member parties of the EPGs tend to be flattened out once MEPs take their parliamentary seats.

Table 4 details mean party group positions as well as two indicators of the programmatic congruence within each group. The ordering of the parties is largely as expected, with Nationalist, Eurosceptic and non-attached parties the most restrictive and assimilationist. The table also supports a number of earlier findings about the EPFs. Control issues divide the centre-right rather than left from right with ALDE parties close to G/EFA parties at the liberal end of the scale. The proximity of SOC and EPP-ED parties on control issues is particularly noticeable if analysis centres on the larger parties. If the group mean is weighted by EP seats, the SOC mean in 2004 actually exceeds

Table 4 1999 and 2004 control and integration policy scores by party group

| | Control policies | | | | | | | |
| | 1999 | | | | 2004 | | | |
	N	Mean	Range	Std. deviation	N	Mean	Range	Std. deviation
Non-att.	7	2.58	20.81	7.53	8	−0.13	10.35	3.39
UEN	5	−0.51	2.33	1.03	7	−0.49	4.78	1.65
IND/DEM	5	−0.87	2.67	1.19	8	0.61	8.96	3.14
GUE/NGL	15	−1.44	3.95	1.47	16	−2.69	6.52	2.06
EPP-ED	24	−1.86	19.0	3.66	41	−1.33	9.02	1.74
SOC	18	−1.91	4.32	1.26	28	−2.50	11.91	2.60
ALDE	16	−2.89	6.02	1.90	29	−3.81	8.28	2.48
G/EFA	16	−3.23	8.60	2.42	16	−4.45	8.97	2.60
	Integration policies							
Non-att.	7	−0.28	9.23	3.39	8	3.02	17.77	5.65
UEN	5	−1.02	2.48	0.99	7	3.73	40.73	13.58
IND/DEM	5	−2.11	12.08	5.19	8	0.72	15.50	4.76
EPP-ED	24	−2.28	23.38	5.04	41	−2.69	39.68	6.55
ALDE	16	−4.06	13.39	3.45	29	−4.05	44.11	7.32
G/EFA	16	−6.25	19.27	4.77	17	−8.08	21.61	5.39
SOC	18	−6.63	15.93	4.82	28	−7.82	20.69	5.26
GUE/NGL	15	−7.18	20.51	5.81	16	−7.13	17.29	4.08

that of the EPP-ED, reflecting the more restrictionist stance of the British Labour Party, the French Socialist Party (PS), the Spanish Socialist Party (PSOE) and the Italian Ulivio. On immigrant integration, however, ALDE parties are, on average, closer to those of the EPP-ED, with SOC and G/EFA parties considerably more multicultural.

Table 4 also suggests that, at least between 1999 and 2004, there was no concerted attempt by the parties belonging to the major EPGs to appropriate far-right positions in EP elections. The mean scores for non-attached, Nationalist and Eurosceptic parties all shift to a more assimilationist position in 2004 with the IND/DEM parties also becoming more restrictionist. In contrast, the mean for all other EPGs remains stable or moves towards greater liberalism and multiculturalism. Yet Table 4 also hints that EPGs and EPFs are troubled by a lack of programmatic congruence. The range and standard deviation statistics for 1999 are already quite high, particularly for integration policies and by 2004 there is increased disunity within the transnational parties. The range covered widens for six out of seven party groups on the control and integration axes. These indications of programmatic disunity within EPGs raise the possibility that national socioeconomic and political conditions strongly influence the control and integration stances of parties in EP elections, therefore blurring ideological distinctions on migration issues.

To test this, we ran multivariate regression analysis on the 1999 and 2004 manifestos to assess whether EPG membership has a significant effect on the control and integration scores of national parties when national variables are also taken into account. These variables, following Hix and Noury (2007), were designed to capture possible socioeconomic, cultural and political influences on party positions on immigration (see Appendix for measurement details of the independent variables). High levels of unemployment, far-right party success and asylum applications are likely to increase public pressure on politicians to adopt restrictionist measures, whereas an onerous pensions burden, sizeable existing migrant community and liberal political culture (here measured by the level of foreign aid) will all tend to result in less restrictive policies. The effect of economic growth is more ambiguous: high growth rates might be associated with more expansive labour migration policies but so too might low economic growth as employers seek to cut wage costs. In addition to these national variables, we also included a dummy variable for the election year and a variable measuring the programme length following earlier studies' identification of manifesto length as a possible source of erroneous party placement (Gabel and Huber 2000).

The first regression model takes the following form:

$$Y_p = \alpha + \beta_1 ASYLUM_p + \beta_2 MIGRANTS_p + \beta_3 UNEMPLOYMENT_p +$$
$$\beta_4 GROWTH_p + \beta_5 PENSIONS\ BURDEN_p + \beta_6 FOREIGN\ AID_p$$
$$+ \beta_7 FAR\text{-}RIGHT_p + \beta_8 YEAR_p + \beta_9 PROGRAMME\ LENGTH_p + \epsilon_p$$

where Y is the dependent variable, α is a constant, β_1 to β_9 are regression coefficients, ϵ is an error term and each party is indexed by p. The dependent variables are the immigration control and migrant integration scores. In model 2, we also checked for any relationship between the respective EPF position and the national party score. The third model adds EPGs to the regression model through the use of dummy variables representing every group, with the SOC group as the baseline. The fourth model uses dummy variables for the member states to assess the impact of state-specific influences not measured by the national variables in models 1–3.

Table 5 shows the results of our regression analysis of control and integration policy. The significant national predictors of control policies in model 1 are asylum applications and foreign aid. In each case, higher levels of the dependent variable result in more liberal policies. Of the national variables only far-right success has a significant (and as expected negative) relationship with integration positions. Document length has a significant negative relationship with both control and integration scores. Overall, however, it is striking that national socioeconomic, cultural and political variables fail to provide a strong explanation of the variance in control and integration policies with the adjusted R^2 of model 1 in Table 5 very low.

In contrast to the generally weak explanatory power of national variables, the manifesto position of the respective EPF emerges as significant for control and integration positions. Its inclusion in model 2 also leads to a greater proportion of variation in the dependent variable being explained although the adjusted R^2 of model 2 on integration positions is still low. Model 3 substitutes the party groups for the EPF positions, testing which positional differences are statistically significant with national variables held constant. EPGs prove on the whole to be reasonably good predictors of control and integration policies despite the earlier evidence of programmatic incongruence. In other words, knowing which EPG a party belongs to allows us to make more accurate predictions of its position on immigration control and immigrant integration than information about background national variables. It is also noticeable that once the EPF position (model 2) and the EPGs (model 3) are added to the analysis, far-right party success is no longer significant. Once membership of TPFs and EPGs is taken into account, far-right pressure does not seem to bring about a turn towards assimilationist policies. To check the robustness of these findings, model 4 replaces the national variables of the first three models with dummy variables for EU member states to control for other nation-specific characteristics not covered by the national variables in the first three models to check whether these alter the party group relationships. However, in no table does a significant relationship uncovered in model 3 cease to be significant in model 4.

The results, to a large extent, confirm the conclusions drawn from Table 4. The gap between EPP-ED and SOC parties on control issues is not statistically significant looking at the data from the 1999 and 2004 elections. By contrast, if the ALDE group is used as the baseline, the greater restrictionism of SOC and EPP-ED parties is significant at 10 per cent and 1 per cent respectively. This

Table 5 OLS regression of migration control positions on EPF positions and country level variables

	Immigration control				Immigrant integration			
	(1)	(2)	(3)	(4)	(1)	(2)	(3)	(4)
Constant	2.033	2.385	1.106	-2.620***	-2.448	1.086	-2.042	-2.088
	(2.747)	(2.800)	(2.559)	(0.761)	(5.801)	(6.151)	(5.341)	(1.603)
Asylum applications	-616.714**	-361.151	-669.750***		444.846	512.265	460.470	
	(248.631)	(243.566)	(233.966)		(525.131)	(527.215)	(488.409)	
Migrant stock	3.284	2.711	4.683		-7.349	-2.657	-5.009	
	(3.775)	(3.431)	(3.459)		(7.974)	(7.434)	(7.220)	
Unemployment rate	-5.260	-7.677	-5.689		-0.551	9.016	-0.550	
	(6.847)	(6.843)	(6.281)		(14.462)	(14.848)	(13.113)	
Growth rate	-6.895	-18.905	-7.892		10.364	-7.119	-6.727	
	(21.435)	(21.503)	(19.816)		(45.273)	(46.549)	(41.366)	
Pensions burden	-13.160	-6.073	-6.033		-9.204	-16.582	1.647	
	(14.195)	(14.506)	(13.093)		(29.980)	(31.496)	(27.332)	
Foreign aid	-207.016**	-299.140***	-158.434*		-112.143	-139.215	-120.842	
	(92.981)	(95.772)	(88.992)		(196.384)	(206.182)	(185.772)	
Far-right success	4.877	-1.829	2.138		11.926*	10.179	5.018	
	(3.142)	(3.251)	(2.932)		(6.636)	(7.050)	(6.120)	
Year	-0.306	-0.467	-0.397	-0.382	0.111	-0.918	-0.288	-0.581
	(0.443)	(0.436)	(0.409)	(0.369)	(0.936)	(0.948)	(0.855)	(0.776)
Document length	-0.001*	0.000	0.000	0.000	-0.002**	-0.002	-0.001	0.000
	(0.000)	(0.001)	(0.000)	(0.000)	(0.001)	(0.001)	(0.001)	(0.001)
EPF position		0.358***				0.334***		
		(0.084)				(0.094)		
SOC			-0.404	-0.625			-4.752***	-5.031***
			(0.550)	(0.514)			(1.148)	(1.082)

(Table continued)

Table 5 Continued

	Immigration control				Immigrant integration			
	(1)	(2)	(3)	(4)	(1)	(2)	(3)	(4)
ALDE			-1.592***	-1.642***			-1.722	-1.904*
			(0.583)	(0.537)			(1.216)	(1.130)
G/EFA			-2.195***	-2.327***			-3.618***	-4.519***
			(0.612)	(0.594)			(1.277)	(1.251)
GUE/NGL			-0.533	-0.948			-4.278***	-5.330***
			(0.626)	(0.617)			(1.306)	(1.299)
UEN			0.770	0.706			4.936**	4.027**
			(0.980)	(0.878)			(2.047)	(1.848)
IND/DEM			1.865**	1.411*			2.334	1.066
			(0.837)	(0.832)			(1.748)	(1.752)
Non-attached			2.729***	2.216***			3.375**	2.967*
			(0.791)	(0.783)			(1.651)	(1.649)
Adjusted R-squared	0.055	0.153	0.211	0.207	0.012	0.064	0.194	0.246
Observations	230	163	230	255	230	163	230	255

Notes: Dependent variable: national party score on migration control and migrant integration index.
Method: OLS linear regression. Standard errors in parentheses. In model 3, EPP-ED is the baseline. In model 4, dummy variables for EU member states are included but estimates of these variables are not reported.
*Significant at 10 per cent. **Significant at 5 per cent. ***Significant at 1 per cent.

once more underscores that although Christian Democrats/Conservatives do not diverge significantly from Socialist parties on immigration control, the issue does divide the centre-right. The greater restrictionism of the EPP-ED parties does not mean, however, that there is little to distinguish them from parties farther to the right as the difference between the Christian Democratic/Conservative parties and the non-attached and Eurosceptic parties is statistically significant (at 10 per cent and 5 per cent respectively).

As expected, Christian Democratic/Conservative, Nationalist, Eurosceptic and non-attached parties are on average less multicultural than the Socialist, Green and left parties in the EP. The position of the Liberals is less clear on the integration scale. A significant difference between the EPP-ED parties and those in ALDE only emerges in model 4 and if ALDE parties are used as the baseline, SOC and GUE/NGL parties adopt significantly more multicultural positions (at 5 per cent and 10 per cent respectively). This confirms the evidence from Table 4 that ALDE parties are closer to their counterparts in the EPP-ED on the issue of migrant integration than on immigration control. Again there is little evidence from the migrant integration scale of the centre-right shifting to the positions of competitors to the right. Nationalist and non-attached parties adopt significantly more assimilationist programmes than Christian Democratic/Conservative parties (both at 5 per cent).

CONCLUSION

In summary, our analysis of EP manifestos suggested that centre-right parties within the same EPG do adopt congruent programmatic positions on immigration. Admittedly, there is a considerable amount of variation in national control and integration positions which is not explained by transnational affiliations. In view, though, of the wide intra-EU differences on socioeconomic and cultural variables, the connection between immigration and sovereignty, the weakness of the EPFs and the identity dilution within the EPP and ELDR, centre-right parties brought together by transnational links adopt surprisingly similar stances on control and integration which also broadly correspond to the manifestos of their respective transnational party federation. One possible interpretation would be to view this programmatic congruence as an indication of the Europeanization of party politics (Ladrech 2002) whereby the policy orientations of member state parties are shaped by their contacts within EPFs. That EP elections continue to be fought as second order national elections dominated by national issues, however, weakens this argument. Instead, the unexpectedly high consistency of party scores within EP groups seems to suggest that immigration is not a cross-cutting issue that smudges ideological distinctions. In other words, ideology, and not just national interests, does appear to provide a guide for parties' programmatic responses to immigration. Moreover, the manifesto data offered little support for a systematic attempt by the transnational centre-right to co-opt the threat of the far-right through a shift to more restrictionist and assimilationist positions. On the whole, the positions of Christian Democrats/Conservatives remain distinct from those of the parties located further to the right.

The structuring effect of ideology on immigration is not straightforward, however. While manifesto placements largely corresponded to the positioning of the transnational parties in Lahav, McElroy and Benoit, and Hix and Noury's earlier studies, one crucial exception was uncovered. Our analysis indicated that on questions of immigration control, differences emerge not between Christian Democrats/Conservatives and Socialists, but between both of these groups and the less restrictionist Liberals and Greens. On integration issues, the order of the parties reproduces more closely left–right scale divisions with Christian Democratic/Conservative, and to a lesser extent Liberal, parties less enthusiastically multicultural than their Socialist and Green competitors. Differentiating between policies towards would-be migrants and those aimed at resident foreigners and ethnic minorities, therefore, revealed nuanced differences in party positioning, thereby supporting Givens and Luedtke's identification of a different political logic underpinning control and integration issues. This suggests that future studies of partisan attitudes and policies on migratory issues, at both the national and transnational level, need to apply this distinction more consistently to understand how ideology influences party responses to immigration.

APPENDIX 1. CONSTRUCTION OF IMMIGRATION CONTROL AND IMMIGRANT INTEGRATION SCALES

Liberal control	Restrictive control	Multicultural	Assimilationist
Labour migration positive v4082	Labour migration negative v4083	Multiculturalism positive v607	Multiculturalism negative v608
Human rights v2012	Immigration non-economic negative v6011	Support for immigrants and foreigners v7053 Social justice v503	National way of life positive v601
Control scores = total % restrictive control – total % liberal control		Immigrant integration scores = total % assimilationist immigrant policy – total % multicultural immigrant policy	

For further description of the content of these categories, see Wüst and Volkens (2003).

APPENDIX 2. DESCRIPTION OF INDEPENDENT VARIABLES

Asylum appli-   The average number of asylum applications in each member
cations   state over the five years up to the election year as a proportion
                 of the total population. Source: Eurostat.

Migrant stock   The number of foreign-born residents of a nation as a
                 proportion of the total population at the time of, or at the
                 nearest available year to, an EP election. Source: Various UN
                 Migration Reports.

Unemploy-   The average standardized unemployment rate in each member
ment rate   state over the five years up to the election. Source: UNECE
                 Statistical Division Database.

Growth rate   The average GDP per capita growth rate over the five years up
                 to the election. Source: UNECE Statistical Division Database.

Pensions   The number of people aged 65 and over as a proportion of the
burden   population. Source: Eurostat.

Foreign aid   The level of foreign aid in each member state as a proportion of
                 its gross national income. Source: OECD, Eurostat.

Far-right success	The support for parties of the far-right in each member state at the last national election before the respective EP election.
Document length	The total length of the manifesto measured in quasi-sentences.

NOTES

1 After 2004, the EFGP became the European Green Party (EGP). For consistency, we use the earlier name.
2 All statistics here from Eurostat http://epp.eurostat.ec.europa.eu/. Accessed 6/06/07.
3 Lahav fails to provide figures for Green MEPs on the question of greater/less immigration.
4 We are very grateful to Abdul Noury for providing us with the MEP Immigration Index dataset.
5 Euromanifestos Project, MZES/University of Mannheim, pre-release 1979–2004 (February 2007). We are very grateful to Andreas Wüst for making this data available.
6 See Milner and Judkins (2004) for a similar construction of a (non-left–right) scale based on manifesto data.
7 Hix and Noury's MEP migration scores have been reversed for ease of comparison.

REFERENCES

Bale, T. (2008) 'Turning round the telescope. Centre-right parties and immigration and integration policy in Europe', *Journal of European Public Policy* 15(3): 315–30.

Bardi, L. (2006) 'EU enlargement, European Parliament elections and transnational trends in European parties', *European View* 3: 13–19.

Budge, I. *et al.* (eds) (2001) *Mapping Policy Preferences. Estimates for Parties, Electors and Governments 1945–1998*, Oxford: Oxford University Press.

Cooper, A.H. (2002) 'Party-sponsored protest and the Movement Society: the CDU/CSU mobilises against citizenship law reform', *German Politics* 11(2): 88–104.

Dauvergne, C. (2004) 'Sovereignty, migration and the rule of law in global times', *Modern Law Review* 67(4): 588–615.

Gabel, M.J. and Huber, J.D. (2000) 'Putting parties in their place: inferring party left–right ideological positions from party manifesto data', *American Journal of Political Science* 44(1): 94–103.

Geddes, A. (2003) *The Politics of Migration and Immigration in Europe*, London: Sage.

Giugni, M. and Passy, F. (2006) 'Introduction: Four dialogues on migration policy', in M. Giugni and F. Passy (eds), *Dialogues on Migration Policy*, Lanham: Lexington Books, pp. 1–24.

Givens, T. and Luedtke, A. (2005) 'European immigration policies in comparative perspective: issue salience, partisanship and immigrant rights', *Comparative European Politics* 3: 1–22.

Hammar, T. (ed.) (1985) *European Immigration Policy: A Comparative Study*, Cambridge: Cambridge University Press.

Hix, S. (2001) 'Legislative behaviour and party competition in the European Parliament: an application of nominate to the EU', *Journal of Common Market Studies* 39: 209–34.

Hix, S. and Lord, C. (1997) *Political Parties in the European Union*, Basingstoke: Macmillan.

Hix, S. and Noury, A. (2007) 'Politics, not economic interests: determinants of migration policies in the European Union', *International Migration Review* 41(1): 182–205.

Ladrech, R. (2002) 'Europeanization and political parties: towards a framework for analysis', *Party Politics* 8(4): 389–404.

Lahav, G. (1997) 'Ideological and party constraints on immigration attitudes in Europe', *Journal of Common Market Studies* 35 (3): 377–406.

Lahav, G. (2004) *Immigration and Politics in the New Europe. Reinventing Borders*, Cambridge: Cambridge University Press.

Lahav, G. and Messina, A. (2005) 'The limits of a European immigration policy: elite opinion and agendas within the European Parliament', *Journal of Common Market Studies* 43(4): 851–75.

McElroy, G. and Benoit, K. (2007) 'Party groups and policy positions in the European Parliament', *Party Politics* 13(1): 5–28.

Milner, H.V. and Judkins, B. (2004) 'Partisanship, trade policy and globalization', *International Studies Quarterly* 48(1): 95–119.

Sandström, C. (2004) 'The European Liberal Democratic and Reform Party: from co-operation to integration', in P. Delwit, E. Kulahci and C. Van Walle (eds), *The Europarties: Organisation and Influence*, Brussels: ULB, pp. 155–82.

Schain, M. (1988) 'Immigration and changes in the French party system', *European Journal of Political Research* 16(6): 597–621.

Spencer, I. (1997) *British Immigration Policy Since 1939: The Making of Multicultural Britain*, London and New York: Routledge.

Triadafilopoulos, T. and Zaslove, A. (2006) 'Influencing migration policy from inside: political parties', in M. Giugni and F. Passy (eds), *Dialogues on Migration Policy*, Lanham: Lexington Books, pp. 171–92.

Wüst, A.M. and Volkens, A. (2003) *Euromanifesto Coding Instructions*, Mannheimer Zentrum für europäische Sozialforschung Working Paper No. 64.

Politics matters: a conclusion

Tim Bale

In 2006 *Eurobarometer* asked respondents throughout the EU-25 whether they agreed or disagreed that immigrants contributed much to their country. There were big differences according to occupation and education: only around four out of ten people in managerial positions disagreed compared to nearly six out of ten manual workers; the difference between those who left school before 16 and those educated past their 20th birthday was almost exactly the same. There were also, as Table 1 shows, big differences between countries – not only between the EU-15 and new member states, but within the EU-15, some of whose centre-right parties we examine in this volume.

Another obvious difference was ideological. As previous research has indicated, some of it referred to elsewhere in this volume – see especially the contributions on France and the Netherlands – those Europeans who consider themselves right-wing are clearly less sanguine about migration than their fellow citizens who think of themselves as on the left. Even if political parties' role in public policy on immigration and integration, then, is reduced to their being 'conduits of public opinion' (see the introduction to this volume), we would therefore expect those parties on the centre-right – Christian democrats, conservatives and market liberals – to feed the feelings of 'their voters' into the process and, presuming the process is even minimally responsive to their efforts, tip it in a more restrictive direction.

But parties are more than merely conduits. They help to structure as well as reflect voter opinion – not only in terms of what citizens think but also what they think about (see Thomassen 2005): they respond to pressure but they also help to cue, channel and even ramp it up. Even if there were no 'rational' incentives for them to stake out positions in advance of those held by their supporters (see Iversen 1994), the fact that they may well do so should come as no surprise. Parties are, after all, populated by individuals who are themselves ideological, sharing the gut instincts of their supporters – and sometimes even more so. The somewhat populist image of a 'political class' of mainstream, essentially centrist,

Table 1 Proportion of people disagreeing that 'immigrants contribute a lot' to their country, 2006

By country	% disagreeing
New member states	64
Germany	63
Italy	53
EU-25	52
Denmark	52
EU-15	50
France	46
UK	45
Netherlands	41
Ireland	30
Sweden	16
By ideological self-placement	
Right-wing	58
Centrist	53
Left-wing	44

Source: *Eurobarometer* 66 (2007).

leaders that spends most of its time holding back or even selling out atavistic party activists and an only slightly more reasonable electorate is highly misleading. Tests of May's so-called law of curvilinear disparity – the scientific version of this image – suggest, with very few exceptions (see Kitschelt 1989; Kennedy *et al.* 2006), that there is no such thing: activists can be moderates just as determined to do well in elections as to preserve ideological purity, while élites are often true believers (see Norris 1995; Narud and Skare 1999; Widfeldt 1999). Inasmuch, then, as those élites, especially when they are in government, are able to steer the ship of state, they are likely to try and steer it in their preferred direction.

We all know, of course, that, to pursue the old analogy, the state is very much a supertanker not a speedboat – a ship that takes time to respond to touches on the tiller and which, especially in Europe, has to take account of the administrative and legal sea in which it sails. We also know that the command structure, such as it is, of the state is far less clear-cut than its nautical analogue: the captaincy is likely to be collective, forced to work with imprecise charts, a vague and changing idea of destination, and a crew that can be relied upon neither to co-ordinate its work nor to translate orders from the bridge to actions in the engine room, even presuming there is enough fuel to make them effective. And all the while the passengers, many of whom believe that the vessel is about to run aground and – like some of the crew – think they could do a better job, are shouting insults and advice. Yet, for all that, it seems intuitively unlikely that whoever is in charge – albeit nominally and temporarily – has little or no bearing on policy-making and policy change.

This leads to the first question raised in the introduction to this volume. Are parties more important to migration policy than they are traditionally given credit for, and should policy and party people pay more attention to each other in this and perhaps other areas? But we also asked other, related questions. How much is the role and behaviour of centre-right parties in particular more than a function of the threat posed by parties on their far-right flank? And what are the internal tensions and dilemmas they face? Clearly our efforts can only produce a first-cut, but what have we found?

DO PARTIES MAKE A POLICY DIFFERENCE?

On the question of the role that parties play in making and shifting state policy on immigration control and immigrant integration, perhaps the most obvious example is one of the countries covered by Green-Pedersen and Odmalm. Their account of the divergence in policy between Denmark (where policy has tightened considerably since the centre-right took office in 2001) and Sweden (where it is only just beginning to show signs of tightening after the victory of the centre-right in 2006) clearly suggests that parties do indeed make a difference. The Social Democratic government that lost power in Denmark was clearly under pressure, and, of course, no one can say for sure how it would have responded to increased anxieties about radical Islam and the continuing climb of the Danish People's Party (DPP), but few would argue that the policy mix pursued by the centre-right administration that replaced it would have been quite so enthusiastically pursued. Certainly, Sweden's admittedly more powerful centre-left did nothing to emulate its Nordic neighbour across the Kattegat.

The most detailed evidence of party involvement – and disputes – over migration policy comes in the process-tracing exercise carried out by Geddes in order to examine a classic dilemma in the literature, namely continued mass immigration despite attempts to control it. Geddes does not ignore the other players in the process – business groups, the Church and charities – but shows how both worked alongside a small Christian Democratic party that was able to use its membership of a potentially fissiparous coalition to dilute proposals that came about, not as an inevitable response to objective conditions or even public anxiety about those conditions, but because of the partisan promises of two of its fellow coalition partners. That the latter were able to make the running was also due to what appears to have been a conscious decision of the senior partner in the coalition to allow them their head (see below).

Party politics also made a difference, according to Boswell and Hough, in Germany – although often the difference is more significant at the level of outputs rather than outcomes. The CDU–CSU government that ran the Federal Republic throughout most of the 1980s and 1990s made several attempts to make more of a reality of Germany's self-image as 'not a country of immigration'; most of them may have been in vain, but not through want of trying. Likewise, it is clear from their account that once in opposition the CDU–CSU was able to use its growing veto power to, in its view, mitigate the attempts of the SPD–Green coalition that took over under Gerhard Schröder to extend citizenship and rationalize labour migration.

In France, where governments enjoy a much freer rein than their German counterparts, policy seems to vary according to who is in charge. Matters are slightly more complicated, however, by the fact that the country's semi-presidential system means that they turn not just on party but on personality. Marthaler's contribution is an illustration of this, showing how French policy on immigration and integration has been heavily influenced in recent years by the ambitions, thinking and response to public opinion of the man who is now its president. If the politics of migration is, like all politics, the interplay of institutions, ideas and individuals, then the literature – even that on France – has perhaps concentrated too much on the first two and underplayed the third.

Van Kersbergen and Krouwel concentrate more on party competition and positioning than they do on government policy-making, partly because they take it as read that the change of government that occurred after the post-Fortuyn election of 2002 prompted big changes in government policy that might otherwise not have occurred. The liberal-conservative VVD, which uniquely was part of both the outgoing and the incoming government, had, when in coalition with the Dutch Labour Party, found it all but impossible to shift migration policy. Once together with the Christian Democrats (and very briefly with the populist LPF) it oversaw policy change – change that has placed the Netherlands, along with Denmark, in the vanguard of European states determined not only to improve control but to insist on the improved integration of those (already) allowed in (see Joppke 2007). Put bluntly, while it is misleading to think that there was little public anxiety about such matters pre-9/11 and pre-Pim Fortuyn, and to think that Dutch governments took no practical notice of it before 2002, changes in state policy – or at least the palpable acceleration of such changes that were already occurring – required a change of government.

This volume does, however, contain one contribution that casts doubt on the difference made by the partisan occupation of office. Smith argues that in both the UK and Ireland contemporary and historical experience suggests that, for all the rhetorical jousting (more a feature in the UK than in Ireland), migration policy has not varied much (nor would not) according to which party or coalition were in power. In the UK, partly because it is so concerned not to cede too great an advantage to the Conservative Party on the issue of immigrant control, Labour has for decades tried to sound (if not always act) as tough as the Tories, while the Tories have always been wary of pursuing their populist impulses too far lest they alienate moderate opinion and damage what used to be called 'race relations'. That said, Conservative governments have often acted, especially in their first year or two in office, to tighten controls – a pattern that may be repeated when they next get into government. In Ireland, the consensus identified by Smith is more permissive and, some would say, pragmatic. It would seem (and understandably so, given Ireland's economic renaissance and the relative lack of public anxiety on the issues) that most mainstream parties take an 'if it ain't broke, don't fix it' stance, unless and until something does appear to need fixing (as with the changes to the Citizenship Law in 2004), in which case they combine to fix it fairly rapidly.

Finally, on this question, Duncan and Van Hecke's contribution on the transnational centre-right obviously has less to tell us about the actuality of party influence on policy. But it may tell us something about the potential for it as policy becomes more subject to decision-making at the EU level. If they are right, and if behaviour in the European Parliament reflects the positions of the transnational federations and parliamentary party groups (which is admittedly a big if), then we should expect to find that party makes less of a difference when it comes to immigration control and more of a difference when it comes to integration policy, with centre-right parties significantly less enthusiastic than their Green, left and centre-left counterparts about multiculturalism.

IS IT ALL DOWN TO RADICAL RIGHT-WING POPULISTS?

On the question of the centre-right's move to shift policy in a more restrictive and more assimilationist (or at least less multiculturalist) direction being driven largely by prompting from the far-right, the contributions to this volume at least question and qualify the common wisdom. Policy being a response to the far-right is probably most evident in France, where, of course, radical rightists stand virtually no chance of winning seats in parliament, let alone the presidency itself. In her attempt to contextualize the policy changes wrought by Nicolas Sarkozy, Marthaler suggests that many of them derive from the candidate's understanding of what would give him, and the party he managed to pull together around himself, the best chance of winning the Presidential election in 2007 – one seen in the context of the previous contest that saw the Front National give the mainstream right (and left) something between a scare and a bloody nose. Sarkozy believed not so much that the FN was likely to make further advances but that, by going on to Le Pen's territory in word as much as in deed, he could usefully bring back millions of voters who had lent the FN their support in 2007. Intra-party politics, however, was just as important: adopting both legislation and a tone that distinguished him from the much smoother, more establishment de Villepin also helps to explain Sarkozy's moves. So too does the defeat of the Constitutional Treaty, where concerns about immigration were considered to have lent support to the victorious no camp. Such considerations appear to have played a part in his dropping, or at least downplaying, his earlier concern to balance – British-style – a concern to beef up control with a stress on combating discrimination and promoting integration. Yet Marthaler also highlights throughout the importance of public opinion, and in particular the fact that Sarkozy, by acting and sounding tough on immigration, knows that he is appealing not just to French people who classify themselves as on the far-right but to the much larger number who see themselves in the right and centre of the political spectrum.

Another case where, on the face of it, radical right-wing populists have helped to push policy in a more restrictive direction without formally entering government is in Denmark. But, as Green-Pedersen and Odmalm show, the critical juncture occurred not when the centre-right parties made it into power in 2001 and were obliged to rely on the Danish People's Party for legislative support but instead in the early to mid-1990s. First, the two centre-right parties broke with the government over easing asylum policy for Bosnian refugees. Then the leader of the conservative Venstre (future Prime Minister Anders Fogh Rasmussen) decided that a focus on immigration could help him to overcome the social democratic government that was proving difficult to attack on the socioeconomic front. Since taking and holding on to power (from 2001 up to and including the election in November 2007), Denmark's centre-right, as Green-Pedersen and Odmalm show, has profoundly altered the course of the country's immigration and integration policy – all the more so when compared to Sweden, where the populist right has had much less electoral impact and, by the same token, cannot explain various centre-right parties occasionally flirting with a harder line on migration and multiculturalism over the last decade. Clearly maintaining a legislative (though not an executive) coalition has meant that the centre-right in Denmark has had to look over its shoulder on such issues. But for Green-Pedersen and Odmalm, it was a development on the left flank that was just as significant, namely the defection of the Social Liberals from the bourgeois to the Social Democrat camp in 1993 – a decision that removed the coalition constraint which until then had prevented the centre-right from mobilizing on migration issues.

The other case in which radical right-wing populist parties have made a difference is the Netherlands, where such parties stand as good a chance as any of their counterparts in other countries of making it into parliament. But again their contribution to policy change has to be contextualized and qualified. There, as van Kersbergen and Krouwel show, Pim Fortuyn (and now others) tapped into, legitimated and enlarged a well of resentment and anxiety about migration and multiculturalism that now helps to structure political competition as much as the traditional class cleavage and its largely socioeconomic issue dimension. Interestingly, however, they also make clear that Dutch centre-right parties stand to benefit from taking a tough stance on the 'foreigners issue' because they are 'the traditional owners of law and order as well as nationalist issues' with voters who by and large favour such a stance. They also show that one of the parties they examine, the conservative-liberal VVD, flirted with the 'foreigners issue' long before the Fortuyn revolt but was constrained by worries over internal unity and the negative impact on its (unusual) coalition with the Dutch Labour Party. That the second constraint came off was no less important than the presence of LPF ministers in the cabinet after 2002 in moving the VVD towards a more restrictive and less multiculturalist line. It is also clear from van Kersbergen and Krouwel's account that a similar move did not pose the Christian Democrats as much of a problem as one might have predicted, their leadership finding little difficulty in reaching back into the party's own traditions to justify a harder line.

Italy, of course, presents an interesting case in that the harder line pursued by a centre-right government can be traced unambiguously to radical right-wing populists (or former radical right-wing populists) who were part of the coalition. Indeed, Geddes's account makes it clear that – at least in the initial stages – Berlusconi and his Forza Italia colleagues virtually left Bossi's Lega Nord (still stridently populist) and Fini's Alleanza Nazionale (trying to transform itself into a more mainstream conservative party) to get on with working up new immigration legislation themselves. This may have been because the prime minister had other more pressing matters to attend to – some interpret his entry into politics mainly as an attempt to ensure the protection of his commercial interests and legal freedom. But almost certainly it owed a great deal to his concern to avoid a repeat of the Lega walkout that effectively brought down his previous government. Even once the internal bargaining that eventually saw the legislation seriously diluted had begun, Forza Italia appears to have avoided interfering. Indeed, it seems to have relied on its other coalition partner, the Christian Democratic Ccd–Cdu, to ensure that the economic interests of its supporters in continued immigration were catered for. Again, though, we should note that in supporting the idea that 'something must be done' about immigrants and immigration and then trying (albeit perhaps half-heartedly) to do it, Forza Italia was aiming not so much to spike the guns of parties on its right flank as cater to the concerns of its own supporters who, the polling reproduced by Geddes shows, were just as worried about the issue as supporters of those other parties.

Our other case studies suggest that pressure generated by the far-right had very little or no impact on the increasingly hard line taken by the parties concerned. Boswell and Hough stress that Germany's centre-right politicians, especially given the numbers coming in and the obvious 'failure' to integrate so many of the country's foreign population, were driven to act by their own, ideological, reading of the situation. Politicizing migration might also help them to regain some of the voters lost not to the far-right but to the SPD. Likewise, in the UK, Smith finds little evidence to suggest that the Conservative Party was or is overly concerned about losses to its right, simply convinced that it had an advantage over the Labour government on the issue, though one it had to be careful (especially as that government took an increasingly restrictive stance itself) not to push too far lest it reinforce its image as the 'nasty' party.

Meanwhile, taking the bird's eye view offered by studying Europe's transnational party federations, Duncan and Van Hecke reinforce the impression that centre-right parties are more restrictive than those on the left, though, owing to the latter's increased stress on control, the difference is more noticeable on immigrant integration. But they see no signs of parties on the centre-right being dragged any closer to far-right positions. If more policy in this area does get made not just at the European level but via a more communitized process where parliament becomes a player, it will not be easy to put down any toughening of control or integration policies to the influence of extreme politicians pushing their supposedly reluctant mainstream counterparts into action.

WHAT ARE THE TENSIONS AND DILEMMAS EXPERIENCED BY CENTRE-RIGHT PARTIES?

On the question of internal dilemmas, we found plenty. They are most clearly crystallized and explicitly laid out by Boswell and Hough, who build on work on political opportunity structure to typologize the risks faced by centre-right parties seeking to politicize immigration control and immigrant integration policy. Aside from the possibility that such a move will increase the salience of an issue that may actually favour competitors further to the right, they posit three risks: first, a risk to the party's 'value legitimacy' – a sense that its rhetoric and programme remains in the same essentially moderate, catch-all space occupied by most of its supporters; second, a risk to its 'programmatic coherence' – a sense that what it does on these issues does not undermine its policies in other, often related areas; third, a risk to its 'practical credibility' – a sense that the party is able to deliver on what it promises. The CDU–CSU has been tempted, both by conviction and hopes of strategic advantage, to take a consistently harder line but it has had to be careful. While public opinion in general is unlikely to condemn the party for its ethno-nationalist rhetoric, pushing matters too far can cause problems with its more liberal and church-based support. Meanwhile, calls and attempts to toughen Germany's line risk disrupting relationships with foreign countries, contradicting moves towards a more liberal economic policy, and the country's traditional support for further Europeanization. Lastly, attempts to be business- and, of course, coalition-friendly, have undermined (and may continue to do so) the parties' ability to match tough words with action, as will Germany's culture of consensus and compromise.

Dilemmas also abound in the Dutch case. Indeed, so extreme have they been in this policy area that they have led to the disintegration of the country's for-midable and (failing a grand coalition of the sort that currently governs the country) seemingly pivotal conservative-liberal party, the VVD. The party's pro-blems exemplify one potential conflict in centre-right parties, namely the one between an impulse towards liberalism (primarily but not solely in the economic sphere) and an impulse towards cultural and social conservatism. For the VVD, as van Kersbergen and Krouwel's analysis of the clustering of parties and public opinion makes clear, it has proved increasingly difficult to reconcile the two impulses under the one roof, leading on two occasions now to high-profile poli-ticians not simply leaving and slamming the door behind them but setting up shop in new premises. Geert Wilders going to take up the torch of Pim Fortuyn was perhaps predictable and the damage possibly temporary, but the departure of Rita Verdonk may be a more serious blow. On the other hand, matters are unlikely to be plain sailing for the CDA, especially if it wishes to carry on moving in a more neo-liberal economic direction; its policy on, for example, the freedom to found and maintain religious schools and its encouragement of voluntary self-organization may come under pressure if anxieties about Islamic separatism carry on increasing.

France's centre-right party does not, it seems, currently suffer too much from internal division on immigration control, integration and asylum, although there were objections from within the UMP government to the 2007 legislation allowing for DNA testing of applicants for migration on the grounds of family unification. Again, though, it is possible to see problems on the horizon. If, for instance, Sarkozy really is the economic liberal some still like to hope he is, there could be a clash between this instinct and the desire to control entry, even if the latter is geared more to the labour market as Sarkozy clearly wants. And if, now he has won the presidency, he returns to the need to modify the republican commitment to race-blind policies in order to more effectively combat discrimination and promote integration and dialogue – or simply to enable the state to get a better idea of the problems it faces by collecting improved information – he could face a backlash from within.

For Italy's centre-right, now out of power, the internal contradictions were mainly inter-party (i.e. inter-bloc) rather than intra-party. As Geddes shows, the Christian Democratic party within the *Casa delle Libertà*, the Ccd–Cdu, managed – between the talk and decision phases – to mitigate some of its partners' plans, with the support not just of the Roman Catholic hierarchy and (associated) migrant charities but also of organized business interests, some of which were almost certainly speaking for constituencies represented by Forza Italia and the populist Lega Nord. Even the latter, he shows, was prepared to swap concessions in substance for more repressive symbolic proposals such as naval intervention and biometric testing. Meanwhile, Gianfranco Fini's desire to reposition himself (and his party) as the leader of the centre-right in the post-Berlusconi and post-Forza Italia era (assuming that comes) meant that he was prepared to countenance the granting of extended rights to immigrants to promote integration. Again (and one can see this in the counter-reaction that Fini's suggestion provoked within his own party and outside it), there may be problems in the future as *Alleanza* continues its halting progress towards centre-right 'respectability'. The recent furore over Romanian/Roma immigrants in Italy tempted Fini to accuse the newcomers of 'prosituting their womenfolk, approving the kidnapping of children and believing that theft was morally justified', suggesting – claimed *The Economist* (8 November 2007), which reported his remarks – that 'the supposedly reformed leader of the former neo-fascists... appears to think that race-hate oratory will enhance his prospects'.

Green-Pedersen and Odmalm's contribution does not tell us much about the dilemmas and tensions faced by the Danish centre-right over its government's tightening of policy, although one would presume that some in the business community would have concerns. Certainly, there were fears – only partially realized – that both government parties would lose votes in 2007 to the New Alliance which, at least initially, pitched itself as a home for those voters who wanted centre-right policies on much else but were tired of, not to say embarrassed about, relying on the xenophobic DPP. Their examination of the four centre-right parties in Sweden that managed to knit together the pre-electoral coalition that won power in 2006, however, again illustrates that immigration and integration can be a potentially troublesome area for that side of the political spectrum. Rather than allow it to disrupt their carefully contrived 'Alliance for Sweden', they downplayed it to the point of disappearance during the campaign. Interestingly, however, their victory has resulted in substantive changes to policy which Green-Pedersen and Odmalm consider significant, and a sign that the two countries will not remain quite as far apart from each other on the issues as, in part dictated by the realities of coalition-building, they have been.

In the other comparative contribution (on the UK and Ireland), however, Smith does dig into the tensions faced by centre-right parties, particularly when in opposition. In both countries, those parties have found it difficult in recent years to disagree with government policy without risking being portrayed as either more extreme than they want to be (as in the UK) or simply wasting their time (as in Ireland). Given reduced anxiety about asylum-seekers in particular, the debate has tended to shift to economic migration, for which both the Conservatives and Fine Gael acknowledge the need – and which is, of course, impossible to promise to stop when most of it comes from the EU. Although some in the Conservative Party continue to argue that immigration is a button that should be pressed because the Tories retain a clear lead on the issue in opinion polls, the watchword now appears to be proceed with caution. It may enthuse voters – many of whom, contrary to common wisdom, would never consider them as core supporters of the party – but it also risks setting back the leadership's relatively successful attempt since 2005 to 'decontaminate' the Tory brand and attract more centrist support. The answer to the dilemma thus posed seems to lie in banking the Tories' tougher reputation on the issue and moving the attack on to the government's supposed lack of competence and credibility rather than principle. Fine Gael, albeit operating in a country where there appears to be less concern than in the UK, has also taken the same 'valence politics' approach. Interestingly, however, none of what Smith characterizes as Ireland's three centre-right parties seems interested in emulating the more restrictive policies of some of its fellow member states – although nationalism in Ireland is traditionally important, there seems to be no mileage in breaking what is a permissive consensus around the arrival of thousands of migrants.

The dilemmas for parties at the transnational level explored by Duncan and Van Hecke can seem less pressing, but only if one continues to cling to the arguably outdated idea that what European federations and parliamentary parties do and say has little real impact. The most obvious of these is the need to ensure some minimal congruence between stances taken 'domestically' and those adopted to achieve not just transnational harmony but also concrete legislation at a European level. Interestingly, Duncan and Van Hecke conclude that there already appears to be a basis for such congruence. Whether, though, this can last as more policy is made at the EU level – and especially if the media in member states break the habit of a lifetime and pay more attention to the potential contradictions and alliances thrown up – remains to be seen.

PUTTING IT ALL TOGETHER

The contributions to this volume suggest, then, that there are a number of common tensions faced by centre-right parties seeking to make policy and compete electorally on immigration control and integration. A hard line can often be reconciled with a tradition of defending the nation and its culture from external threats, and also seems to make sense in many countries, given evident public anxiety. But there is both a business case and a religious (or at least charitable or humane) case for a more liberal policy. Moreover, the latter can also make sense from an electoral and particularly a coalitional point of view. The contributions also suggest that centre-right parties, although clearly they have to take into account the electoral performance – potential and actual – of the populist radical right, are more than capable of thinking, talking and acting for themselves on immigration control and integration. Finally, the contributions suggest that it may well be worthwhile remembering that parties have a potentially significant impact on policy in this area – and that they will continue to do so even as it progresses beyond the nation-state.

To date, the evidence for parties making a difference to public policy has largely been gathered from, and argued about in, the political economy tradition (see, for example, Bradely *et al.* 2003; Allan and Scruggs 2004; Amable *et al.* 2006; Nygård 2006). But it can be found elsewhere, outside of the public and particularly welfare spending that lends itself so easily to quantitative investigation. Even though the results of a first pass by other scholars are mixed (see Givens and Luedtke 2005), policy on immigrant control and integration is, we believe, one such field. The twenty-first century has seen a great deal of policy change. Clearly, that change can in part be traced back to interest groups or Europeanization. But it also results from the control (and the quest for control) of government by parties – institutions that respond and contribute not just to public opinion but to the physical flows and cultural clashes (perceived and real) that underlie it. Politics matters.

REFERENCES

Allan, J.P. and Scrugss, L. (2004) 'Political partisanship and welfare state reform in advanced industrial societies', *American Journal of Political Science* 48(3): 496–512.

Amable, B. Gatti, D. and Schumacher, J. (2006) 'Welfare-state retrenchment: the partisan effect revisited,' *Oxford Review of Economic Policy* 22(3): 426–44.

Bradley, D., Huber, E., Moller, S., Nielsen, F. and Stephens, J.D. (2003) 'Distribution and redistribution in postindustrial democracies', *World Politics* 55(2): 193–228.

Givens, T. and Luedtke, A. (2005) 'European immigration policies in comparative perspective: issue salience, partisanship and immigrant rights', *Comparative European Politics* 3(1): 1–22.

Iversen, T. (1994) 'The logics of electoral politics: spatial, directional, and mobilizational effects', *Comparative Political Studies* 27(2): 155–89.

Joppke, C. (2007) 'Transformation of immigrant integration: civic integration and antidiscrimination in the Netherlands, France and Germany', *World Politics* 59: 243–73.

Kennedy, F., Lyons, P. and Fitzgerald, P. (2006) 'Pragmatists, ideologues and the general law of curvilinear disparity: the case of the Irish Labour Party', *Political Studies* 54(4):786–805.

Kitschelt, H. (1989) 'The internal politics of parties: the law of curvilinear disparity revisited', *Political Studies* 37(3): 400–21.

Narud, H.M. and Skare, A. (1999) 'Are party activists the party extremists? The structure of opinion in political parties', *Scandinavian Political Studies* 22(1): 45–65.

Norris, P. (1995) 'May's law of curvilinear disparity revisited: leaders, officers, members and voters in British political parties', *Party Politics* 1(1): 29–47.

Nygård, M. (2006) 'Welfare-ideological change in Scandinavia: a comparative analysis of partisan welfare state positions in four Nordic countries, 1970–2003', *Scandinavian Political Studies* 29(4): 356–85.

Thomassen, J. (2005) *The European Voter: A Comparative Study of Modern Democracies*, Oxford: Oxford University Press.

Widfeldt, A. (1999) 'Losing touch? The political representativeness of Swedish parties, 1985–1994', *Scandinavian Political Studies* 22(4): 307–26.

Commentary: Why political parties matter

Martin A. Schain

In this brief analysis, I will seek to develop a series of propositions about the relationship between immigration and political parties that derive from the vast literature on both parties and immigration. I will argue that political parties have been a driving force in the development of immigration policy in Europe, but that there are specific dynamics that apply to parties of the centre-right. Although it is often argued that immigration has an impact on political parties and party competition, it is not – as Anthony Messina has argued – 'an independent variable floating above the political process' (Messina 2007: 55). Indeed, it is through the agency of political parties that the issues of immigration are often politicized (Schain *et al.* 2002: intro.).

Tim Bale is certainly correct, when he writes in the introduction to this volume that:

> the political science communities working on asylum and immigration, on the one hand, and parties, on the other, have traditionally sat at separate tables. Leading migration scholars have rightly nodded to the need to understand how the arrival of newcomers and their families impacts on attitudes and electoral politics ... But very few treat the parties that fight those elections as a vital source of state and European Union (EU) policy – policy which for some time now has been moving towards an emphasis on restriction and cultural integration that borders on the coercive.
>
> (Bale 2008: 316)

This omission is strange if we consider that in every European country political parties – or processes dominated by political parties – are responsible for the way issues of immigration are framed, how they are shaped, and are primarily responsible for how and where they are placed on the political agenda. Even in the United States, where national parties are less capable of developing national agendas, presidential priorities (and therefore presidential party networks) are important for the understanding of the development of immigration policy (Schain 2006a).

POLITICAL PARTIES AND IMMIGRATION

Immigration matters for political parties for several unavoidable reasons that are related to the political opportunity structure. The first is that immigration ultimately contributes to the expansion of the electorate. The timing of the impact of immigration may be over a relatively brief period of time, or over several generations, depending on requirements for voting and the openness of naturalization processes. Thus, in the United States before the First World War, many states permitted immigrants to vote before they had formally become citizens, and throughout the EU residents from other EU states can vote and run for office in some or all local elections in the countries in which they reside. Citizens from 54 Commonwealth countries and Ireland, as well as immigrants from 15 Dependent Territories are eligible to vote in all elections (and run for office) in the UK, once they have established residency and registered to vote.[1]

The structure of the electorate changes for other reasons as well, of course. Each year, new voters enter the potential electorate by passing the threshold age of eligibility, while still others enter the actual electorate by moving from abstention to voting. Therefore, aside from attracting supporters of other parties, political parties have several other opportunities to alter their relative position within the party system.

What differentiates immigrant voters (and potential voters) from the others, however, is that they become electoral participants without having been previously socialized either by family experience and heritage, or by having previously experienced major national events that have shaped the voting patterns of native voters (Andersen 1979: ch. 1). In this sense they are far more 'available' for mobilization by all major political parties, and their electoral impact can alter balances within the party system for generations to come. For example, the 'New Deal Coalition' built by Franklin Roosevelt in the United States in 1932 was largely built on new voters, among whom were large numbers of new immigrants who had recently been naturalized, as well as their first-generation children who had been born American citizens (Andersen 1979: 41–2).

Although this implies an impact upon the parties and the party system, parties are far from being passive actors in this process. Indeed, as in the American case, they can be active mobilizers of newly enfranchised immigrant groups, and can integrate mobilization into their strategic outlook. Viewed from this perspective, immigration is an opportunity, particularly for minority parties. This helps to explain why George Bush decided, during the presidential election campaign of 2000, to shift the Republican Party away from the hard anti-immigration position that it had taken four years earlier. Confronted by the gains that the Democrats had made in California among Mexican voters, the presidential candidate began to give short speeches in Spanish (Gimpel and Kauffman 2001). Although there was little hope of the Republicans attracting a majority of Latino voters, by 2004 they had succeeded in reducing the Democratic advantage.

Alternatively, political parties can use immigration as a different kind of opportunity, to shift committed native voters from one party to another.

Rather than focusing on immigrants as potential voters, this strategy usually implies a focus on questions of national identity, and the challenge to national identity posed not only by newly arrived immigrants but by their integration into the national community as well. Here, the opportunity is not the immigrants themselves, but the problem that they pose, and their usefulness in altering the electoral balance (Money 1999).

Thus, it does not follow that immigration issues will necessarily be framed as an electoral question. The way political parties understand 'electoral considerations' can involve different kinds of policy considerations, depending on whether they project the immigration issue as a challenge to identity for voters they anticipate to be anti-immigrant, or as a means of mobilizing a potential immigrant electorate. Both patterns have clearly been present in the politics of countries in Europe as well as the United States. However, if the former focus has dominated the thinking of political parties in Britain and France in recent years, the latter focus has been more dominant among political parties in the United States. If the first pattern has often been identified as the politics of identity, the second has been characterized as ethnic politics, the 'pandering' to the sensibilities of ethnic or naturalized voters.

Each of these strategic views of immigrants and immigration also implies a different policy perspective and outcome. The second implies the support of policies that are generally pro-immigration and pro-immigrant. Sensitivity to immigrant interests sometimes sets in motion a process that leads to more open immigration, particularly from those countries from which immigrants have previously arrived. The first implies policies oriented towards greater control and exclusion, even in the context of economic conditions that could benefit from increases of immigrant labor.

One question raised by this analysis is why the importance of immigrant electoral influence should be more important in the United States, and the framing of immigration as a challenge to national identity more important in Europe. The difference may be partially related to differences in what Michèle Lamont has called 'moral communities' (Lamont 2000: 9), or in differences in historical experiences with immigration (Citrin and Sides 2006). Nevertheless, in both Europe and the United States the vast majority of those polled are consistently opposed to increased immigration. It has been argued that how political parties decide to mobilize voters may be related, not to the size of the immigrant population, but to its spatial distribution among legislative constituencies. In contrast to European countries, high percentages of immigrant populations are relatively widely distributed in the United States, providing significant gains (or losses) for those parties that succeed in mobilizing (or fail to mobilize) them (Schain 2006b).

CENTER-RIGHT PARTIES AND IMMIGRATION

In general, issues of immigration have divided both the left and the right in most countries. Parties of the left have been inclined to support immigration and immigrants because they are a source of working-class support. On the other hand, parties of the left have often supported restrictionist and exclusionary policies, first because employers have often used immigrant labor to suppress wages and to break strike movements; second (and linked to this), reaction to immigrants by native working-class voters has often made parties of the left electorally vulnerable.

Parties of the center-right have also been divided about issues of immigration, but for different reasons. If business interests have almost always favored immigration for the same reasons that labor interests have opposed it, the identity wings of center-right parties have been inclined to see immigrants as a challenge to national identity. The center-right ignores its identity wing to its electoral peril, since it then becomes vulnerable to challenges in these terms from its right – the extreme right.

On balance, it would appear that immigration poses a more severe challenge for the center-right than for the left, primarily because the left is generally more likely to benefit from the integration of newly enfranchised immigrant voters. For the center-right, on the other hand, while there may be some positive electoral benefits from immigration, the most substantial benefit is for its business wing. The problem, then, is to please its business interests, without at the same time alienating its identity wing (Tichenor 2002: 169–75).

SALIENCE, POLITICIZATION AND PARTY SYSTEMS

Thus far, it seems that, because immigration divides the left and the center-right in different ways, the differences between left and right on this issue may be less important than the differences within each camp. Increasing the political salience of immigration issues, however, has a different impact on the left and on the center-right.

When parties of the left have increased the salience of immigration, they have generally done so in order to enhance the mobilization of ethnic electorates. When parties of the left have supported restriction, they have often done so to develop a consensus with the center-right in an attempt to depoliticize the issue (as in Britain in the 1970s). On occasion, parties of the left have used the identity issue to mobilize native voters (the Democratic Party in the South of the United States between 1900 and 1965, for example), but this has become more difficult as increasing numbers of immigrants have arrived for settlement. Thus, although the working-class reaction to newly enfranchised immigrants has certainly been a problem for parties of the left, it has been relatively rare that the left has supported restriction and exclusion.

For the center-right, however, increased salience generally means reduced influence of its business wing, which not only supports immigration, but generally works quietly through the administrative system. For the center-right, politicization has meant the use of identity issues to challenge the left, but also to challenge the business wing on an issue on which it is most vulnerable.

Of course, the strategic decisions of the left and the center-right are made in the context of a party system, in which the decisions of one influence those of the other. The emergence of a party of the extreme right vastly complicates this strategic relationship, for several reasons. First, the populist right has an impact on the electorates of both the left and the right. Where the extreme right has made an electoral breakthrough, it has generally done so at the expense of the established parties of the center-right. On the other hand, it has also appealed to a potential electorate of the left, particularly among young working-class men. In almost every country where the radical right has achieved an electoral breakthrough in recent years, it has become the party that has attracted the highest percentage of working-class votes (Schain *et al.* 2002: part 3).

However, because of its strategic position within the party system, the extreme right is capable of ensuring that the center-right parties are incapable of gaining office. By dividing the electorate of the right, both nationally but – more important – in specific spatial areas, it leverages bargaining power, not unlike what powerful Communist parties did in France and Italy during the post-war period (Schain 2006c).

In this way, the extreme right – even where it has not gained governmental power – has developed agenda-setting influence that goes far beyond what its percentage of the vote would indicate. While the left has not been immune from this influence, the impact has been primarily on the center-right, and has prevented center-right parties and governments from developing more flexible and/or open policies on immigration/integration.

In these ways, political parties of the center-right are agents of policy development. They are certainly constrained by their own electorates, and the conflicting interests that help to define the center-right. They are also constrained by the dynamics of the party system, primarily in the context of elections. Scholars have given some attention to the agency of political parties with regard to immigration policy. However, most of the attention has been reserved to parties of the radical right. Parties of the center-right have been far more responsible for the shaping and development of immigration policies but have received far less attention.

NOTE

1 This eligibility is explained on the website of the UK Electoral Commission: www.electoralcommission.org.uk.

REFERENCES

Andersen, K. (1979) *The Creation of a Democratic Majority 1928–1936*, Chicago: University of Chicago Press.
Bale, T. (2008) 'Turning round the telescope: centre-right parties and immigration and integration policy in Europe', *Journal of European Public Policy* 15(3): 315–30.

Citrin, J. and Sides, J. (2006) 'European immigration in the people's court', in C.A. Parsons and T.M. Smeeding (eds), *Immigration and the Transformation of Europe*, Cambridge: Cambridge University Press.

Gimpel, J.G. and Kauffman, K. (2001) 'Impossible dream or distant reality? Republican efforts to attract Latino voters', *Center for Immigration Studies Reports.*

Lamont, M. (2000) *The Dignity of Working Men: Morality and the Boundaries of Race, Class and Immigration*, Cambridge, MA: Harvard University Press.

Messina, A.M. (2007) *The Logics and Politics of Post-WWII Migration to Western Europe*, Cambridge: Cambridge University Press.

Money, J. (1999) *Fences and Neighbors: The Political Geography of Immigration Control*, Ithaca, NY: Cornell University Press.

Schain, M.A. (2006a) 'Immigration policy', in A. Menon and M.A. Schain (eds), *Comparative Federalism: The European Union and the United States in Comparative Perspective*, Oxford: Oxford University Press.

Schain, M.A. (2006b) 'The politics of immigration in France, Britain and the United States: a transatlantic comparison', in C.A. Parsons and T.M. Smeeding (eds), *Immigration and the Transformation of Europe*, Cambridge: Cambridge University Press.

Schain, M.A. (2006c) 'The extreme right and immigration policy-making: measuring direct and indirect effects', in V. Guiraudon and G. Lahav (eds), *Immigration Policy in Europe: The Politics of Control*, London and New York: Routledge.

Schain, M., Zolberg, A. and Hossay, P. (eds), (2002) *Shadows Over Europe: The Development and Impact of the Extreme Right in Western Europe*, Basingstoke and New York: Palgrave Macmillan.

Tichenor, D. J. (2002) *Dividing Lines: The Politics of Immigration Control in America*, Princeton: Princeton University Press.

Index